THE DIRECTORY

OF INTERIOR

DESIGN

**A PROFESSIONAL
CREATIVE RESOURCE**

THE DIRECTORY

OF INTERIOR

DESIGN

ARCHITECTURE & DESIGN
FOR COMMERCIAL & PUBLIC SPACES
IN EUROPE & ASIA

OFFICES & SPACE PLANNING

RETAILING

PUBLIC AND INSTITUTIONAL

LEISURE & ENTERTAINMENT

HOTELS & RESTAURANTS

EXHIBITIONS & TRADE FAIRS

DID

The *Directory of Interior Design* is published by
DID S.A.R.L. La Vieille Maison, Villemétrie
Senlis 60300, France
☎ (33) 44 60 06 54 - Fax (33) 44 60 08 77

Paris Office
DID, 4, rue d'Enghien, 75010 Paris
☎ (33) 1 47 70 03 30 - Fax (33) 1 48 24 04 84

London Office
DID, 30-40 Elcho Street, London SW11 4AU
☎ (44) 71 228 3468 - Fax (44) 71 228 9661

Publisher
Christopher Curtis

Associate Publishers
Christopher Gates
Véronique Kolasa
Hervé Morel
Yves Ferandou

Book design
Design House. London

Production
Luc Raimond Dit Yvon/Bruno Orer
Typesetting : Composetting, Paris.
Colour Separations : Graphotec, Paris.
Printing : Le Govic, Nantes. Binding : Mame, Tours.

The Directory of Interior Design
ISBN 2-88046-099-9

Worldwide Book Trade distribution
Rotovision S.A. Route Suisse 9, CH-1295 Mies,
Switzerland
☎ (41) 22 755 3055 - Fax (41) 22 755 4072
Telex 414 246 rovi ch

US Book Trade Distribution
Rotovision c/o Watson Guptill
1515 Broadway, New York, NY 10036
☎ (1) 212 764 7300 - Fax : (1) 212 536 5359

INTERNATIONAL OFFICES

Austria
Sonja Jamkojian-Huber, Gruengasse 12/2,
1050 Vienna
☎ (43) 1 587 0524 - Fax (43) 1 587 0524

Benelux
Sedip, Mr P. de Vanssay/Mrs E. Wibaut, rue
Vanderkindere 318, 1180 Brussells, Belgium
☎ (32) 2 343 4499 - Fax (32) 2 343 7951

Denmark, Norway, Sweden
Mr Michael Hargreave, Christianehoj 50, 2860 Soborg,
Denmark
☎ (45) 31 69 89 85 - Fax (45) 33 33 00 45

Finland
Leena Royna Anttila, Liikejulkaisut oy, PO Box 50,
SF-02611 Espoo
☎ (358) 509 3011 - Fax (358) 59 2049

France
Le Book Editions, Véronique Kolasa, 4, rue d'Enghien,
75010 Paris
☎ (33) 1 47 70 03 30 - Fax (33) 1 48 24 04 84

Germany
Siegmund Verlag, Christian Siegmund, Buxtehuder
Strasse 31b, D-2151 Moisburg
☎ (49) 41 65 66 09 - Fax (49) 41 65 68 83

Italy
Visual Books Srl, Maria Teresa Boselli, Via Durini 9,
20122 Milan
☎ (39) 2 793 973 - Fax (39) 2 7600 5302

Giannino Malossi, Via Marcona 80, 20129 Milan
☎ (39) 2 742 5368 - Fax (39) 2 738 7117

Spain
Rovira Asociados Editores S.A., Joan Rovira, Calle
Galileo 288, 08028 Barcelona
☎ (34) 3 490 57 34 - Fax (34) 3 490 16 62

United Kingdom & Eire
Christopher Gates, 30-40 Elcho Street,
London SW11 4AU
☎ (44) 71 228 9488 - Fax (44) 71 228 9661

North America
Brenda Curtis, 140 Cabrini Boulevard, Suite 129
New York, NY 10033
☎ (1) 212 740 1140 - Fax (1) 212 927 0791

CONTENTS PAGE

INTRODUCTION

A new department store in Barcelona, a hotel development in Singapore, a bank in Frankfurt, a restaurant in Tokyo : the need for high quality interior design and architecture is increasing dramatically.

Developers are demanding not only that commercial and public buildings function efficiently, but also that they operate profitably, and both factors are central to modern design.

But there are other considerations... the pressure on space, the increasing variety of building materials and the perpetual call for inventiveness and individuality. In this context, there has been a rapid growth in the number of design and architectural practices offering specialist services and skills.

For professionals making decisions about how commercial and public buildings look and perform, there is now a real need for a practical and reliable reference book which can function as a showcase for leading exponents in this complex field.

The Directory of Interior Design (DID) has been developed to meet this need. It is the first international guide to architects and designers specialising in interiors. DID offers a visually exciting and unique view of outstanding commercial design. We are proud to introduce you to DID. We believe it will be invaluable.

INTRODUCTION

Un grand magasin à Barcelone, un hôtel à Singapour, une banque à Francfort ou bien un restaurant à Tokyo : le besoin d'une architecture intérieure répondant à des critères de plus en plus sophistiqués devient de plus en plus pressant.

Les promoteurs exigent que les espaces commerciaux et publics soient non seulement fonctionnels, mais aussi rentables, et ces deux facteurs constituent le cœur des nouvelles données du design contemporain.

Mais il y a d'autres considérations : les contraintes de l'espace, la diversité croissante des matériaux de construction, l'éternelle demande de créativité et de personnalisation, chaque nouvel aménagement constituant aujourd'hui un vecteur de communication.

Dans ce contexte, on constate une croissance rapide du nombre de cabinets d'architectes et de designers offrant des services et des compétences spécialisés. Pour tous les décideurs s'est fait sentir le réel besoin d'un ouvrage de référence qui puisse présenter un panorama des principaux professionnels et des grandes tendances de ce domaine complexe et en pleine évolution.

Le DID (Directory of Interiror Design) a été créé pour répondre à ce besoin. Il s'agit du premier guide international consacré aux intérieurs et destiné à l'ensemble des professionnels du secteur.

Nous sommes fiers et heureux de vous le présenter.

EINLEITUNG

Ein neues Kaufhaus in Barcelona, ein Hotelkomplex, der in Singapur errichtet wird, eine Bank in Frankfurt, ein neues Restaurant in Tokio : der Bedarf an hochqualitativem Design und erstklassiger Innenarchitektur steigert sich auf dramatische Weise. Bauherren und Erschließer verlangen von gewerblichen wie von öffentlichen Gebäuden nicht nur effiziente Funktionserfüllung, sondern vielmehr auch das Abwerfen einer gesunden Rendite in der tagtäglichen Nutzung. Beide Faktoren sind ein zentrales Anliegen moderner Innenarchitektur. Doch es gibt auch andere Erwägungen, die ins Kalkül gezogen werden müssen... erdrückende Grundstückspreise mit dem Zwang zu optimaler Raumnutzung, eine immer größer werdende Vielfalt an Baustoffen und der ewige Ruf nach Ingenuität und Individualität. In diesem Zusammenhang gesehen nimmt es nicht Wunder, daß die Zahl der niedergelassenen Architektur- und Designfirmen, die sich auf ganz spezifische Fachbereiche beziehungsweise Dienstleistungen spezialisiert haben, in dramatischer Weise gestiegen ist.

Für Entscheidungsträger, die sich von Berufs wegen mit dem Aussehen, der Leistungsfähigkeit und der Funktionalität gewerblicher und öffentlicher Gebäude zu befassen haben, ist das Bedürfnis ebenso real wie auch zwingend, auf ein praktisches und zuverlässiges Nachschlagewerk zurückgreifen zu können, das sich als Orientierungshilfe und schaufenstergleicher Wegweiser zu den führenden Exponenten dieses so komplexen Gesamtfeldes erweist.

Das Directory of Interior Design (DID) wurde ganz speziell im Hinblick auf diese Bedarfslücke entwickelt. Es ist ein völlig neues Verzeichnis, das sich als erster wirklich internationaler Wegweiser zu Architekten und Designern vorstellt, die sich auf den Innenbereich spezialisiert haben. Als solches bietet das DID - Verzeichnis einen weiten Blick auf herausragende gewerbliche Designleistungen - visuell erregend und einzigartig in seiner Art.

Nicht ohne Stolz präsentieren wir Ihnen DID im ersten Verzeichnisjahrgang. Wir sind sicher, daß es für Sie von unschätzbarem Wert sein wird.

INTRODUCCION

Un nuevo hotel en Barcelona, una nueva sucursal de unos grandes almacenes en Singapur, una entidad bancaria en Franfurt, un restaurante en Tokio ; la exigencia de una alta calidad de diseño y arquitectura de interiores está acrecentándose imparablemente.

El desarrollo cultural y económico no demanda únicamente que los comercios, edificios públicos funcionen perfectamente, sino también utilizar el factor de un moderno y racional diseño de interiores para obtener un mayor aprovechamiento de todas las posibilidades.

Pero también existen otras consideraciones... la presión espacial, la creciente variedad de materiales de construcción y la constante demanda de novedades y singularidades. En este contexto, existen la necesidad de una base de consulta rápida y eficaz para encontrar la propuesta más adecuada entre un importante bloque de profesionales de la arquitectura y del diseño de interiores que brindan sus servicios y especialidades.

Para la toma profesional de decisiones sobre el como iniciar una aproximación a un proyecto de diseño de interiores de espacios comerciales o públicos, el poder consultar otras muchas realizaciones es una necesidad real y disponer de un buen libro de referencia que también puede tener la función de exposición para los más representativos profesionales y empresas de este completo sector.

The Directory of Interior Design (DID), ha sido pensàdo y desarrollado para satisfacer esta necesidad. Es la primera guia internacional de arquitectos y diseñadores especializados en interiores.

DID ofrece una panorámica interesante y única del más brillante diseño comercial.

Nos sentimos muy orgullosos de presentarle el DID. Esperamos que será muy positivamente valorado.

INTRODUZIONE

Un nuovo grande magazzino a Barcellona, un complesso alberghiero a Singapore, una banca a Francoforte, un ristorante a Tokyo : la domanda di arredamenti e di architettura di alto livello è in vertiginosa crescita.

I committenti esigono non solo che gli edifici commerciali e pubblici funzionino efficientemente, ma anche che operino con profitto, ed entrambi i fattori sono al centro del design moderno.

Ma ci sono altre considerazioni... il problema degli spazi, la crescente varietà dei materiali per costruzione e la perpetua richiesta di inventiva ed individualità. In questo contesto, si è assistito a un rapido incremento nel numero degli studi di progettazione e d'architettura che offrano servizi specialistici e qualificati.

Per i professionisti che decidono le caratteristiche estetiche e funzionali degli edifici commerciali e pubblici si prospetta ora l'esigenza di una guida di consultazione pratico e di sicuro affidamento, che possa servire da vetrina per gli esponenti più importanti in questo complesso settore.

La "Directory of Interior Design" (DID) è stata ideata per venire incontro a questa esigenza. Si tratta della prima guida internazionale per architetti e progettisti specialisti d'interni. DID offre un panorama unico e stimolante dal punto di vista visivo del design commerciale di alta qualità.

E' con giustificato orgoglio che presentiamo DID al publico. Siamo convinti che risulterà un sussidio di inestimabile valore.

INTRODUCTION 序文

バルセロナの新しい百貨店、シンガポールでのホテル開発、フランクフルトの銀行、東京のレストラン――質の高いインテリア・デザインと建築への需要は激しく増加しています。

開発業者は、商業・公共の建物が効果的に機能するだけではなく、利益を生み出すことを要求し、その双方が現代のデザインの中核要素を織り成します。

しかし考慮すべきことは他にもあります。空間不足、種類を増すばかりの建築素材、それにいつの世も変わることのない創意と個性の必要性。このため、専門家によるサービスと技術を提供するデザイン・建築会社の数が急速に増えてきました。

商業・公共の建物の外観や機能をどんなものにしようか、と考えるプロの方々にとって、この複雑な分野での主要な実例を見せるショーケースとして機能する実用的で信頼の置ける参考書が今や絶対に欠かせません。

インテリア・デザイン人名録「DID」は、そんな要求に応じて生まれました。本書は、建築家と内装を専門とするデザイナーを扱った初めての国際的なガイドです。「DID」は、刺激的でユニークな素晴らしい商業デザインの姿をお目にかけます。

私たちは自信を持って「DID」をお勧めします。必ずや読者の役に立つことと思います。

HOW TO USE THIS BOOK

The Directory of Interior Design - DID - is a new and unique resource for people involved in commissioning architecture and design for commercial and public spaces in Europe and the Far East.

It provides you, the professional, with a visual reference to leading design and architectural practices which have undoubted creative skills, and experience in the international market place. DID enables you to view a wide variety of outstanding work from across Europe, Asia and North America, together with comprehensive company data.

DID works on a double page portfolio system. Each design and architectural practice has filled two pages with examples of their work and has provided the key facts you will need to assess their status, experience, and company philosophy.

The work illustrated, the Specialisation symbols, and the Recent Clients list will give you an instant guide to the type of projects the practice undertakes. Full address details and names of key contacts are provided.

You can access information about each practice in a number of ways, using the comprehensive indexing system.

The Speciality Index will enable you to select design and architectural businesses that offer the particular area of expertise you require. Full information about the six Specialisations and their symbols, which are used throughout DID, are detailed below.

The Geographic Index provides a comprehensive guide to all participants, including full addresses and the range of specialisations each offers.

At the back of the book, there is an Alphabetic Index and a large name and address Listing of other leading design and architectural practices in Europe and North America.

We believe that DID will be invaluable when selecting appropriate candidates for your next project.

OFFICES AND SPACE PLANNING

Interior planning and design for commercial, financial, professional, industrial and scientific spaces.

RETAILING

All retail activities in Goods and Services, including Shopping Malls, Super and Hyper Markets, Department, independent and multiple Stores, Petrol Stations, Showrooms, Banks, Building Societies, Estate Agencies and Travel Agencies.

PUBLIC AND INSTITUTIONAL

All government and private sector spaces serving the public including Cultural facilities, Health and Education, and Transportation.

LEISURE AND ENTERTAINMENT

Sports and Fitness Facilities, Leisure Centres and Theme Parks, Cruise Ships, Boats and Marinas, Spas, Clubs, Cinemas and Auditoriums.

HOTELS AND RESTAURANTS

Hospitality spaces including all types of Hotels, Motels, Restaurants, Fast Food chains, Pubs, Bars, Cafés and Catering facilitites.

EXHIBITIONS AND TRADE FAIRS

All aspects of Trade Fairs, Conferences, Conventions and Exhibitions ; Film, Television and Theatre Set Design and Lighting.

MODE D´EMPLOI

Le DID (Directory of Interior Design) est un outil de travail nouveau et unique destiné aux personnes concernées par les commandes de travaux d'architecture et de design d'espaces commerciaux ou publics en Europe et en Extrême-Orient.
Il vous informe, vous, l'ensemble des professionnels, avec des exemples visuels, sur les principaux cabinets d'architecture et de design qui ont une incontestable créativité et l'expérience du marché international. Le DID vous permet de visualiser une grande variété de travaux remarquables en Europe, en Asie et en Amérique du Nord, ainsi que des renseignements clairs sur les entreprises.
Le DID se présente comme un système de porte-folio double-page. Chaque atelier de design et d'architecture a rempli deux pages avec des exemples de ses réalisations et donné les clés dont vous aurez besoin pour évaluer son importance, son expérience et sa philosophie.
Les réalisations illustrées, les symboles des spécialisations, la liste des clients récents vous donnent tout de suite une idée du type de projets que l'atelier conçoit et entreprend. On y trouve tous les détails sur l'adresse et le nom des responsables à contacter.
Grâce à un système d'index clair, vous avez accès à de nombreuses informations sur chaque cabinet.
L'index des spécialisations vous permet de sélectionner les entreprises d'architecture et de design qui offrent le champ d'expérience dont vous avez besoin.
L'index géographique constitue un guide clair de ces entreprises et comprend l'adresse complète, et les spécialisations de chacun.
A la fin du livre, vous trouverez un index alphabétique et une vaste liste des noms et adresses d'autres cabinets importants de design et d'architecture d'Europe et d'Amérique du Nord.
Nous sommes persuadés que le DID vous sera indispensable pour la sélection des partenaires appropriés à votre prochain projet.

BUREAUX ET AGENCEMENT D´ESPACE
Bureaux de direction, espaces commerciaux, industriels et scientifiques, cabinets juridiques et médicaux.

COMMERCES DE DÉTAIL
Toutes activités de distribution et de services, y compris galeries commerciales, super et hypermarchés, grands magasins, stands, banques, agences immobilières, etc.

ÉTABLISSEMENTS PUBLICS INSTITUTIONNELS
Tous secteurs d'activités publiques et d'État, y compris la Santé et l'Éducation, les centres de conférence, les moyens de transport et établissements culturels, etc.

LOISIRS ET SPECTACLES
Centres sportifs et de remise en forme, centres de loisirs et parcs d'attraction, bateaux de croisières, bateaux et ports de plaisance, stations thermales, pubs, bars/cafés, clubs, cinémas, salles de concert, etc.

HÔTELS ET RESTAURANTS
Tous types d'hôtels, motels, restaurants, chaînes de fast-food, etc.

EXPOSITIONS ET GALERIES
Stands d'exposition et de conférence, décors de cinéma, télévision, théâtre, éclairage, etc.

COMO UTILIZAR ESTE LIBRO

El DID - Directory of Interior Design - es la nueva y única fuente para las empresas y profesionales vinculados con la arquitectura y el diseño de espacios.

Proporciona una referencia visual de destacados profesionales de gran experiencia y reconocido nivel creativo en el mercado.

Este libro descubre a la vez información que difícilmente se puede obtener reunida y coordinada en alguna otra parte, facilitando una amplia y variada visión de los trabajos más sobresalientes recientemente desarrollados internacionalmente.

DID pretende ser un libro de consulta y elección de candidatos para la realización de futuros proyectos, ofreciendo a los potenciales clientes la posibilidad de una primera aproximación a los profesionales y empresas brindándoles información gráfica de sus realizaciones, dimensión de los equipos, credenciales, especializaciones... En el DID se presentan las empresas y profesionales de la arquitectura y diseño de interiores mediante una doble página con el sistema portfolio, presentando trabajos seleccionados por ellos mismos, indicando los datos necesarios para exponer su experiencia, capacidades y filosofía de empresa.

Estos trabajos ilustrados gráficamente ; los símbolos de Especialiación, la relación de últimos clientes, ofrecen una visión inmediata del tipo y clase de proyectos y obras que pueden realizar.

DID, además, proporciona muchos datos, con señas, nombres y contactos clave mediante un fácil y comprensible índice por diferentes epígrafes. El sistema inicial es por el Indice de Especializaciones, por el cual se selecciona el área concreta que se busca. La información completa sobre las seis especializaciones y sus símbolos está reflejada en el Indice de la página XX.

El Indice por Países proporciona una comprensiva información de todos los participantes. Existe asismismo el Indice Alfabético con una extensa relación de nombres y datos de otros importantes arquitectos y diseñadores en activo de Europa y EE. UU.

OFICINAS Y DISTRIBUCIÓN ESPACIO

Despachos de dirección, espacios comerciales, industriales y científicos, gabinetes jurídicos y médicos.

COMERCIOS AL DETALLE

Todas las actividades de distribución y de servicios, incluido las galerías comerciales, super e hipermercados, grandes almacenes, stands, bancos, agencias imobiliarias, etc.

ESTABLECIMIENTOS PÚBLICOS INSTITUCIONALES

Todos los sectores de actividades públicas y de organismos del Estado, incluyendo la Sanidad y la Educación, los centros de conferencias, los medios de transporte y los establecimientos culturales, etc.

OCIO Y ESPECTÁCULOS

Centros deportivos y de puesta en forma, centros de ocio y parques de atracciones, cruceros, barcos y puertos de recreo, estaciones termales, pubs, bares/cafés, clubs, cines, salas de concierto, etc.

HOTELES Y RESTAURANTES

Todo tipo de hoteles, moteles, restaurantes, cadenas de fast-food, etc.

EXPOSICIONES Y GALERÍAS

Stands de exposición y conferencias, decorados de cine, televisión, teatro, iluminación, etc.

COME USARE QUESTA A GUIDA

DID (Directory of Interior Design) e un nuovo e unico strumento di informazione per i potenziali clienti di studi di architettura e arredamento, coloro cioe che sono coinvolti nelle decisioni relative alla scelta di uno studio per l'architettura e l'arredamento di spazi commerciali e publici in Europa e in Estremo Oriente. DID, che si rivolge ai professionisti, vi fornisce informazioni e immagini dei principali studi che hanno indubbie capacita creative e esperienza del mercato internazionale. DID rende possibile il confronto tra una grande varietà di realizzazioni di alta qualita in Europa, Asia e Nord America.
DID è strutturata in un sistema di doppie pagine, ciascuna delle quali e dedicata ad uno studio d'architettura o d'interni, e ne illustra i piu significativi lavori e contiene i dati essenziali per conoscerne l'organizzazione, l'esperienza, la filosofia, lo stile.
Le illustrazioni dei lavori eseguiti, i Simboli di

specializzazione, e la lista dei Clienti Recenti vi danno una rapida lettura del tipo e alla dimensione dei progetti che gli studi sono in grado di realizzare. E possibile avere informazioni su ciascuno studio usando diversi indici.
L'indice principale, l'indice delle Specializzazioni, vi mette in grado di selezionare il tipo di studio professionale piu adatto alle vostre esigenze. Tutte le informazioni sulle sei Specializzazioni e i loro Simboli, sono riportate di seguito.
L'indice Geografico riporta tutte le informazioni sugli studi i cui lavori sono publicati su DID, e le specializzazioni offerte. Completano le vie di accesso alle informazioni un Indice Alfabetico e una lista dei pricipali studi di architettura e di interni in Europa e in Nord America.
Noi crediamo che DID vi sara di grande aiuto nel selezionare i candidati al vostro prossimo progetto.

UFFICI E SPACE PLANNING
Progettazione d'interni per spazi commerciali, finanziari, professionali, industriali e tecnico-scientifici.

NEGOZI
Tutte le attività di vendita al dettaglio di beni e servizi, compresi complessi di negozi, super e ipermercati, grandi magazzini, negozi autonomi e catene, stazioni di servizio, showroom, banche, società di costruzioni, agenzie immobiliari e agenzie di viaggio.

ISTITUZIONI ED ENTI PUBBLICI
Spazi statali e privati adibiti a impianti pubblici, compresi i servizi culturali e didattici, sanità e trasporti.

TEMPO LIBERO E SPETTACOLO
Impianti sportivi, centri di divertimento, parchi a soggetto, navi da crociera, marine e litorali, club, cinematografi e auditorium.

HOTEL E RISTORANTI
Spazi ricettivi, come alberghi, ristoranti in alberghi e motel, catene di fast-food, pub, bar e caffè, servizi di catering.

FIERE E MOSTRE
Tutti gli aspetti di fiere, convegni, congressi ed esposizioni. Progettazione di scenografie cinematografiche, televisive e teatrali, inclusa l'illuminazione.

HINWEISE ZUM GEBRAUCH DIESES BUCHES

Als einzigartiges Branchenverzeichnis stellt das Directory of Interior Design - DID - eine völlig neue Informationsquelle für alle dar, die auf dem gewerblichen und öffentlichen Sektor mit der Ausschreibung und Vergabe von Bauprojekten dieser Art in Europa und im Fernen Osten zu tun haben. Als Kenner der Materie und Fachmann finden Sie hier den visuellen Wegweiser zu den führenden Architektur- und Designbüros, deren Erfahrung und Können international außer Zweifel steht. Das DID -Buch ermöglicht Ihnen die Einsichtnahme in unterschiedlichste, herausragende Arbeitsbeispiele aus ganz Europa, Asien und Nordamerika - komplett mit umfassenden, einschlägigen Firmenangaben. Das DID - Porträtbuch ist nach doppelseitigem Portfolioformat aufgebaut. Auf je einer Doppelseite präsentieren sich die hier aufgeführten Architektur- und Designfirmen mit Arbeitsbeispielen und Schlüsseldaten und -fakten, die Sie brauchen, um Status, Erfahrung und philosophischen Standort einer jeden sich präsentierenden Firma beurteilen zu können. Die bebilderten Arbeitsbeispiele, die Symbole für Spezialgebiete und die aktuelle Klientenliste vermitteln Ihnen einen sofortigen Einblick in den Leistungsumfang jeder Firma und in die Art der durchgeführten Projekte. Natürlich finden Sie auch die vollen Anschriften und die Namen der wichtigsten Kontaktpersonen.

Die umfangreiche Indexierung ermöglicht Ihnen den direkten Zugriff zu Sachinformationen über jede Firma, und das auf unterschiedlichen Ebenen. Der Specialty-Index läßt Sie exakt diejenige Architektur- oder Designfirma auswählen, die ziel- und bedarfsgerecht genau die Erfahrungen mitbringt, die Sie suchen.

Der geographische Index bietet mit seiner Angabe der kompletten Postanschriften, und Aufführung der Spezialgebiete jeder vorgestellten Architektur- und Designfirma einen umfassenden Wegweiser zu allen Verzeichnispartizipanten.

Der am Schluß des Buches aufgeführte alphabetische Index enthält mit seiner großen Zahl von Namen und Adressen eine Fülle von Hinweisen auf andere führende Architektur- und Designfirmen in Europa und Nordamerika.

Bei Ihrer Suche nach geeigneten Kandidaten für Ihr nächstes Vergabeprojekt wird sich das DID -Buch sicherlich als ein Helfer von unschätzbarem Wert erweisen.

BÜRO- UND GEBÄUDEPLANUNG

Innenarchitektur und Design für Kommerz-, Finanz-, Geschäfts-, Industriegebäude und Forschungsinstitute.

HANDELSUNTERNEHMEN

Sämtliche Einzelhandelstätigkeiten für Waren und Dienstleistungen einschliesslich Einkaufszentren, Super- und Hypermärkten, Warenhäusern, Einzelgeschäften und Geschäftsketten, Tankstellen, Ausstellungsräumen, Banken, Bauunternehmen, Grundstücksmaklern sowie Reisebüros.

ÖFFENTLICHE GEBÄUDE UND INSTITUTIONEN

Sämtliche öffentlichen oder privaten Gebäude, die der Öffentlichkeit dienen, einschliesslich Gebäude für Kulturelle-, Gesundheits-, und Erziehungszwecke, sowie Transport.

FREIZEITZENTREN

Sport- und Fitnessanlagen, Vergnügungszentren und Parks, Kreuzer, Schiffe, Bäder, Clubs, Kinos und Auditorien.

HOTELS UND RESTAURANTS

Gaststätten, einschliesslich sämtlicher Arten von Hotels, Motels, Restaurants, Schnellimbissketten, Pubs, Bars, und Kaffees, sowie Delikatessenhändlern.

MESSESTÄNDE UND GALERIEN

Sämtliche Aspekte von Messen, Konferenzen, Kongressen und Ausstellungen, Film-, Fernseh- und Bühnengestaltung und Beleuchtung.

▶ この本の使い方

インテリア・デザイン人名録「DID」は、ヨーロッパと極東で商業・公共スペースの建築デザインを依頼しようという方々に向けた最新にして類のない情報源です。

プロである読者諸氏はこの本で、国際市場で創造的な技術と経験を誇る第1級のデザインと建築の実例を、目で見て参照していただけます。「DID」は、ヨーロッパと北アメリカ全域からの傑出した作品を豊富にお目にかけると共に、各社の詳細なデータをお届けします。

「DID」は1件2ページの作品集システムをとっています。それぞれのデザインと建築例に2ページをさき、作品例と、彼らの業界での地位や経験、会社の方針など評価には欠かせない鍵となる情報を収めました。

図解した得意分野の記号と、最近の顧客リストは、その事業がどんなタイプの仕事を手がけているのかが即座に分かるガイドの役割りを果たします。正確な住所と連絡先も明記してあります。

それぞれの実例に対して、詳細な索引システムを使用して何通りもの情報の得方ができます。

Speciality Index（専門分野の索引）では、あなたが求める特定の分野に専門技術を提供するデザイン・建築会社を選択することができます。「DID」の全般で使用した6つの得意分野とその記号に関しては、20ページの索引で詳細な情報が得られます。

Geographic Index（地理的索引）では、記載社全部の正確な住所、連絡をとるべき人名、得意とする専門技術など詳細な案内が得られます。

巻末にはアルファベット順の索引があり、ヨーロッパ及び北アメリカにある他の一流デザイン・建築会社の名前と住所が膨大なリストにしてあります。

あなたが次のプロジェクトへの適切な候補者を選ぼうとする時、「DID」は貴重な役割りを果たすことでしょう。

INTERIOR DESIGN

BY JEREMY MYERSON AND WENDY SMITH

Virgin Megastore on the Champs-Elysées, Paris, designed by UK consultancy Peter Leonard Associates. The transformation of architect Andre Arfvidson's austere French bank of the 1930s into a modern retail environment exemplifies the cultural trend in Europe to recycle old buildings with imaginative refurbishment.

IN THE 1990s

Some years ago London-based architectural guru Dr Frank Duffy of DEGW surveyed the world design scene and famously asserted that _"architecture is now a branch of interior design."_

At the time, his statement was regarded as no more than an amusing heresy by those who upheld the dominant values of the mother profession of architecture. But developments during the past decade – a time of spectacular creative and commercial growth for the profession of interior design – have had the effect of turning Duffy's words into a self-fulfilling prophecy.

It has taken a complex combination of several economic, cultural, social and technological strands of development to bring the environmental designer and interior architect into the international limelight.

In different parts of the world, different factors have been responsible. Certainly different industrial sectors have led the way in showing the contribution that better interior design can make not only to improved commercial performance in the office or retail sectors, but to improved cultural life in civic buildings, public spaces and amenities.

The technological impetus which has brought computer-aided design techniques into the design studio, offering great productivity on large schemes and a more scientific, rational approach to the discipline, is another key factor in the emergence of interior design consultancy as a major force within the business and construction worlds.

The cultural trend to recycle old buildings, paying greater attention to heritage and conservation, has undoubtedly played its part in giving interior designers major refurbishment commissions.

But all the interior design activity we have seen in Europe, North America and the Pacific Rim has been stimulated by the direction of underlying economic trends. The economic barometers have all been pointing in the right direction to sustain the level of growth.

ECONOMICS

Certainly the world market for design and architectural services has been growing at an impressive rate.

Reliable industry estimates now put the level of fees earned from design and architectural work – fees which have been separated out from much bigger construction and corporate identity budgets – at £6bn worldwide. North America is the biggest market, accounting for roughly £3bn in fees; Europe accounts for £2bn and is tipped for the most rapid growth due to forthcoming trade harmonisation in 1992; meanwhile the Far East accounts for £1bn and is a region of enormous potential given recent political and trade initiatives.

If you divide the £6bn up into disciplines, then the lion's share goes to commercial architecture (£4.1bn) and interior design including retail (£1bn). Product and graphic design account for just under £1bn in fee income. The environmental designer and interior architect is now working in a £5bn plus fee market which is growing all the time, and handling budgets for building and refurbishment that can be estimated to be in excess of £50bn.

Why has this level of activity come about? The simplest explanation can be found in the growing affluence of nations – in the greater wealth available to upgrade environments and invest in better living, working and leisure facilities. And the simplest insight into this process can be gained by comparing trends in population with growth in GNP (gross national product).

If you take trends in population over a five year-period, say 1982 to 1987, only the USA recorded a 30 per cent leap from 226 million people to 301 million. Elsewhere growth was largely static. Japan's population grew by three per cent, the UK and Spain by just one per cent. West Germany's population actually fell slightly – from 61.6 million to 61.1 million.

But GNP trends tell a different story. Every nation tracked over the same period showed a significant increase: the USA by 47 per cent, Spain by 42 per cent (suggesting its new economic freedom after years of Franco domination), the UK by 40 per cent, Japan by 35 per cent and West Germany by 20 per cent.

North America £3bn Europe £2bn South-East Asia £1bn

Fee income from design and architectural services by geographical area

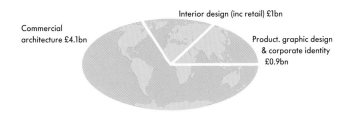

Commercial architecture £4.1bn Interior design (inc retail) £1bn Product. graphic design & corporate identity £0.9bn

Fee income from design and architectural services by design discipline

POPULATION TRENDS AND GROSS NATIONAL PRODUCT GROWTH OVER 5 YEAR PERIOD 1982-87

POPULATION

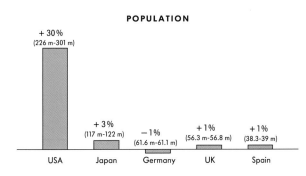

+ 30% (226 m-301 m) USA
+ 3% (117 m-122 m) Japan
– 1% (61.6 m-61.1 m) Germany
+ 1% (56.3 m-56.8 m) UK
+ 1% (38.3-39 m) Spain

GNP (Gross National Product)

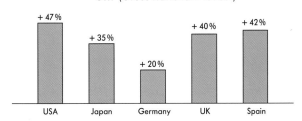

+ 47% USA
+ 35% Japan
+ 20% Germany
+ 40% UK
+ 42% Spain

GROWTH IN MERGERS AND ACQUISITIONS 1982-87

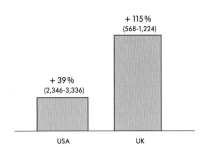

+ 39% (2,346-3,336) USA
+ 115% (568-1,224) UK

Growing affluence in the US and elsewhere has given retailers the confidence to spend on their environments: the Saks Fifth Avenue flagship department store in New York has been renovated by Walker Group/CNI to generate 30 per more selling space.

The message is clear: while populations have remained largely static – contributing, incidentally, to a demographic time bomb which will see employers everywhere frantically upgrading their offices during the 1990s in a bid to attract the ever-dwindling band of young people coming into the job market – national economies have been generating more wealth.

Growing affluence has given companies all over the world – whether department stores, hotel chains or office developers – the confidence to invest in more sophisticated interior design.

There has also been a pull from the ultimate end user. People, after all, are becoming better educated, more travelled and more demanding than ever before. Ron Van Pelt, principal with American architects and planners WAT&G International, puts it succinctly : *"The travelling public – whether it be for business or pleasure – wants more bang for its buck and better service."*

Of course one has come to expect a New World scenario of evergrowing consumer demands in the States, where, as Van Pelt outlines, *"The American dream is still a reality for those who strive for it. Look at the immigrants of the 70s and 80s – the Indo-Chinese. They're our next succeeders. There's this constant striving to be part of a strong and burgeoning middle class. We don't have the social blocks and class structures that you find elsewhere."*

However it's much the same story in the Old World of class-ridden Europe. Take Spain, for example. Salvador Ballarin, senior architect with McColl Spain, explains : *"The Spanish economy is racing. The quality of life for the Spaniard has gone right up. After Franco came democracy and that took four or five years to settle in. Now we have more foreign investors, more freedom, EEC membership and more information about the rest of Europe."*

Ballarin continues : *"And then there's our black economy – the black money has to be got rid of. How is this done? By shopping, or, if you have a company, by shovelling it back into the interior design of your business. It can't go on the bank balance."*

Salvador Ballarin reckons that the interior design market in Spain is growing by 10 to 15 per cent per annum. Until a recent downturn in retailing and an over-saturation of office development upset the applecart, the British interior design industry boasted even more spectacular expansion – an average of about 30 per cent a year during the latter half of the 1980s. (That rate of growth has now slowed to less than 10 per cent, below Spain's rate of expansion.)

In 1988, the 100 largest design and architectural firms in Britain – which has the greatest concentration of design consultancies in the world – earned £450m. The following year that figure was £525m. Interiors work accounted for a very substantial proportion of that income.

Contributing to the design boom in Britain was a pronounced

acceleration in both corporate and retail activity during the 1980s. The number of corporate acquisitions increased by 115 per cent over a five-year period during the decade, the number of registrations of private companies grew by 44 per cent, and the number of companies going public grew eight-fold. These figures had important longterm implications for the office property market, given the growing importance of interior design to the successful implementation of corporate identity.

Meanwhile, in UK retailing, operators of both small and large stores boosted the value of sales by margins of 60 to 100 per cent in the 1980s.

That pattern has been repeated to a varying degree around the world. Corporate mergers and acquisitions in the USA grew by 39 per cent in the 1980s, while Japan recorded a 6 per cent increase in firms listed on the Stock Market and West Germany showed a 7 per cent rise. American retailers also flourished: they increased average sales per sq. ft. by 33 per cent, while over the same period the number of Japanese wholesale and retail outlets grew by 22 per cent.

Aside from office and retail sectors, exhibitions and special events also boomed – giving many valuable commissions to architects and designers all over the world. Japan's number of international conferences rose by 74 per cent during the 1980s. Meanwhile, according to a report by City analyst James Capel, Britain's exhibitions industry motored at an annual growth rate of 15 per cent during the 80s to become worth in excess of £500m.

TRENDSETTERS

But even if the economic barometers are all in the right direction, it takes courage and conviction on the part of trendsetting organisations and their design teams to create mould-breaking interior design.

A brief survey of recent innovations reveals that important developments can be found in all three major markets for interior design.

The Pacific Rim, however, is the most misunderstood in terms of innovation – at least according to Ken Walker, president of US designers Walker Group/CNI, which services the Far East from a Tokyo office.

"Australia and New Zealand show sophisticated European standards in hotels, stores and offices", explains Walker. *"In Hong Kong you'll see design used as a marketing tool and some civilised offices. But they're the exceptions. In Japan, for all its technology, the workplace is horrible, positively neanderthal. Only multinational companies have a humanistic approach to the work environment."*

So if the offices are unspeakable, where is the cutting edge in Japanese interior design? *"Retail and hotels"*, says Walker. *"The Japanese are keen on new international ideas and they treat new ideas like objects. Everything is built to bump up against everything else. Tokyo has absolutely no sense of contextual design. The Japanese will take something by Walker or Nigel Coates or Frank Gehry or Philippe Starck, and simply build a succession of competing novelties."*

These novelties also have a short life cycle. The English architect Nigel Coates, who has worked extensively in Japan on such interior schemes as Caffe Bongo and the Hotel Otaru Marritimo, talks ruefully of how clients start making major alterations before the designer has even left for the airport.

A key reason to commission someone like Coates or Philippe Starck to work on a corporate headquarters, says Walker, is simply to build image. Certainly it has worked for the Tokyo makers of Asahi beer: Starck has put a giant publicity-grabbing archi-

Leisure and retail are setting the trends in the Far East. Caffe Bongo in Tokyo (above), designed in 1986 by Branson Coates Architecture, demonstrates the Japanese penchant for commissioning visual novelties from overseas designers. The BMW showroom in Hong Kong (right), designed by RSCG Conran Design Pacific, reflects the role of the multinationals in upping design standards around the Pacific Rim.

tectural phallus on the top of their building. Ken Walker, however, commends such companies as Sony and Nissan as the real trend-setters. *"Japanese car makers in particular have turned their showrooms into ideas centres"*, he remarks.

Japanese companies have also showed their paces in Hong Kong, according to Patrick Bruce, managing director of RSCG Conran design Pacific. He cites the work of such Japanese stores as Yaohan and Daimaru as accomplished ; and when Seibu joins the Japanese retail influx into Hong Kong, standards will be further enhanced. Apart from retail schemes and the uniformly high standard of office interiors by such multinationals as IBM and Hewlett Packard, design accolades in the region go to the hotels which are springing up, says Bruce.

He admits confidence among hoteliers in Hong Kong has been knocked by the Tianamen Square fall-out, but he insists that confidence will return and singles out Hong Kong's Grand Hyatt as *"an opulent design statement."*

The Far East's outstanding interior scheme for Bruce, however, isn't a hotel. It is Singapore's Changi Airport which he commends for its *"design excellence and relevant ambience."* The designers were Chaix and Johnson, an American firm with a Singapore office.

Back in America, trendsetting work has also emerged in the airport terminal. The essay in light, space and sculpture that is the United Airlines Terminal at Chicago's O'Hare Airport has commended Murphy/Jahn's interior scheme to those travellers fortunate enough to pass through it. But the most concentrated US design efforts are currently in hotels and leisure.

Ron Van Pelt of WAT&G International points to the US phenomenon of what he calls *"second cititess – they are developing their own trade shows and convention centres and the spin-off from that is the development of smaller 300 to 400-bed hotels of a high quality to put all these people up."*

Meanwhile, the leisure industry is also hotting up, says Van Pelt. The buzzword, he explains, is *"fantasy"*. Key developments here: mega-resorts with strong theme-parks, outdoor and multi-restau- rant elements; and *"boutique resorts"*, desperately expensive, low profile, exclusive 150-200 bed places where the thinking classes go to hide themselves away from the hoi polloi.

Lynn Wilson of Lynn Wilson Associates agrees that vacation leisure is the interiors boom area in the USA. *"The world has shrunk, there's more travel and a whole new generation of people are committed to spend now, pay later"*, she says.

But what about office design ? The inner-city corporate facility market is stabilising, explains Wilson, after major problems. *"The office market has been overbuilt in the past ten years, there has been indiscriminate financing, weak feasibility studies, and projects flooding onto the market and competing for the same clients."*

Problems such as these are not over, given the precarious state of the US economy. Indeed Ken Walker warns that the oportunites in US interior design in the 1990s will be *"more about gaining market share than gaining market growth."* That point is borne out by Arthur Gensler, head of Gensler Associates, America's largest interior design firm. *"The US market for interiors is unlikely to grow as dramatically as, say, Japan's or Europe's so we're happy to follow our US multinational clients overseas."*

That is precisely what is happening. In 1989, for instance, Gensler set up in London as a springboard into Europe in the 1990s. An astute move, certainly, because Europe has not only been a fountainhead of design creativity in recent years but it is set to capture an increasing share of the world interiors market this decade.

You don't have to look far to see evidence of an extraordinary blossoming of European interior design.

France and Spain have probably been the most spectacular, but Britain has also been at the centre of things.

The French have enjoyed the special advantage of enlightened state patronage that designers usually only dream about. But interior and furniture designers in France at least showed the talent to capitalise on the opportunities presented by the *"grands projects"* initiated by Mitterrand and his culture minister Jack Lang during the 1980s.

Government money was poured into a succession of ambitious public building schemes as a pump-priming exercise to make Paris a world leader in art, architecture and design, and set an exemple to the rest of France. Unknown avant garde designers such as Marc Held, Jean-Michel Wilmottte, Ronald Cecil Sportes and Philippe Starck were even invited to redesign the private presidential apartments of the Elysée Palace.

The results were staggering. French designers became world famous figures, none more so than Starck and Wilmotte.

Provincial mayors all over France began initiating their own mini versions of the *grands projets*. The French have now begun to emerge on the world stage as serious design business leaders – a development reflected by the recent acquisition of Conran Design Group, the best known brand name in interior design, by French communications giant RCSG.

The scale of French ambitions should not be under-estimated. According to Jean-François Bentz, architect of the takeover and chairman of the newly formed RSCG Conran Design, *"To be in the top five design groups worldwide, it will take an investment of £20 million to develop an international network over the next five years."*

Other French designers have similar aspirations to capture a larger share of the world design market. Design Stratégie of Paris, for instance, has recently formed an international network by

The intriguing Bar Velvet in Barcelona designed by leading architect Alfredo Arribas (above) reflects the liberated artistic spirit of Spanish design. Scandinavian design has a more empirical approach: Norwegian architect Niels Thorp's SAS building near Stockholm (above right) is a brilliant demonstration of green, democratic values.

teaming up with British group Minale Tattersfield. Environmental design is part of the offer to clients, and Design Stratégie director-general Philippe Rasquinet explains : *"France has now got a very good image abroad, particularly in America and Australia. Paris is renowned for its fashion, architecture and lifestyle. Mitterrand, Chirac and Jack Lang generated panache and now we're turning it into a marketable commodity."*

Spanish designers may not yet have the international business drive of their French counterparts, but there is no doubt that Spain has been the scene for much artistic innnovation in interiors – a lot of it centred on Barcelona and deriving from the cultural traditions and outlook of the Catalonian psyche. Salvador Ballarin of McColl Spain says the leading edge work has been in *"trendy bars and restaurants, media and financial companies."*

Clearly the Spanish way with interiors is highly eclectic and individualistic, a reflection of the unfettered spirit of post – Franco democracy and an antidote to the more formal procedures of Northern Europe and America. Nobody epitomises the spirit of Spanish interior design more strongly than architect Alfredo Arribas, who is described by design commentator Patrick Kelly as *"probably Spain's hottest property in interior design. A weaver of dreams, he has a talent for turning unpromising spaces into delightful fantasies, at once exciting and intimate."*

It was Arribas who created the self-consciously intriguing Bar Velvet in Barcelona and crashed a real plane fuselage into the side of Louie Vega, Europe's biggest discotheque on Spain's Costa Dorada. Spain is unlikely to slip from the global spotlight, given the 1992 Barcelona Olympics and Seville World Expo, even if – to the chagrin of locals – more and more international architects are being brought on to the design projects associated with these events.

Whisper it not in Milan, but Barcelona's reputation for design innovation – at least until some of its creative adrenalin dried up – irrevocably altered the balance of style power between Spain and Italy. The Italians have enjoyed the design leadership of Europe for so long that the challenge from Paris and Barcelona was not fully appreciated until it was upon them.

Ironically it has been in the area of product design that an entire generation of Italian architects – Achille Castiglioni, Ettore Sottsass, Anna Castelli Fieri and Vico Magistretti among them – have chosen to make their names. But working in the proximity of some of the world's finest furniture and lighting companies, such as Flos, Artemide, Cassina and Zanotta, many Italian organisations have commissioned a high standard of interior design – among them Olivetti and fashion giant GFT (which has just commissioned Aldo Rossi to design its new Turin headquarters).

The Latin approach to design is in contrast to the more businesslike, empirical Anglo Saxon model. The interiors boom in the UK, for instance, has not been due to an innate visual literacy of clients. Rather, it has been due to the emergence of a new generation of design managers working in major corporations and public bodies: the patronage of environmental designers by such figures as Jane Priestman at British Rail, Dick Peterson at BAA (the airports authority), Tony Key at British Telecom and Jeremy Rewse-Davies at London Transport spawned many ground-breaking commissions – some of which have yet to see the light of day.

Coupled with that, many private British companies in the office and retail sector raised the design flag – from the much – emulated Next store chain to the corporate headquarters of electrical conglomerate Emess PLC. The beautiful handcrafted office of Emess in London's St James Street, designed by David Davies Associates, marks a zenith in the use of environment as an expression of corporate identity.

Germany, meanwhile, does not have Britain's sophistication in retail design. But according to German designer Dieter Sieger of Sieger Design, the office sector reflects true Teutonic values. *"It's very quality-oriented in Germany with more long-term investment in high quality materials. The design is more classic and solid than the UK, where companies are forever changing."* Sieger singles out kitchen maker Bulthaup and lighting firm Erco as examples of German companies with an excellent design philosophy.

In many ways Germany shares design characteristics with Scandinavia – a belief in quality, timelessness and environmental accountability. One of the most influential environments in recent years has been the interior of the new SAS (Scandinavian Airline Systems) building outside Stockholm, designed by Oslo architect Niels Thorp. This features a naturally lit interior "street" which links facilities for off-duty air crews and administrative staff: it is technologically advanced, green, aesthetically pleasing and on a human scale. It has been inspected and re-inspected by designers from all over the world.

PROCESS

The way interior design work is commissioned and executed varies from country to country, and is anyway in a constant cycle of professional change. However there are a number of emerging trends worthy of discussion. Dr Frank Duffy of DEGW makes the distinction between the North American and European approach to designing interiors.

The North American model splits the responsibility between the building shell designer and the interior designer; this, he explains, allows a good, robust building to be used and reused several times in its lifetime, to be fitted out in different ways by different interior designers. But this is a repugnant idea to many German and Scandinavian architects who get a commission to design a building and want to see it all the way through to the finest details. This European approach will often include custom-design for furniture and accessories inside the building.

The conflict between the grand vision of the architect and the more specialised art of the interior designer has been a feature of environmental design for the past 30 years, ever since the Ameri-

Chairman's office at London advertising
agency Ogilvy & Mather: British
architect Tom Pike, an interiors specialist,
designed custom furniture for the environment.

The stranglehold of design-and-build firms on projects in Japan has made interiors consultancy work - such as the renovation of Tokyo's Isetan flagship store by Walker Group/CNI (far left) - all the harder. Everywhere, though, lighting consultants are rising to prominence: Tobacco Dock in London (left) was lit by Lighting Design Partnership.

can designer Florence Knoll first originated many of the scientific principles of interior space-planning.

The initiative ebbs and flows between designers and architects depending on economic and technological circumstance. In the 1980s, architects in Britain, for example, had so many new-build projects to occupy them that interior designers made great inroads into retail, leisure and office work. Now, as recession hits the UK construction industry, architects are fighting to win refurbishment and interiors work back.

Tom Pike is a British architect concentrating entirely on interiors, but says he is a rare animal. His scheme for the chairman's office of advertising agency Ogilvy & Mather in London even features custom-designed furniture pieces. But unless new-build schemes pick up, Pike will be joined by more and more architects in search of interiors work.

In Continental Europe, things are slightly different in that – unlike British design education, which has shaped an independent interior design profession – most people who design interiors are trained architects in the first place. There is, in Spain and Italy in particular, a concern to cross design boundaries – a more fluid, renaissance approach to interior design in which many different influences are brought to bear. It is refreshing to think that Milan-based Perry King and Santiago Miranda should not only design products and graphics but also produce innovative showrooms for furniture firm Marcatre.

The process in the Far East is different again, particularly in Japan where Ken Walker explains that *"design-and-build firms will throw in the interior design for free if they get the contract to build a store."* In that climate it makes the job of selling independent retail design consultancy very hard. Walker admits it has taken six years of hard slog to make the breakthrough now evident in such Walker schemes as the Isetan department store in Tokyo.

Patrick Bruce of RSCG Conran Design Pacific points out that the power of the design-and-build package in the region, particularly in the public sector, has "forced architects and interior designers to form alliances with reputable contractors." Who gets to do the work - architect or designer - depends on the nature of the project. A retro-fit in an existing building will favour the designer; a new building will give the architect a better chance.

One notable feature of the Hong Kong scene – which is also evident in the UK and USA – is the growing degree of specialisation on a multi-disciplinary building design team. Hotel specialists are a growing force, as are lighting consultants and acousticians.

Lighting designers first emerged in the USA as experts on energy saving in the years following the oil crisis of 1973. During the 1980s they found a further market in the UK as retail, leisure and museum design schemes grew ever more sophisticated. Now the lighting specialism is part of an established repertoire – especially in hotel design, which requires, says Richmond Design chairman Bob Lush, *"the skills of a film director."*

Ron Van Pelt of WAT&G International describes a typical US hotel project : *"Hotels are multi-disciplinary events. The architect will come in first and may well recommend who is to be the interior designer and lighting consultant. In an ideal world it would be best to have the ID on board at the schematic design phase and the lighting man at the next phase. He's very important but he usually doesn't get the attention he deserves."*

FUTURES

Lighting designers are guaranteed a far greater role in the future because energy-saving and environmental issues will provide the main *leitmotif* of the 1990s. Already interior designers in Europe are struggling with ways to conserve energy and materials. But it is a horrendously complex issue, as Rodney Cooper, senior partner of Building Design Partnership, explains: *It is not about choosing particular bits of hardwood or telling your mechanical engineers not to put CFCs in the air-conditioning system. The green issue is so complicated that it is going to take major scientific minds to work out what is the best mode of action to create a green policy."*

This policy remains some way off, despite extensive research in a number of places. Other scenarios look more firmly plotted, most notably technological development. Electronic innovations

A concern to add variety and soul to the basic geometry of Modernism in the 1990s is reflected in these two schemes by London-based architects Harper Mackay for the ing fashion store (top) and the advertising agency offices of Still Price Court Twivy D'Souza (above).

will mean more interactive interiors, with the thread of new technology stretching right from the equipment used to design schemes in the studio, through to the end user.

In retailing, checkout computer links will be able to analyse the exact return on every square foot of space and every item on the shelf. Meanwhile teleshopping will provide an alternative to the traditional shopping trip, says James Woudhuysen, European director of Fitch-RS' Exploratory Design Laboratory. But when you do venture into a mall, it will, he says, be more opulent and dramatic than before, a real sensory experience.

In stylistic terms, crystal-gazers predict that interior design will pull in a number of different directions reflecting the splintering of the mass market of the 70s and 80s into a number of niches. There will be the pull of local vernacular styles, with an emphasis on ethnic handcrafts and materials, counterbalanced by the imperative of the homogenous look initiated by multinationals who trade all over the world.

If there is a central focus to forthcoming trends then it is "human scale": in Germany, Dieter Sieger talks of adding some soul and atmophere to the basic geometry of Modernism and making design more people-centred. Meanwhile, British environmental psychologist David Tong of Building Use Studies suggests that, in future, employees will want far more personal control over their workplace. Out will go controlled environments with high speed lifts and air conditioning systems ; staircases, lights you can switch off and windows you can open will return.

But the biggest changes in interior design are linked to economic and political events. The post-1992 Europe will create a single market of 320 million people, 200 million of them within three hours travelling distance of each other. Their spending power will be greater than the entire American economy – and the interior design opportunities in the creation of a new retail, transport   and

financial services infrastructure are immense. Little wonder that so many US architectural and design practices have opened offices in London.

WAT & G International is among them. They see opportunities in the European travel industry : *"The Europeans have a strong resort tradition which got frozen in time with the old spa hotels. Then there was the resurgence in the 1960s and 70s with Benidorm and the rest which all went terribly wrong. At best they were urban environments in a resort setting. Maybe we'll see them all pulled down. Europeans, like Americans, are expecting better for their money."*

Aside from the European Community, there is also the not inconsiderable matter of the liberation of the Eastern European economies. That will inevitably yield more interiors work as hard currencies are sorted out. Already Lynn Wilson is talking to the Yugoslavian governement about its hotels, while UK architectural firm DY Davies has signed a deal with a state-owned Prague design institute to carry out joint design ventures in Czechoslovakia.

Everywhere you look, the interior design business is on the move. Patrick Bruce points to the number of world trade centres going up in the Far East which will bring in much exhibition work within four or five years. He also observes that the current glut of office space in Hong Kong is likely to depress rentals and so reduce operating costs for companies. The net result could be the release of more capital expenditure for interior fit-outs.

Optimism like this characterises the leading figures in interior design, those who commission it, design it, build it and implement it. It augurs well for the 1990s.

Jeremy Myerson is contributing editor of *Design Week* and the author of a number of books, including a new series of guides to the classics of twentieth century consumer design.

Wendy Smith is consultant editor of *Office Environment* and a contributor to the *Financial Times* and *Interior Design UK*.

GEOGRAPHIC INDEXES

UNITED KINGDOM AND EIRE

INTERIOR CONSULTANCY SERVICES LTD   133

Tyttenhanger House
St Albans, Herts AL4 OPG
☎ (0)727 23633 - Fax (0)727 26488
Tx 299169 JAYBEE G

INTRADESIGN INC   135

c/o Robinson Conn Partnership
68 Alma Road
Windsor, Berkshire
☎ (0)753 830055 - Fax (0)753 850913

JOHN HERBERT PARTNERSHIP LIMITED   137

8 Berkeley Road, Primrose Hill
London NW1 8YR
☎ (0)71 722 3932 - Fax (0)71 586 7048

LYNN WILSON ASSOCIATES INC   141

McColl/Wilson, London
☎ (0)71 935 4788 - Fax (0)71 224 3424

McCOLL GROUP INTERNATIONAL   145

64 Wigmore Street
London W1H 9DJ
☎ (0)71 935 4788 - Fax (0)71 935 0865

124/125 Princes Street
Edinburgh EH2 4AD
☎ (0)31 220 3322 - Fax (0)31 220 4454

MICHAEL PETERS GROUP, RETAIL ARCHITECTURE AND INTERIORS   147

3 Olaf Street, Holland Park
London W11 4BE
☎ (0)71 229 3424 - Fax (0)71 221 7720

PD DESIGN COMPANY LIMITED   149

The Grange
Wigston
Leicester LE8 1NN
☎ (0)533 810 018 - Fax (0)533 813 010

PENNINGTON ROBSON LIMITED   151

Tea Warehouse, 10A Lant Street
London SE1 1QR
☎ (0)71 378 0671 - Fax (0)71 378 0531

RICHMOND INSTON   157

52-70 Shorts Gardens
London WC2H 9AB
☎ (0)71 379 6556 - Fax (0)71 240 1915

ROBERT BYRON ARCHITECTS   159

78 Fentiman Road
London SW8 1LA
☎ (0)71 735 0648 - Fax (0)71 735 1843

RPW DESIGN PARTNERSHIP   161

77 Weston Street
London SE1 3RS
☎ (0)71 378 8001 - Fax (0)71 403 6386

RSCG SOPHA DESIGN   163

RSCG Design Group : RSCG Conran Design, London
☎ (0)71 631 0102 - Fax (0)71 255 2049
Tx 265 490

SHEPPARD ROBSON   165

77 Parkway - Camden Town
London NW1 7PU
☎ (0)71 485 4161 - Fax (0)71 267 3861
Tx 22157

ttsp   175

90-98 Goswell Road
London EC1V 7DB
☎ (0)71 490 8899 - Fax (0)71 490 5845

56 Queen Square
Bristol B51 4LF
☎ (0)272 25 22 07 - Fax (0)272 25 22 08

TIBBATTS & CO. DESIGN GROUP LIMITED   177

1 St-Paul's Square
Birmingham, B3 1QU
☎ (0)212 33 28 71 - Fax (0)212 36 87 05
Tx 336947 TIBCO G

TILNEY LUMSDEN SHANE LIMITED 179

5 Heathmans Road
London SW6 4TJ
☎ (0)71 731 6946 - Fax (0)71 736 3356

TRICKETT ASSOCIATES/ TRICKETT & WEBB 181

The Factory, 84 Marchmont Street
London WC1N 1HE
☎ (0)71 388 6586 - Fax (0)71 387 4287

WIMBERLY ALLISON TONG & GOO 185

87 Elystan Street
London SW3 3PA

WOLFF OLINS/HAMILTON 187

22 Dukes Road
London WC1R 9AB
☎ (0)71 387 0891 - Fax (0)71 388 2460
Tx (0)71 261 438

YRM INTERIORS 189

24 Britton Street
London EC1M 5NQ
☎ (0)71 253 4311 - Fax (0)71 250 1688
Tx 21692 YRMG

 EIRE - Tel Code: 353

A & D WEJCHERT ARCHITECTS 57

23 Lower Baggot Street
Dublin 2
☎ (0)1 610 321 - Fax (0)1 610 203

CONTINENTAL EUROPE

BELGIUM - Tel Code: 32

SIMONI INTERIEUR N.V. 169

Hentjenslaan 9A
3511 Kuringen Hasselt
☎ (0)11 25 35 02 - Fax (0)11 87 21 00

WHITE DESIGN 183

White & Partners
Avenue L. Gribaumont, 1
11500 Brussels
☎ (0)2 772 43 10 - Fax : (0)2 772 43 08

DENMARK - Tel Code: 45

MICHAEL PETERS GROUP, RETAIL ARCHITECTURE AND INTERIORS 147

GI Lundtoftevej 1A
2800 Lyngby/Copenhagen
☎ (0)42 88 85 55

FRANCE - Tel Code: 33

A.C.R. ARCHITECTURE INTÉRIEURE 53

36, bd de la Bastille
75012 Paris
☎ 1 43 40 47 52/1822 - Fax 1 43 41 08 01

A.D.S.A. & PARTNERS 55

74, rue du Faubourg-St-Antoine
75012 Paris
☎ 1 43 46 90 58 - Fax 1 43 47 28 47

ADDISON DESIGN CONSULTANTS LIMITED 59

16, rue St-Denis
92100 Boulogne
☎ 1 30 21 95 31

AGENCE BERNARD GRENOT 61

79 bis, rue Madame
75006 Paris
☎ 1 45 48 70 45 - Fax 1 45 44 18 86

ARCAM ALAIN CARRÉ DESIGN 63

11, rue Paul Lelong
75002 Paris
☎ 1 42 60 36 60 - Fax 1 42 61 79 03

ARCHIMÈDE (GROUPE VITRAC DESIGN) 65

60, rue d'Avron
75020 Paris
☎ 1 40 24 08 00 - Fax 1 40 24 08 12

ARCHITECTURES 67

Château l'Escadrille
33390 Cars-Bordeaux
☎ 57 42 15 18

ARCHITECTURE INTÉRIEURE ALAIN MARCOT 69

5, rue Richepanse
75008 Paris
☎ 1 47 03 46 00 - Fax 1 42 97 51 83

ARCHITRAL 71

28, rue Broca
75005 Paris
☎ 1 45 35 04 04 - Fax : 1 43 36 38 98
Tx BARRAU 205 616

ARTRIUM SARL 73

43, rue Monge
75005 Paris
☎ 1 43 26 47 80 - Fax : 1 46 34 07 69
Tx : 219 000 + Q86038 ARTRIUM

ASYMÉTRIE 75

16, rue des Minimes
75003 Paris
☎ 1 43 56 22 20 - Fax 1 43 56 75 67

ATELIER JEAN-LUC CÉLEREAU 77

13-15, rue de la Verrerie
75004 Paris
☎ 1 40 29 95 05 - Fax 1 40 29 00 96

B.E.D. 81

50-54, rue de Silly
92513 Boulogne-Billancourt Cedex
☎ 1 49 09 75 75 - Fax 1 49 09 73 79

BERBESSON RACINE ET ASSOCIÉS 85

1, villa Juge
75015 Paris
☎ 1 45 77 87 48 - Fax 1 45 77 78 34

BRIGITTE DUMONT DE CHASSARD 89

108, rue Vieille-du-Temple
75003 Paris
☎ 1 42 77 06 50 - Fax 1 42 77 65 70

BUREAU D´ÉTUDES ARCHITECTURALES BACHOUD HECHT 91

6 bis, rue Leconte-de-Lisle
75016 Paris
☎ 1 45 20 78 04 - Fax 1 45 20 60 62
Tx 270 105 F

C.S.I.A. CHRISTOPHE SEGUIN INTERNATIONAL ART 93

27, rue Buffault
75009 Paris
☎ 1 42 81 38 05

CABINET AARKA 95

1, rue Théodule-Ribot
75017 Paris
☎ 1 47 66 33 64 - Fax 1 48 88 93 05

Agence Nice France
Résidence Le Majestic
4, bd de Cimiez
06000 Nice
☎ 93 80 72 71

CORAME 99

5, bd Poissonnière
75002 Paris
☎ 1 42 36 19 91 - Fax 1 42 36 28 28
Tx 215 056

CRABTREE HALL PROJECTS LIMITED 103

Crabtree Hall / Plan Créatif
10, rue Mercœur
75011 Paris
☎ 1 43 70 60 60 - Fax 1 43 70 96 29

DESIGN ARCHITECTURAL 107

15 bis, rue du Général-de-Gaulle
94480 Ablon-sur-Seine
☎ 1 45 97 43 41 - Fax 1 45 97 27 52
Tx 264 918

DESIGN SOLUTION 113

65, rue Rambuteau
75004 Paris
☎ 1 42 77 03 63 - Fax 1 42 72 93 11

ÉRIC LIEURÉ 119

89, fg St-Antoine
75011 Paris
☎ 1 43 42 39 49 - Fax 1 43 45 08 62

HART-LABORDE 127

174, avenue Charles-de-Gaulle
92200 Neuilly-sur-Seine
☎ 1 46 24 76 89 - Fax 1 47 45 50 42
Tx HARTLAB 620 049 F

LYNN WILSON ASSOCIATES INC 141

Lynn Wilson Assoc., Paris
☎ 1 40 49 02 34 - Fax 1 40 49 02 73

PPH VOLUME 155

10, rue Duvergier
75019 Paris
☎ 1 40 35 43 45 - Fax 1 40 35 43 47

RSCG SOPHA DESIGN 163

8, rue Rouget-de-Lisle
92130 Issy-les-Moulineaux
☎ 1 40 93 93 94 - Fax 1 46 62 60 72
Tx 631 262

WOLFF OLINS / HAMILTON 187

Wolff Olins
72, rue du Fg Saint-Honoré
75008 Paris
☎ 1 40 07 86 06 - Fax 1 40 07 80 40

GERMANY - Tel Code: 49

BORN & STRUKAMP MESSEBAU GmbH 153

Grossenbaumer Weg 9
4000 Düsseldorf 30
☎ (0)2 11 41 10 25 - Fax (0)2 11 42 40 53

FITCH-RS DESIGN CONSULTANTS 121

Am Seestern 24
4000 Düsseldorf
☎ (0)2 11 59 67 22 / 23 / 25 - Fax (0)2 11 59 15 76

MICHAEL PETERS GROUP, RETAIL ARCHITECTURE AND INTERIORS 147

Bilker Strasse 32
4000 Düsseldorf
☎ (0)2 11 13 35 91

PETER SCHMIDT VEIT MAHLMANN DESIGN GmbH 153

Badestrasse 19
2000 Hamburg 13
☎ (0)40 44 38 67 / 41 76 00 - Fax (0)40 44 68 30

SIEGER DESIGN 167

Schloss Harkotten
4414 Sassenberg 2
☎ (0)5426 2796 / 2816 - Fax (0)5426 3875

STUDIO 2A S.A.S. 173

c/o Blu Consult
Holzstrasse 11
8000 Munich
☎ (0)89 2607799 - Fax (0)89 2607586

ttsp 175

Wilhelm - Leuschner Strasse 7
6000 Frankfurt-am-Main, 1
☎ (0)69 25 33 08 - Fax (0)69 25 33 84

 HOLLAND - Tel Code: 31

EGM ARCHITECTEN BV 115

Laan der Verenigde Naties 9
Postbus 298
3300 AG Dordrecht
☎ (0)78 330660 - Fax (0)78 140071

Wijnhaven 14
Postbus 21301
3000 AH Rotterdam
☎ (0)104 132 540 - Fax (0)104 048 491

Geertestraat 2 bis
3511 XE Utrecht
☎ (0)30 322 352 - Fax (0)30 321730

HIDDE CONSULTANTS 129

Herengracht 162
1016 BP Amsterdam
☎ (0)20 38 21 37 - Fax (0)20 38 21 38

MICHAEL PETERS GROUP, RETAIL 147
ARCHITECTURE AND INTERIORS

Koningslaan 54
1075 AE Amsterdam
☎ (0) 20 758 551

ITALY - Tel Code: 39

MICHAEL PETERS GROUP, RETAIL 147
ARCHITECTURE AND INTERIORS

Via Dante 4
20121 Milan
☎ (0)2 7202 0181

STUDIO 2A S.A.S 173

Via Novara 13
20013 Magenta
Milan
☎ (0)2 979 3177 - Fax (0)2 979 4276

SPAIN - Tel Code: 34

ARCHIMÈDE 65
(GROUPE VITRAC DESIGN)

Madrid : B.F.L. S.A.
☎ (9)1 593 8317 - Fax (9)1 446 2219

BIAIX S.A. - 87
ARCHITECTURA INTERIOR

Rambla Cataluña No 90
08008 Barcelona
☎ (9)3 215 8967 - Fax (9)3 487 2810

DECO STIL S.A. 105

c/o Santa Ana, 2
08002 Barcelona
☎ (9)3 301 02 48/02 90 - Fax (9)3 412 33 38

FITCH RS DESIGN CONSULTANTS 121

FITCH RS
Serrano 240-5°
28016 Madrid
☎ (9)1 457 0784 - Fax (9)1 457 2079

MANBAR 143

Via Augusta 61
08006 Barcelona
☎ (9)3 218 6450 - Fax (9)3 217 3437

McCOLL GROUP INTERNATIONAL 145

Marques de Riscal no 6, 1
28010 Madrid
☎ (9)1 308 2764

MICHAEL PETERS GROUP, RETAIL ARCHITECTURE AND INTERIORS 147

Velazquez 24, 5D
28001 Madrid
☎ (9)1 575 3964

PENNINGTON ROBSON LIMITED 151

Plaza Santa Eulalia, 7-6°
07001 Palma de Mallorca
☎ (71)72 07 44 - Fax (71)72 04 41

 SWEDEN - Tel Code: 46

PENNINGTON ROBSON LIMITED 151

Pennington Robson/Rupert Gardner AB
Sibyllegatan 53
11443 Stockholm
☎ (0)8 665 1910 - Fax (0)8 662 7026

WHITE DESIGN 183

Box 2502
40317 Göteborg
☎ (0)31 173 460 - Fax (0)31 114 642

SWITZERLAND - Tel Code: 41

ARCHITECTURES 67

Minervastrasse 117
8032 Zurich
☎ (0)1 38 39 117 - Fax (0)1 38 39 117

NORTH AMERICA

CANADA - Tel Code: 1

DESIGN INTERNATIONAL D.I. DESIGN & DEVELOPMENT CONSULTANTS LIMITED 111

110 Bond Street
Toronto, Ontario M5B 1X8
☎ 416 595 9598 - Fax 416 595 0670

UNITED STATES - Tel Code: 1

A.D.S.A. & PARTNERS 55

B.M.E.S. New York
☎ 212 737 3525 - Fax 212 737 3647

ADDISON DESIGN CONSULTANTS LTD 59

112 East 31st Street
New York, NY 10016
☎ 212 532 6166 - Fax 212 532 3288

575 Sutter Street
San Francisco CA 94102
☎ 415 956 7575 - Fax 415 433 8641

CONCEPT DESIGN GROUP, INC 97

615 Piikoi street - Suite 1406
Honolulu
Hawaii 96814
☎ 808 523 7630 - Fax 808 531 1706

COVELL MATTHEWS WHEATLEY ARCHITECTS LIMITED 101

Tribble Harris Li Inc.
730 Fifth Avenue, Suite 604
New York, NY 10019
☎ 212 262 7180

DESIGN. INTERNATIONAL. D.I. DESIGN & DEVELOPMENT CONSULTANTS LIMITED 111

20 South Charles Street
Baltimore, Maryland 21201
☎ 301 962 0505 - Fax 301 783 0816

ÉRIC LIEURÉ 119

Eric Lieuré / Butler Rogers Baskett
381 Park Avenue South
New York, NY 10016
☎ 212 686 9677 - Fax 212 213 2170

FITCH-RS DESIGN CONSULTANTS 121

Fitch Richardsonsmith,
10350 Olentangy River Road, PO Box 360
Worthington, OH 43085
☎ 614 885 3453 - Fax 614 885 4289

INTRADESIGN INC 135

910 North La Cienega Boulevard
Los Angeles, CA 90069
☎ 213 652 6114 - Fax 213 652 6945
Telex 317779

JON GREENBERG & ASSOCIATES INC 139

2338 Coolidge Highway
Berkley, Mich. 48072
☎ 313 548 8080 - Fax 313 548 4640

LYNN WILSON ASSOCIATES INC 141

111 Majorca Avenue
Coral Gables
Florida 33134
☎ 305 442 4041 - Fax 305 443 4276

8500 Melrose Avenue, Suite 201
Los Angeles, Ca. 90069
☎ 213 854 1141 - Fax 213 854 1149

RSCG SOPHA DESIGN 163

RSCG Conran Design
Pacific : Hong Kong
☎ (852) 58 68 26 63 - Fax (852) 58 68 46 58

WIMBERLY ALLISON TONG & GOO 185

2222 Kalakaua Avenue
Honolulu
Hawaii 96815
☎ (1) 808 922 1253 - Fax (1) 808 923 6346

SPECIALITY INDEXES

BORN & STRUKAMP MESSEBAU GmbH — 153

Grossenbaumer Weg 9
4000 Düsseldorf 30, Germany
☎ (0)211 411025 - Fax (0)211 424053

BRIGITTE DUMONT DE CHASSARD S.A. — 89

108, rue Vieille-du-Temple
75003 Paris, France
☎ 1 42 77 06 50 - Fax 1 42 77 65 70

BUREAU D'ÉTUDES ARCHITECTURALES BACHOUD HECHT — 91

6 bis, rue Leconte-de-Lisle
75016 Paris, France
☎ 1 45 20 78 04 - Fax 1 45 20 60 62

C.S.I.A. CHRISTOPHE SEGUIN INTERNATIONAL ART — 93

27, rue Buffault
75009 Paris, France
☎ 1 42 81 38 05

CABINET AARKA — 95

1, rue Théodule-Ribot
75017 Paris, France
☎ 1 47 66 33 64 - Fax 1 48 88 93 05

CORAME — 99

5, bd Poissonnière
75002 Paris, France
☎ 1 42 36 19 91 - Fax 1 42 36 28 28

COVELL MATTHEWS WHEATLEY ARCHITECTS LIMITED — 101

19 Bourdon Place
London W1X 9HZ, England
☎ (0)71 409 2444 - Fax (0)71 493 8998

CRABTREE HALL PROJECTS LIMITED — 103

70 Crabtree Lane
London SW6 6LT, England
☎ (0)71 381 8755 - Fax (0)71 385 9575

DECO STIL S.A. — 105

c/o Santa Ana, 02
08002 Barcelona, Spain
☎ (9)3 301 02 48 / 02 90 - (9)3 301 00 05
Fax (9)3 412 33 38

DESIGN ARCHITECTURAL — 107

15 bis, rue du Général-de-Gaulle
94480 Ablon-sur-Seine, France
☎ 45 97 43 41 - Fax 45 97 27 52

DESIGN HOUSE CONSULTANTS LTD — 109

120 Parkway, Camden Town
London NW1 7AN, England
☎ (0)71 482 2815 - Fax (0)71 267 7587

DESIGN INTERNATIONAL D.I. DESIGN & DEVELOPMENT CONSUTLANTS LIMITED — 111

12 Dryden Street, Covent Garden
London WC2E 9NA, England
☎ (0)71 836 1853 - Fax (0)71 379 4727

DESIGN SOLUTION — 113

20 Kingly Court
London W1R 5LE, England
☎ (0)71 434 0887/0517 - Fax (0)71 434 0269

EGM ARCHITECTEN BV — 115

Laan der Verenigde Naties 9
Postbus 298
3300 AG Dordrecht, Holland
☎ 078 330660 - Fax 078 140071

EPR DESIGN LIMITED — 117

56-62 Wilton Road
London SW1V 1DE, England
☎ (0)71 834 2299 - Fax (0)71 834 7524
Tx: 917 940 PRLON G

ÉRIC LIEURÉ — 119

89, fg St-Antoine
75011 Paris, France
☎ 1 43 42 39 49 - Fax 1 43 45 08 62

FITCH-RS DESIGN CONSULTANTS — 121

Porters South, 4 Crinan Street
London N1 9UE, England
☎ (0)71 278 7200 - Fax (0)71 833 1014

FURNEAUX STEWART — 123

24 Beaumont Mews
London W1N 3 LN, England
☎ (0)71 935 5724 - Fax (0)71 486 0304

RETAILING
COMMERCES DE DÉTAIL
NEGOZI
HANDELSUNTERNEHMEN
COMMERCIOS AL DETALLE

ARCHITRAL 71

28, rue Broca
75005 Paris, France
☎ 1 45 35 04 04 - Fax 1 43 36 38 98

ARTRIUM SARL 73

43, rue Monge
75005 Paris, France
☎ 1 43 26 47 80 - Fax 1 46 34 07 69
Tx: 219 000 + Q 860 38 ARTRIUM

ASYMÉTRIE 75

16, rue des Minimes
75003 Paris, France
☎ 1 43 56 22 20 - Fax 1 43 56 75 67

ATELIER JEAN-LUC CÉLEREAU 77

13-15, rue de la Verrerie
75004 Paris, France
☎ 1 40 29 95 05 - Fax 1 40 29 00 96

BDFS GROUP RETAIL & LEISURE LTD 79

41-43, Mitchell Street
London EC1V 3QD, England
☎ (0)71 253 6172 - Fax (0)71 608 2155

B.E.D. 81

50-54, rue de Silly
92513 Boulogne-Billancourt Cedex, France
☎ 1 49 09 75 75 - Fax 1 49 09 73 79

BERBESSON RACINE ET ASSOCIÉS 85

1, villa Juge
75015 Paris, France
☎ 1 45 77 87 48 - Fax 1 45 77 78 34

BIAIX S.A. ARCHITECTURA INTERIOR 87

Rambla Cataluña No. 90
08008 Barcelona, Spain
☎ (9)3 215 8967 - Fax (9)3 487 2810

BORN & STRUKAMP MESSEBAU GmbH 153

Grossenbaumer Weg 9
4000 Düsseldorf 30, Germany
☎ (0)211 411025 - Fax (0)211 424053

BRIGITTE DUMONT DE CHASSARD S.A. 89

108, rue Vieille-du-Temple
75003 Paris, France
☎ 1 42 77 06 50 - Fax 1 42 77 65 70

BUREAU D'ÉTUDES ARCHITECTURALES 91
BACHOUD HECHT

6 bis, rue Leconte-de-Lisle
75016 Paris, France
☎ 1 45 20 78 04 - Fax 1 45 20 60 62

C.S.I.A. CHRISTOPHE SEGUIN 93
INTERNATIONAL ART

27, rue Buffault
75009 Paris, France
☎ 1 42 81 38 05

CABINET AARKA 95

1, rue Theodule-Ribot
75017 Paris, France
☎ 1 47 66 33 64 - Fax 1 48 88 93 05

CONCEPT DESIGN GROUP, INC 97

615 Piikoi street - Suite 1406
Honolulu, Hawaii 96814, United States
☎ 808 523 7630 - Fax 808 531 1706

CORAME 99

5, bd Poissonnière
75002 Paris, France
☎ 1 42 36 19 91 - Fax 1 42 36 28 28

COVELL MATTHEWS WHEATLEY 101
ARCHITECTS LIMITED

19 Bourdon Place
London W1X 9HZ, England
☎ (0)71 409 2444 - Fax (0)71 493 8998

CRABTREE HALL PROJECTS LIMITED 103

70 Crabtree Lane
London SW6 6 LT, England
☎ (0)71 381 8755 - Fax (0)71 385 9575

DECO STIL S.A. 105

c/o Santa Ana, 2
08002 Barcelona, Spain
☎ (9)3 301 02 48/90 - (9)3 301 00 05 - Fax (9)3 412 33 38

DESIGN HOUSE 109
CONSULTANTS LTD

120 Parkway, Camden Town
London NW1 7AN, England
☎ (0)71 482 2815 - Fax (0)71 267 7587

DESIGN INTERNATIONAL 111
D.I. DESIGN & DEVELOPMENT
CONSULTANTS LIMITED

12 Dryden Street, Covent Garden
London WC2E 9NA, England
☎ (0)71 836 1853 - Fax (0)71 379 4727

DESIGN SOLUTION 113

20 Kingly Court
London W1R 5LE, England
☎ (0)71 434 0887/0517 - Fax (0)71 434 0269

EGM ARCHITECTEN BV 115

Laan der Verenigde Naties 9
Postbus 298
3300 AG Dordrecht, Holland
☎ (0)78 330 660 - Fax (0)78 140 071

EPR DESIGN LIMITED 117

56-62 Wilton Road
London SW1V 1DE, England
☎ (0)71 834 2299 - Fax (0)71 834 7524

FITCH-RS DESIGN CONSULTANTS 121

Porters South, 4 Crinan Street
London N1 9UE, England
☎ (0)71 278 7200 - Fax (0)71 833 1014

FURNEAUX STEWART 123

24 Beaumont Mews
London W1N 3 LN, England
☎ (0)71 935 5724 - Fax (0)71 486 0304

GMW PARTNERSHIP 125

PO Box 1613
239 Kensington High Street
London W8 6SL, England
☎ (0)71 937 8020 - Fax (0)71 937 5815

HART - LABORDE 127

174 avenue Charles-de-Gaulle
92220 Neuilly-sur-Seine, France
☎ 1 42 24 76 89 - Fax 1 47 45 50 42

HIDDE CONSULTANTS 129

Herengracht 162
1016 BP Amsterdam, Holland
☎ (0)20 38 21 37 - Fax (0)20 38 21 38

HODGE ASSOCIATES LIMITED 131

3 Lambton Place
London W11 2SH, England
☎ (0)71 727 8600 - Fax (0)71 727 6195

INTERIOR CONSULTANCY SERVICES LTD 133

Tyttenhanger House
St Albans, Herts AL4 OPG, England
☎ (0)727 23633 - Fax (0)727 26488
Tx: 299 169 JAYBEE G

JOHN HERBERT PARTNERSHIP Ltd 137

8 Berkeley Road, Primrose Hill
London NW1 8YR, England
☎ (0)71 722 3932 - Fax (0)71 586 7048

JON GREENBERG & ASSOCIATES INC 139

2338 Coolidge Highway
Berkley, Mich. 48072, United States
☎ 313 548 8080 - Fax 313 548 4640

McCOLL GROUP INTERNATIONAL 145

64 Wigmore Street
London W1H 9DJ, England
☎ (0)71 935 4788 - Fax (0)71 935 0865

MICHAEL PETERS GROUP, RETAIL ARCHITECTURE AND INTERIORS 147

3 Olaf Street, Holland Park
London W11 4BE, England
☎ (0)71 229 3424 - Fax (0)71 221 7720

PD DESIGN COMPANY LIMITED 149

The Grange, Wigston
Leicester LE8 1NN, England
☎ (0)533 810 018 - Fax (0)533 813 010

PENNINGTON ROBSON LTD 151

Tea Warehouse, 10A Lant Street
London SE1 1QR, England
☎ (0)71 378 0671 - Fax (0)71 378 0531

PETER SCHMIDT VEIT MAHLMANN DESIGN GmbH 153

Badestrasse 19
2000 Hamburg 13, Germany
☎ (0)40 44 38 67/41 76 00 - Fax (0)40 44 68 30

PPH VOLUME 155

10, rue Duvergier
75019 Paris, France
☎ 1 40 35 43 45 - Fax 1 40 35 43 47

ROBERT BYRON ARCHITECTS 159

78 Fentiman Road
London SW8 1LA, England
☎ (0)71 735 0648 - Fax (0)71 735 1843

RSCG SOPHA DESIGN 163

8, rue Rouget de Lisle
92130 Issy-les-Moulineaux, France
☎ 1 40 93 93 94 - Fax 1 46 62 60 72

SHEPPARD ROBSON 165

77 Parkway, Camden Town
London NW1 7PU, England
☎ (0)71 485 4161 - Fax (0)71 267 3861

PUBLIC AND INSTITUTIONAL
ÉTABLISSEMENTS PUBLICS INSTITUTIONNELS
ISTITUZIONI ED ENTI PUBBLICI
ÖFFENTLICHEN GEBÄUDE UND INSTITUTIONEN
ESTABLECIMIENTOS PÚBLICOS INSTITUCIONALES

ARTRIUM SARL 73

43, rue Monge
75005 Paris, France
☎ 1 43 26 47 80 - Fax : 1 46 34 07 69
Tx 219 000 + Q86038 ARTRIUM

ASYMÉTRIE 75

16, rue des Minimes
75003 Paris, France
☎ 1 43 56 22 20 - Fax 1 43 56 75 67

ATELIER JEAN-LUC CÉLEREAU 77

13-15, rue de la Verrerie
75004 Paris, France
☎ 1 40 29 95 05 - Fax 1 40 29 00 96

BDFS GROUP RETAIL & LEISURE 79
LTD

41-43 Mitchell Street
London EC1V 3QD, England
☎ (0)71 253 6172 - Fax (0)71 608 2155

B.E.D. 81

50-54, rue de Silly
92513 Boulogne-Billancourt Cedex, France
☎ 49 01 97 57 5 - 1 49 09 73 79

BUREAU D'ÉTUDES 91
ARCHITECTURALES BACHOUD HECHT

6 bis, rue Leconte-de-Lisle
75016 Paris, France
☎ 1 45 20 78 04 - Fax 1 45 20 60 62

C.S.I.A. CHRISTOPHE SEGUIN 93
INTERNATIONAL ART

27, rue Buffault
75009 Paris, France
☎ 1 42 81 38 05

CABINET AARKA 95

1, rue Théodule-Ribot
75017 Paris, France
☎ 1 47 66 33 64 - Fax 1 48 88 93 05

CORAME 99

5, bd Poissonnière
75002 Paris, France
☎ 1 42 36 19 91 - Fax 1 42 36 28 28

COVELL MATTHEWS WHEATLEY 101
ARCHITECTS LIMITED

19 Bourdon Place
London W1X 9HZ, England
☎ (0)71 409 2444 - Fax (0)71 493 8998

CRABTREE HALL PROJECTS 103
LIMITED

70 Crabtree Lane
London SW6 6LT, England
☎ (0)71 381 8755 - Fax (0)71 385 9575

DESIGN ARCHITECTURAL 107

15 bis, rue du Général-de-Gaulle
94480 Ablon-sur-Seine, France
☎ 1 45 97 43 41 - Fax 1 45 97 27 52

EGM ARCHITECTEN BV 115

Laan der Verenigde Naties 9
Postbus 298
3300 AG Dordrecht, Holland
☎ (0)78 33 06 60 - Fax (0)78 14 00 71

EPR DESIGN LIMITED 117

56-62 Wilton Road
London SW1V 1DE, England
☎ (0)71 834 2299 - Fax (0)71 834 7524

ÉRIC LIEURÉ 119

89, fg St-Antoine
75011 Paris, France
☎ 1 43 42 39 49 - Fax 1 43 45 08 62

FITCH-RS DESIGN CONSULTANTS 121

Porters South
4 Crinan Street
London N1 9UE, England
☎ (0)71 278 7200 - Fax (0)71 833 1014

FURNEAUX STEWART 123

24 Beaumont Mews
London W1N 3 LN, England
☎ (0)71 935 5724 - Fax (0)71 486 0304

GMW PARTNERSHIP 125

PO Box 1613
239 Kensington High Street
London W8 6SL, England
☎ (0)71 937 8020 - Fax (0)71 937 5815

HART - LABORDE 127

174, avenue Charles-de-Gaulle
92000 Neuilly-sur-Seine, France
☎ 1 46 24 76 89 - Fax 1 47 45 50 42

HIDDE CONSULTANTS 129

Herengracht 162
1016 BP Amsterdam, Holland
☎ (0)20 38 21 37 - Fax (0)20 38 21 38

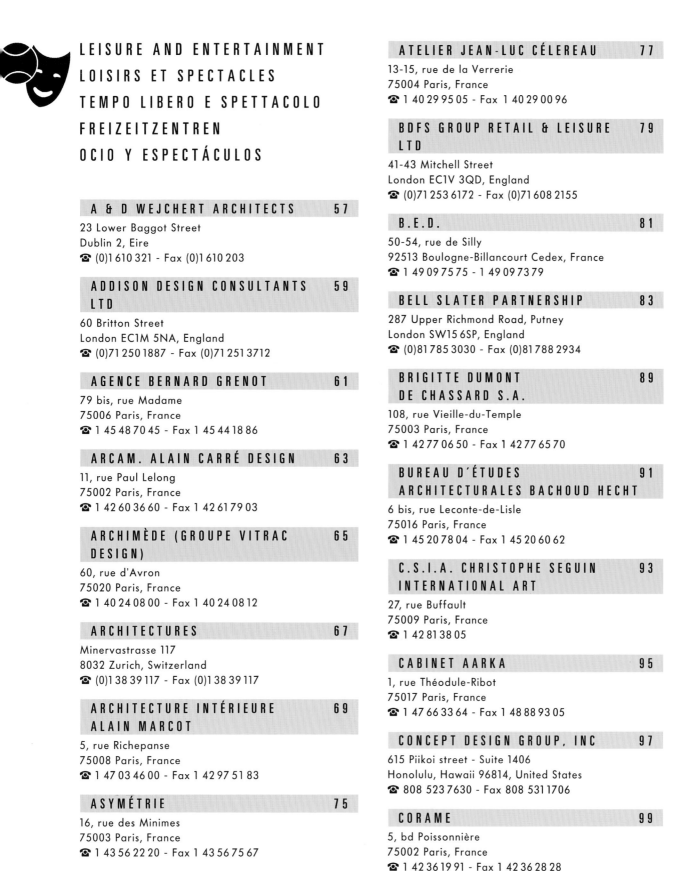

LEISURE AND ENTERTAINMENT
LOISIRS ET SPECTACLES
TEMPO LIBERO E SPETTACOLO
FREIZEITZENTREN
OCIO Y ESPECTÁCULOS

A & D WEJCHERT ARCHITECTS 57
23 Lower Baggot Street
Dublin 2, Eire
☎ (0)1 610 321 - Fax (0)1 610 203

ADDISON DESIGN CONSULTANTS LTD 59
60 Britton Street
London EC1M 5NA, England
☎ (0)71 250 1887 - Fax (0)71 251 3712

AGENCE BERNARD GRENOT 61
79 bis, rue Madame
75006 Paris, France
☎ 1 45 48 70 45 - Fax 1 45 44 18 86

ARCAM. ALAIN CARRÉ DESIGN 63
11, rue Paul Lelong
75002 Paris, France
☎ 1 42 60 36 60 - Fax 1 42 61 79 03

ARCHIMÈDE (GROUPE VITRAC DESIGN) 65
60, rue d'Avron
75020 Paris, France
☎ 1 40 24 08 00 - Fax 1 40 24 08 12

ARCHITECTURES 67
Minervastrasse 117
8032 Zurich, Switzerland
☎ (0)1 38 39 117 - Fax (0)1 38 39 117

ARCHITECTURE INTÉRIEURE ALAIN MARCOT 69
5, rue Richepanse
75008 Paris, France
☎ 1 47 03 46 00 - Fax 1 42 97 51 83

ASYMÉTRIE 75
16, rue des Minimes
75003 Paris, France
☎ 1 43 56 22 20 - Fax 1 43 56 75 67

ATELIER JEAN-LUC CÉLEREAU 77
13-15, rue de la Verrerie
75004 Paris, France
☎ 1 40 29 95 05 - Fax 1 40 29 00 96

BDFS GROUP RETAIL & LEISURE LTD 79
41-43 Mitchell Street
London EC1V 3QD, England
☎ (0)71 253 6172 - Fax (0)71 608 2155

B.E.D. 81
50-54, rue de Silly
92513 Boulogne-Billancourt Cedex, France
☎ 1 49 09 75 75 - 1 49 09 73 79

BELL SLATER PARTNERSHIP 83
287 Upper Richmond Road, Putney
London SW15 6SP, England
☎ (0)81 785 3030 - Fax (0)81 788 2934

BRIGITTE DUMONT DE CHASSARD S.A. 89
108, rue Vieille-du-Temple
75003 Paris, France
☎ 1 42 77 06 50 - Fax 1 42 77 65 70

BUREAU D'ÉTUDES ARCHITECTURALES BACHOUD HECHT 91
6 bis, rue Leconte-de-Lisle
75016 Paris, France
☎ 1 45 20 78 04 - Fax 1 45 20 60 62

C.S.I.A. CHRISTOPHE SEGUIN INTERNATIONAL ART 93
27, rue Buffault
75009 Paris, France
☎ 1 42 81 38 05

CABINET AARKA 95
1, rue Théodule-Ribot
75017 Paris, France
☎ 1 47 66 33 64 - Fax 1 48 88 93 05

CONCEPT DESIGN GROUP, INC 97
615 Piikoi street - Suite 1406
Honolulu, Hawaii 96814, United States
☎ 808 523 7630 - Fax 808 531 1706

CORAME 99
5, bd Poissonnière
75002 Paris, France
☎ 1 42 36 19 91 - Fax 1 42 36 28 28

COVELL MATTHEWS WHEATLEY ARCHITECTS LIMITED 101

19 Bourdon Place
London W1X 9HZ, England
☎ (0)71 409 2444 - Fax (0)71 493 8998

CRABTREE HALL PROJECTS LIMITED 103

70 Crabtree Lane
London SW6 6LT, England
☎ (0)71 381 8755 - Fax (0)71 385 9575

DESIGN ARCHITECTURAL 107

15 bis, rue du Général-de-Gaulle
94480 Ablon-sur-Seine, France
☎ 1 45 97 43 41 - Fax 1 45 97 27 52

DESIGN HOUSE CONSULTANTS LTD 109

120 Parkway - Camden Town
London NW1 7AN, England
☎ (0)71 482 2815 - Fax (0)71 267 7587

DESIGN INTERNATIONAL D.I. DESIGN & DEVELOPMENT CONSUTLANTS LIMITED 111

12 Dryden Street - Covent Garden
London WC2E 9NA, England
☎ (0)71 836 1853 - Fax (0)71 379 4727

DESIGN SOLUTION 113

20 Kingly Court
London W1R 5LE, England
☎ (0)71 434 0887/0517 - Fax (0)71 434 0269

EGM ARCHITECTEN BV 115

Laan der Verenigde Naties 9
Postbus 298
3300 AG Dordrecht, Holland
☎ (0)78 330 660 - Fax (0)78 140 071

EPR DESIGN LIMITED 117

56-62 Wilton Road
London SW1V 1DE, England
☎ (0)71 834 2299 - Fax (0)71 834 7524

FITCH-RS DESIGN CONSULTANTS 121

Porters South, 4 Crinan Street
London N1 9UE, England
☎ (0)71 278 7200 - Fax (0)71 833 1014

GMW PARTNERSHIP 125

PO Box 1613
239 Kensington High Street
London W8 6SL, England
☎ (0)71 937 8020 - Fax (0)71 937 5815

HART - LABORDE 127

174, avenue Charles-de-Gaulle
92000 Neuilly-sur-Seine, France
☎ 1 46 24 76 89 - Fax 1 47 45 50 42

HIDDE CONSULTANTS 129

Herengracht 162
1016 BP Amsterdam, Holland
☎ (0)20 38 21 37 - Fax (0)20 38 21 38

INTERIOR CONSULTANCY SERVICES LTD 133

Tyttenhanger House
St Albans, Herts AL4 OPG, England
☎ (0)727 23633 - Fax (0)727 26488
Tx 299169 JAYBEE G

INTRADESIGN INC 135

910 North La Cienega Boulevard
Los Angeles, CA 90069, United States
☎ 213 652 6114 - Fax 213 652 6945

JOHN HERBERT PARTNERSHIP LTD 137

8 Berkeley Road - Primrose Hill
London NW1 8YR, England
☎ (0)71 722 3932 - Fax (0)71 586 7048

JON GREENBERG & ASSOCIATES INC 139

2338 Coolidge Highway
Berkley, Mich. 48072, United States
☎ 313 548 8080 - Fax 313 548 4640

McCOLL GROUP INTERNATIONAL 145

64 Wigmore Street
London W1H 9DJ, England
☎ (0)71 935 4788 - Fax (0)71 935 0865

MICHAEL PETERS GROUP, RETAIL ARCHITECTURE AND INTERIORS 147

3 Olaf Street, Holland Park
London W11 4BE, England
☎ (0)71 229 3424 - Fax (0)71 221 7720

HOTELS AND RESTAURANTS
HÔTELS ET RESTAURANTS
HOTEL E RISTORANTI
HOTELS UND RESTAURANTS
HOTELES Y RESTAURANTES

BELL SLATER PARTNERSHIP 83

287 Upper Richmond Road, Putney
London SW15 6SP, England
☎ (0)81 785 3030 - Fax (0)81 788 2934

BRIGITTE DUMONT 89
DE CHASSARD S.A.

108, rue Vieille-du-Temple
75003 Paris, France
☎ 1 42 77 06 50 - Fax 1 42 77 65 70

BUREAU D'ÉTUDES 91
ARCHITECTURALES BACHOUD HECHT

6 bis, rue Leconte-de-Lisle
75016 Paris, France
☎ 1 45 20 78 04 - Fax 1 45 20 60 62

CONCEPT DESIGN GROUP, INC 97

615 Piikoi street - Suite 1406
Honolulu, Hawaii 96814, United States
☎ 808 523 7630 - Fax 808 531 1706

CORAME 99

5, bd Poissonnière
75002 Paris, France
☎ 1 42 36 19 91 - Fax 1 42 36 28 28

COVELL MATTHEWS WHEATLEY 101

19 Bourdon Place
London W1X 9HZ, England
☎ (0)71 493 8998 - Fax (0)71 493 8998

CRABTREE HALL PROJECTS 103
LIMITED

70 Crabtree Lane
London SW6 6LT, England
☎ (0)71 381 8755 - Fax (0)71 385 9575

DESIGN HOUSE CONSULTANTS Ltd 109

120 Parkway, Camden Town
London NW1 7AN, England
☎ (0)71 482 2815 - Fax (0)71 267 7587

DESIGN INTERNATIONAL 111
D.I. DESIGN & DEVELOPMENT
CONSUTLANTS LIMITED

12 Dryden Street, Covent Garden
London WC2E 9NA, England
☎ (0)71 836 1853 - Fax (0)71 379 4727

DESIGN SOLUTION 113

20 Kingly Court
London W1R 5LE, England
☎ (0)71 434 0887/0517 - Fax (0)71 434 0269

EGM ARCHITECTEN BV 115

Laan der Verenigde Naties 9
Postbus 298
3300 AG Dordrecht, Holland
☎ (0)7 833 06 60 - Fax (0)7 814 00 71

EPR DESIGN LIMITED 117

56-62 Wilton Road
London SW1V 1DE, England
☎ (0)71 834 2299 - Fax (0)71 834 7524

FITCH-RS DESIGN CONSULTANTS 121

Porters South, 4 Crinan Street
London N1 9UE, England
☎ (0)71 278 7200 - Fax (0)71 833 1014

GMW PARTNERSHIP 125

PO Box 1613
239 Kensington High Street
London W8 6SL, England
☎ (0)71 937 8020 - Fax (0)71 937 5815

HART - LABORDE 127

174, avenue Charles-de-Gaulle
92000 Neuilly-sur-Seine, France
☎ 1 46 24 76 89 - Fax 1 47 45 50 42

HIDDE CONSULTANTS 129

Herengracht 162
1016 BP Amsterdam, Holland
☎ (0)20 38 21 37 - Fax (0)20 38 21 38

INTERIOR CONSULTANCY 133
SERVICES LTD

Tyttenhanger House
St Albans, Herts AL4 OPG, England
☎ (0)727 23633 - Fax (0)727 26488
Tx 299 169 JAYBEE G

INTRADESIGN INC. 135

910 North La Cienega Boulevard
Los Angeles, CA 90069, United States
☎ 213 652 6114 - Fax 213 652 6945

JOHN HERBERT PARTNERSHIP 137
LTD

8 Berkeley Road, Primrose Hill
London NW1 8YR, England
☎ (0)71 722 3932 - Fax (0)71 586 7048

JON GREENBERG & ASSOCIATES 139
INC

2338 Coolidge Highway
Berkley, Mich. 48072, United States
☎ 313 548 8080 - Fax 313 548 4640

EXHIBITIONS AND TRADE FAIRS
EXPOSITIONS ET GALERIES
FIERE E MOSTRE
MESSESTÄNDE UND GALERIEN
ESPOSICIONES Y GALERIÁS

FURNEAUX STEWART — 123

24 Beaumont Mews
London W1N 3 LN, England
☎ (0)71 935 5724 - Fax (0)71 486 0304

GMW PARTNERSHIP — 125

PO Box 1613
239 Kensington High Street
London W8 6SL, England
☎ (0)71 937 8020 - Fax (0)71 937 5815

HART - LABORDE — 127

174, avenue Charles-de-Gaulle
92000 Neuilly-sur-Seine, France
☎ 1 46 24 76 89 - Fax 1 47 45 50 42

HIDDE CONSULTANTS — 129

Herengracht 162
1016 BP Amsterdam, Holland
☎ (0)20 38 21 37 - Fax (0)20 38 21 38

INTERIOR CONSULTANCY SERVICES LTD — 133

Tyttenhanger House, St Albans
Herts AL4 OPG, England
☎ (0)72 723 633 - Fax (0)72 726 488
Tx 299 169 JAYBEE G

JON GREENBERG & ASSOCIATES INC — 139

2338 Coolidge Highway
Berkley, Mich. 48072, United States
☎ 313 548 8080 - Fax 313 548 4640

McCOLL GROUP INTERNATIONAL — 145

64 Wigmore Street
London W1H 9DJ, England
☎ (0)71 935 4788 - Fax (0)71 935 0865

MICHAEL PETERS GROUP, RETAIL ARCHITECTURE AND INTERIORS — 147

3 Olaf Street - Holland Park
London W11 4BE, England
☎ (0)71 229 3424 - Fax (0)71 221 7720

PD DESIGN COMPANY LIMITED — 149

The Grange, Wigston
Leicester LE8 1NN, England
☎ (0)533 810 018 - Fax (0)533 813 010

PETER SCHMIDT VEIT MAHLMANN DESIGN GmbH — 153

Badestrasse 19
2000 Hamburg 13, Germany
☎ (0)40 44 38 67 / 41 76 00 - Fax (0)40 44 68 30

PPH VOLUME — 155

10, rue Duvergier
75019 Paris, France
☎ 1 40 35 43 45 - Fax 1 40 35 43 47

RSCG SOPHA DESIGN — 163

8, rue Rouget de Lisle
92130 Issy-les-Moulineaux, France
☎ 1 40 93 93 94 - Fax 1 46 62 60 72

SIEGER DESIGN — 167

Schloss Harkotten
4414 Sassenberg 2, Germany
☎ (0)54 26 27 96 / 2816 - Fax (0)54 26 38 75

SIMONI INTERIEUR N.V. — 169

Hentjenslaan 9A
3511 Kuringen Hasselt, Belgium
☎ (0) 11 25 35 02 - Fax (0) 11 87 21 00

STUDIO 2A S.A.S. — 173

Via Novara 13
20013 Magenta
Milan, Italy
☎ (0)2 979 3177 - Fax (0)2 979 4276

ttsp — 175

90-98 Goswell Road
London EC1V 7DB, England
☎ (0)81 980 4400 - Fax (0)81 981 6417

TRICKETT ASSOCIATES/ TRICKETT & WEBB — 181

The Factory, 84 Marchmont Street
London WC1N 1HE, England
☎ (0)71 388 6586 - Fax (0)71 387 4287

WHITE DESIGN — 183

Box 2502
40317 Göteborg, Sweden
☎ 31 173 460 - Fax 31 114 642

WOLFF OLINS/HAMILTON — 185

22 Dukes Road
London WC1R 9AB, England
☎ (0)71 387 0891 - Fax (0)71 388 2460

CHEQUEPOINT : Comptoirs de change Paris/province. Aménagement de 15 agences.

PRIMFLEUR : Magasin de fleurs à Paris 1000 m².

DESLEGAN : Agence de publicité à Courbevoie Siège social.

MIKROS Informatique : Aménagement du siège social à Boulogne-Billancourt.

THOMSON : Centre de séminaires et extension du bâtiment aux Mesnuls (Yvelines).

THOMSON : Centre de séminaires et extension du bâtiment aux Mesnuls (Yvelines).

CRÉDIT AGRICOLE : Image de marque des agences (IdF). Réalisation de 60 agences.

DESLEGAN : Agence de publicité à Courbevoie. Immeuble de bureaux.

ACR ARCHITECTURE INTÉRIEURE

HEAD OFFICE

36, boulevard de la Bastille
75012 Paris
☎ 1 43 40 47 52 / 18 22
Fax 1 43 41 08 01

CONTACT

Christian Masselis
Architecte d'Intérieur
Michel Amouroux
Architecte d'Intérieur

SIZE OF COMPANY

Personnel : 10

KEY PERSONNEL

Martine Baillot *Responsable gestion*
Jean-Marie Hertig *Architecte DPLG*
Gilles Maurel *Architecte DPLG*
Philippe Mirailler *Architecte d'intérieur*

AREAS OF SPECIALISATION

40% 10% 30% 20%

RECENTS CLIENTS

Chèquepoint
Hôtel OPEN Juan-les-Pins
Hôtel OPEN Fréjus
Siège social SGE-SOGEA

COMPANY PROFILE

A full time team of interior designers, architects, Illustrators and animators.

We take great care to understand, analyse, and research the needs of our clients, and to meet their objectives.

We aim to maximise the coherence of the creative process right up to the final point of production.

Interior design is a key element of corporate visual identity and global communications. At A C R we feel it our duty to provide relevant solutions to organisations and to help those organisations to understand them clearly.

"Une équipe permanente d'Architectes d'Intérieur, Architectes, Coloristes et illustratrices animés :

– d'une préoccupation très attentive à comprendre, analyser, estimer les besoins et servir les objectifs fixés.

– du souci d'optimiser la cohérence du processus de conception jusqu'à la conclusion tangible de la réalisation.

L'architecture intérieure participe à l'identification visuelle et à la communication globale.

A C R se doit d'apporter aux entreprises et institutions les réponses pertinentes dans le domaine de leur savoir-faire, et le faire savoir.

H.D.M. Siège social

H.D.M. Siège social

H.D.M. Siège social

H.D.M. Siège social

Mairie de Paris

Mairie de Paris

ADSA + PARTNERS

HEAD OFFICE

74, rue du Faubourg-Saint-Antoine
75012 Paris
☎ 1 43 46 90 58
Fax 1 43 47 28 47

INTERNATIONAL OFFICES

U.M.I., Tokyo, Japan
☎ 478 88 77
Fax 478 88 11

B.M.E.S., New York, USA
☎ 212 737 35 25
Fax 212 737 36 47

KEY PERSONNEL

Marc Lebailly
Maïa Wodzislawska
Pierre Paulin
Roger Tallon
Jean-Pierre Grunfeld
Jean-Roger Rioux
Eric Zeller

SIZE OF COMPANY

Personnel: 60

AREAS OF SPECIALISATION

COMPANY PROFILE

Design management for strong and durable communication.

Design management is the answer to establishing a powerful, lasting identity.

Taking into account a company's particular background and positioning objectives, we manage in a coherent manner all aspects of corporate identity: graphics, product design and environmental design.

We contribute to a company's success in an increasingly competitive environment. We help strengthen its corporate identity through in-depth consistency and quality of design.

Our strength: the association of three top names in design. Pierre Paulin, Roger Tallon and Michel Schreiber all guarantee the great creative quality of the agency's services.

Notre vocation: Le Design Management pour une communication forte et durable. Le Design Management, c'est la réponse stratégique à toute volonté de communiquer et de s'inscrire de manière forte et durable dans son environnement.

Nous aidons l'entreprise à maîtriser et à gérer de façon cohérente, en adéquation avec sa culture et ses objectifs de positionnement, tous ses vecteurs d'identité: design graphique, design produit, design d'environnement.

Nous participons à la réussite de l'entreprise dans un univers de plus en plus concurrentiel en l'aidant à: affirmer sa personnalité par la différence, construire un système d'identité structuré, s'inscrire dans la pérennité.

Notre force: la grande qualité créative des prestations de l'agence est garantie par l'association de trois grands noms du design: Pierre Paulin, Roger Talon, Michel Schreiber.

ADDITIONAL INFORMATION

Notre savoir-faire: la synergie des compétences, la complémentarité des disciplines.

Nos départements sont autonomes mais travaillent en synergie afin d'assurer une parfaite cohérence à tous les vecteurs d'identité de l'entreprise ou de l'institution.

Études et communication, design graphique entreprise et institution, design graphique produit et marque: Ekonos, design d'environnement, design produit, design textile.

Lombard & Ulster Bank, Dublin, 1980

Fitzwilliam Lawn Tennis Club, Dublin, 1989

Aillwee Cave Visitors Centre, County Clare, 1979

Sports Centre, University College, Dublin, 1981

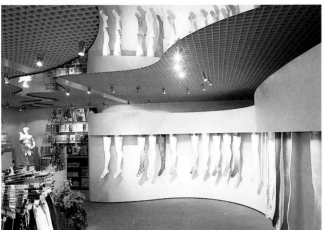

Office Building for Industrial Development Authority, Castletroy, 1983

Fogal, Dublin, 1987

A & D WEJCHERT ARCHITECTS

Standing from left: Hugh Maguire, Denis Connolly, Danuta Kornaus-Wejchert, Andrzej Wejchert, Margaret Hastings, Joo Tze Jong.
Seated: Catherine O'Carroll, Paul Roche, Martin Carey, Ruth Cummins, Patrick Fletcher

HEAD OFFICE

23 Lower Baggot Street
Dublin 2
☎ (0)1 610321
Fax (0)1 610203

AREAS OF SPECIALISATION

30%   20%   25%   10%

15%

CONTACT

Andrzej Wejchert *Partner*
Danuta Kornaus-Wejchert *Partner*
Patrick Fletcher *Associate*
Martin Carey *Associate*
Paul Roche *Associate*

KEY PERSONNEL

Andrzej Wejchert *Partner*
Danuta Kornaus-Wejchert *Partner*

SIZE OF COMPANY

Personnel: 16

RECENT CLIENTS

Irish Life Assurance plc
Green Property plc
Industrial Development Authority
Department of Health
Department of Education
FAS (Formerly AnCo)
Fogal
Fitzwilliam Lawn Tennis Club
I.T.I.

COMPANY PROFILE

A. & D. Wejchert, Architects is a Multidisciplinary Practice combining architecture, interior design and landscaping. We feel that it is essential to interweave both fabrics, the design of buildings with their interior image, as they compliment each other and enrich the overall effect. The same applies to landscaping which very often is part of the interior design.

We provide also the services of interior consultancy in already existing buildings. Our approach to design and its implementation is consistently orientated towards innovations, exploring the appropriate use of technology and materials for given conditions of context and client requirements. At the same time cost limits, in all our work, are strictly observed.

ADDITIONAL INFORMATION

Triennial Gold Medal RIAI for Administration at U.C.D.
"Europa Nostra" Diploma for Aillwee Cave Visitors Centre.
National Trust of Ireland Award 1984 Public Building Category: Sports Building, U.C.D.
Sunday Independent Arts Award for the outstanding achievement for industrial architecture for the AnCo Training Centre at Loughlinstown, County Dublin.
Commendation by the RIAI Gold Medal Jury for period 1977-1979 for Aillwee Cave Access Building, and for period 1980-82 for sport building V.C.D.

BP: world-wide retail identity; proto-type site, London, UK.

BP: New-Build "Station of the Future"; Milton Keynes, UK.

Lucky Stores: new supermarket concept: "Advantage", California, USA.

Citicorp: retail identity for Citicorp Savings Bank, USA.

House of Fraser: store re-design programme, Birmingham, UK (1986).

House of Fraser: Manchester, UK(1990).

Lucky Stores: "Advantage", California, USA.

Jobac - Mercasa: new supermarket concept: "Viva"; Valencia, Spain.

ADDISON DESIGN CONSULTANTS LIMITED

HEAD OFFICE

60 Britton Street
London Ec1 M 5NA
☎ 071 250 1887
Fax 071 251 3712

CONTACT

Kate Manasian

INTERNATIONAL OFFICES

Paris ☎ (33-1) 30 21 95 31
Contact: Christopher Weeden

Singapore ☎ (65) 225 37 66
Fax (65) 225 49 91
Contact: Jonathan Bonsey or
Lynn Hall

San Francisco ☎ (415) 956 7575
Fax (415) 433 8641
Contact: Rick Bragdon or
Margaret Widelock

New York ☎ (212) 532 6166
Fax (212) 532 3288
Contact: Richard Lewis or
Charles Norton

SIZE OF COMPANY

Personnel: 200 +.

AREAS OF SPECIALISATION

RECENT CLIENTS

As illustrated plus:
Abbey National Building Society, UK
American Isuzu, USA
Commercial Bank of Greece, Greece
Dickens and Jones, UK
Fiorucci, Europe
Ganz-Hunslet, Hungary
London underground Limited, UK
Marchmont, France
Moss Bros, UK
Pizza Hut inc, USA
Safeway, UK
Scotts Shopping Centre, Singapor
Shell - world-wide

COMPANY PROFILE

We see design as a process that uncovers what is unique about each of our clients.
As a leading worldwide design consultancy, we work in multi-disciplinary teams
with clients in all sectors of business, on large and small scale projects, to create
and design identities, products, printed materials, packaging and environments.
Our expertise covers a wide range of disciplines: architecture, ergonomics,
research and planning, name creation, graphic, industrial and interior design.
Our strength in problem solving is based on our experience and understanding
of the market, focusing our client's needs, and providing a creative, thoroughly
detailed, cost effective and relevant solution.
Our objective is to enhance the value of our client's activities and to contribute
to the quality of the world in which we all live.

Nous considérons le design comme un procédé capable de mettre en valeur la
singularité de chacun de nos clients.
Au rang des leaders internationaux dans le monde du design, nos équipes multidisciplinaire travaillent avec des clients de tous secteurs d'activité, sur des projets à petite et grande échelle. Notre expertise couvre un large éventail de disciplines : architecture, ergonomie, recherche et plannification, création de nom,
création graphique, design industriel et d'intérieur.
Notre force est basée sur notre expérience et notre compréhension du marché.
Notre attention est concentrée sur les besoins de notre clientèle et nous permet
d'apporter des solutions créatives, rentables, adéquates et amplement détaillées.
Notre objectif est d'ajouter de la valeur aux entreprises pour qui nous travail-
lons et de contribuer à la qualité du monde dans lequel nous vivons tous.

Vemos el diseño como un proceso que revela las cualidades únicas de nuestros clientes.
Somos una consultoría de diseño, de ámbito mundial y trabajamos en equipos
multidisciplinarios con clientes en todos los sectores profesionales y comerciales
en proyectos pequeños y grandes. Nuestra competencia abarca una extensa
gama de disciplinas, arquitectura, ergonomía, investigación y planificación,
creación de nombres, gráfica, diseño industrial y de interiores.
Nuestra capacidad para resolver problemas se basa en nuestra experiencia y
comprensión del mercado, enfocando sobre las necesidades de nuestros clientes
y proporcionando una solución creativa, muy detallada, relevante y económica-
mente eficaz.
Nuestro objetivo es anadir al valor de las actividades nuestros clientes y contri-
buir a la calidad del mundo en el que vivimos

Espace Présidence CBC à Paris-La Défense, 1990

Bureau Direction CBC, 1990

Banque B.U.O. avenue George-V, Paris, 1989

Banque B.U.O., 1990

Banque B.U.O. Poste de travail, 1989

Hall CBC La Défense, 1990

Banque Shearson-Lehman-Hutton, Paris 8ᵉ, 1989

Détails murs peints, parking SORIF Boulogne, 1989

AGENCE BERNARD GRENOT

Bernard Grenot

HEAD OFFICE

79 bis, rue Madame
75006 Paris
☎ (1) 45 48 70 45
Fax (1) 45 44 18 86

CONTACT

Bernard Grenot

KEY PERSONNEL

Bernard Grenot *Diplômé ENSAD*
OPQAI - SNAI
Christophe Kubicki *Architecte DPLG*

AREAS OF SPECIALISATION

RECENT CLIENTS

Banque de l'Union Occidentale
    (BUO), Paris
Compagnie Générale de Bâtiment et
    de Construction, La Défense
    (10 000 m²)
Hall Gaz de France, Paris
Aéroport de Bordeaux (restaurants)
Hôtel-restaurant 5 étoiles, Chester,
    Grande-Bretagne
Agence Spatiale Européenne, Paris
Banque Shearson-Lehman-Hutton,
    Paris (17 00 m²)
Apple Computer Lyon,
Compagnie Financière de CIC, Paris

COMPANY PROFILE

Design and realization of interiors (public spaces - private, professional offices).
Corporate identity, ergonomics and functionalism of working areas,
environmental aesthetics (offices - banks - reception areas).
Interior design and decor of prestige locations (hotels - restaurants).
Design of high-tech environments (airports - video - conference rooms).
Murals, interior and exterior wall colouring, frescos, polychromy (offices,
industrial and government buildings, schools).

L'agence Bernard Grenot : conception et réalisation des aménagements
intérieurs (locaux publics - locaux professionnels et privés).
Identité d'entreprise, image de firme, ergonomie et fonctionnalité des espaces
de travail, esthétique de l'environnement (bureaux - banques - espaces
d'accueil).
Architecture intérieure et décoration de cadres prestigieux (hôtels-restaurants).
Concepts d'espaces de haute technicité (Aéroports-Salles de visioconférences).

Animations murales et coloration de surfaces intérieures et extérieures - murs
peints - fresques - polychromies (tertiaire, bâtiments industriels, administratifs,
scolaires).

Daïmaru : Genius Gallery Kobe - Architecture et Image.

Galerie de Bohême : Show-room. Tokyo.

Lacoste : France et International.

Lissac : Architecture et Image.

Daïmaru : Genius Gallery Kobe - Architecture et Image.

Loto National : Concept France.

ARCAM S.A.

ARCHITECTURE & IMAGE

HEAD OFFICE

Arcam S.A.
Groupe Alain Carré
11, rue Paul Lelong
75002 Paris
☎ 1 42 60 36 60
Fax 42 61 79 03
Telex 215 661

KEY PERSONNEL

Marc Damème *Associate Director*
Patrice Blanchot *Development*

SIZE OF COMPANY

Personnel: 75

AREAS OF SPECIALISATION

RECENT CLIENTS

Lloyd Continental
Lacoste
Lissac
Daïmaru - Japon
Loto national

COMPANY PROFILE

As consultant specialists in the development and management of commercial space and areas, ARCAM can create and apply design concepts for France, as well as for international projects.

Part of the Alain Carre Design Group, ARCAM associates its experience and talent with other Group activities such as corporate identity, product design, packaging graphics and stands.

Composed of architects, interior designers and techniciens, ARCAM approaches and analyses each project globally. We are well known internationally, especially in Japan.

Conseil en développement et en management d'espaces commerciaux, ARCAM crée des concepts et les applique en France et à l'étranger.

Intégré au Groupe Alain Carré Design et Etudes, ARCAM associe ses compétences aux autres activités du Groupe : identité visuelle, produit packaging et stands.

Composé d'architectes, techniciens et architectes d'intérieur, ARCAM appréhende chaque projet dans sa globalité, notre méthodologie est reconnue à l'étranger, notamment au Japon.

ADDITIONAL INFORMATION

Alain Carré, Japon.

Groupe Vitrac Design - Siège social, Paris

N.M.P.P. - Siège social, Paris, 1990

N.M.P.P. - Siège social, Paris, 1990

Groupe Vitrac Design - Siège social, Paris

CIC Paris - Mise en valeur de façade de succursale, Paris, 1990

S.A.D. - Stand "Luz de Cidade", Paris, 1990

ARCHIMEDE

Juan Trindade
Directeur de Création

Sylvie Perrin
Études-Communication

Jean-Louis Husson
Responsable Commercial

HEAD OFFICE

Groupe Vitrac Design
60, rue d'Avron
75020 Paris
☎ 1 40 24 08 00
Fax 1 40 24 08 12

CONTACT

Sylvie Perrin
Jean-Louis Husson

INTERNATIONAL OFFICES

TOKYO : PRO INTER
☎ 81 34 81 80 31
Fax 81 34 81 80 33

MADRID : BFL S.A.
☎ 34 1 593 83 17
Fax 34 1 446 22 19

KEY PERSONNEL

Juan Trindade *Directeur de Création*
Jean-Louis Husson
Responsable Commercial
Sylvie Perrin *Études-Communication*

SIZE OF COMPANY

AREAS OF SPECIALISATION

 26 % 18 % 12 % 17 %
15 % 12 %

RECENT CLIENTS

CIC Paris, missions de conseil
Groupe André, façades "Halles aux Vêtements"
Air Inter, nouveau bâtiment "Réservation"
Nouvelles Messageries de la Presse Parisienne (NMPP), nouveau siège social
COPRA, immeuble (architecte : J.J. Ory)
Groupe Hoche, ensemble immobilier
Steria, signalétique siège social

COMPANY PROFILE

Archimede is the interior design division of the Vitrac design group. Its approach is to analyse in depth the client's identity and profile. Once the key elements have been defined, these are translated in terms of forms, volumes, materials and colours. Archimede undertakes the preliminary studies, sketches out the framework of the project, and organizes the implementation from concept to production.

Archimède est le département Design d'Environnement du Groupe Vitrac Design. La méthodologie de travail d'Archimede est fondée sur l'étude approfondie de l'identité de son client (entreprise ou institution) afin de définir les principaux messages qui seront traduits en termes de formes, volumes, matières, couleurs, etc. Archimède assure les études préalables, l'élaboration des lignes directrices du parti architectural et le développement du projet depuis sa conception jusqu'à sa réalisation.

ADDITIONAL INFORMATION

Juan Trindade was the winner of the 1990 Interior Design Oscar awarded by the S.N.A.I. (S.A.D.).
The Vitrac design group is structured to offer all the skills necessary for successful environmental and product design : (product design, graphic and packaging design, environmental design, large-scale modelling, styling, photography).

Juan Trindade a reçu en 1990 l'Oscar de la Meilleure Architecture Intérieure décerné par le S.N.A.I. dans le cadre du S.A.D.

Johannes Holenstein

HEAD OFFICE

Minervastrasse 117
8032 Zürich
Switzerland
☎ (0)1 38 39 117
Fax (0)1 38 39 117

INTERNATIONAL OFFICES

FRANCE
Château l'Escadrille
33390 Cars-Bordeaux
☎ 57 42 15 18

SAUDI-ARABIA
Abdel Rahmal Al Outaibi
Jeddah
☎ (2) 65 31 811

MALAYSIA
978, JLN-SS-15/4C,SBG-Jaya
47500 Petaling Jaya
☎ (03) 73 39 189

KEY PERSONNEL

Johannes Holenstein

AREAS OF SPECIALISATION

RECENT CLIENTS

Government of Kuwait
Royal Family of Saudi-Arabia
Marc Rich + Co
UTA-Airlines France
Electrowatt Engineering LTD

COMPANY PROFILE

Johannes Holenstein is the Swiss architect-designer whose name has joined the ranks of Omega, Cartier, Mercedes and Yves Saint Laurent. Succeeding these illustrious names he was awarded the Grand Prix Triomphe in Paris on 24th April 1986.

This "oscar of European aesthetics" is an award for excellence and supreme creation within the realm of European culture – this is what the former Nobel prize winner René Cassin intended – when in 1970 he founded the Comité de l'Excellence Européenne. The Internationally Active Holenstein received his lau-

Bureaux LE FIGARO, Paris.

Bureaux LE FIGARO, Paris.

ARCHITECTURE INTÉRIEURE
ALAIN MARCOT

Entrée Tour Perspectives SEMEA XV, Paris.

Accueil Thalassothérapie Sables-d'Olonne.

Entrée Tour Reflets SEMEA XV, Paris.

Accueil Hôtel Mercure, Sables-d'Olonne.

HEAD OFFICE

5, rue Richepanse
75008 Paris
☎ 1 47 03 46 00
Fax 1 42 97 51 83

CONTACT

Alain Marcot

KEY PERSONNEL

Mathilde Berger
Jean-Pierre Allouard
Michel Gauchet

SIZE OF COMPANY

Personnel PSVM : 10

AREAS OF SPECIALISATION

RECENT CLIENTS

Le Figaro
L'Indicateur Bertrand
Semea XV
Accor (Sofitel, Mercure)

COMPANY PROFILE

Tous les programmes qui traitent de l'aménagement et de l'organisation des espaces intérieurs nous passionnent. Donner à chaque projet son identité est notre souci prioritaire.

Notre compétence s'exerce également dans le suivi de la réalisation pour créer des lieux dans lesquels nos clients sont heureux de vivre et de travailler.

We are very enthusiastic about any project involving interior refurbishment and design. Our main aim is to give each project its own identity.

We are equally skilled in the implementation of our designs, ensuring that we create environments in which our clients are happy to live and work.

ADDITIONAL INFORMATION

Création de mobiliers.

Furniture Designers.

FNAC musique de l'Opéra-Bastille, Paris, 1990

FNAC musique de l'Opéra-Bastille, Paris, 1990

FNAC du CNIT, La Défense, Paris, 1989

Magasin Darty Rosny 2, Rosny-sous-Bois, 1988

Magasin Grand Optical La Défense, Paris, 1989

Siège social du groupe GPS La Défense, Paris, 1989

ARCHITRAL

Gérard Barrau
Président-Directeur Général

HEAD OFFICE

28, rue Broca
75005 Paris
☎ (1) 45 35 04 04
Fax (1) 43 36 38 98
Telex BARRAU 205 616

CONTACT

Gérard Barrau

KEY PERSONNEL

Gérard Barrau
Président-Directeur Général

SIZE OF COMPANY

Personnel : 60

AREAS OF SPECIALISATION

✐ 10%   ▢ 80%   ᛞ 10%

COMPANY PROFILE

A French company, and a leader in the environmental design field, ARCHITRAL realizes your company's projects and turns your marketing strategies into reality. Its services include :
1) Analysis of the potential (positioning of products, customer segmentation),
2) Merchandising study and development,
3) Creation of workable, high performance concepts,
4) Financial projections (investments and return on investments),
5) Commercial engineering,
6) Realization and general contracting of the project.

The 150 spaces conceived and realized by ARCHITRAL each year are our guarantee of a top level of service, combining creativity with a hard-headed practical approach. In order to achieve this, ARCHITRAL works to develop real partnerships with its clients, which prove to be both long lasting and productive.

Société française, leader dans le domaine du design d'environnement, ARCHITRAL concrétise les projets d'entreprise, et rend tangibles les stratégies marketing. Son intervention comprend :
1) l'analyse des potentialités (zone de chalandise, segmentation clientèle),
2) l'étude et la planification merchandising,
3) la création de concepts performants,
4) la prospective financière (investissements et retour sur investissements),
5) l'ingénierie commerciale,
6) la réalisation et la maîtrise d'œuvre des projets.

Les 150 espaces, conçus et réalisés chaque année, sont la garantie d'une prestation de haut niveau, prestation alliant créativité et rationalité. Pour ce faire, ARCHITRAL entretient avec ses clients une véritable relation de partenariat, qui s'inscrit dans les faits et dans la durée.

ADDITIONAL INFORMATION

Grand Prix du Design d'Environnement 89 (Stratégies) pour la FNAC du CNIT, La Défense Paris.
Winner of the Grand Prix du Design d'Environnement' 89 (stratégies) for the FNAC of the CNIT at La Défense, Paris.

Artrium, siège social, Paris, 1986

Operator TDF, aménagement d'un show-room CNIT-La Défense, 1989

Ferco-Liebert, aménagement d'un show-room CNIT-La Défense, 1989

ARTRIUM SARL

HEAD OFFICE

43, rue Monge
75005 Paris
☎ 1 43 26 47 80
Fax 1 46 34 07 69
Télex 219 000 + Q86038 ARTRIUM

CONTACT

Joumana Fayad
Adolphe Youssevitch

KEY PERSONNEL

Joumana Fayad *Gérante*
Adolphe Youssevitch *Directeur de Création*
Marielle Bapst *Chef de Projet*

AREAS OF SPECIALISATION

 50 % 20 % 10 % 20 %

RECENT CLIENTS

Vitrine de France
Facom
TDF - Operator TDF
Merlin-Gérin
Centre Botticelli

COMPANY PROFILE

A young, creative, motivated and high-achieving team of ESAG graduates form the heart of Artrium.

Our primary goal is to analyse and meet the client's needs on a custom-design basis.

The team's small size allows us to be flexible, efficient, and to believe passionately in every job we are responsible for.

Our special relationships with larger design companies have led and will continue to lead to improved synergy and a wider network of opportunities.

Artrium rassemble une jeune équipe de diplômés de l'ESAG. Elle met un point d'honneur, pour chaque étude, à l'analyse personnalisée des souhaits, besoins et objectifs de ses clients.

Son but principal est de concrétiser un compromis idéal, un partenariat abouti et permanent.

La taille d'Artrium, et les liens étroits développés avec des structures importantes dans le secteur du design d'environnement lui permettent de réagir avec souplesse et efficacité sur tous types de projets, et de les mener à bien depuis leur conception jusqu'à la réalisation.

Aegina, centre de soins esthétiques, Paris, 1985

Operator TDF, stand d'exposition, SICOB/SIRCOM, Paris, 1990

Clinique des Lilas

Magasin Alfredo Caral (Madrid)

Exposition Boucheron, Musée André Jaquemard

Magasin Christophe

Comité Colbert (centre Pompidou)

ASYMÉTRIE

HEAD OFFICE

16, rue des Minimes
75003 Paris
☎ 1 43 56 22 20

CONTACT

Bernard Fric

KEY PERSONNEL

Bernard Fric
Dominique Kelly

SIZE OF COMPANY

Personnel : 10

AREAS OF SPECIALISATION

RECENT CLIENTS

Louis Vuitton
Comité Colbert
Aérospatiale
Hermès
Boucheron
Espace Expansion
Boussac
Carrefour
Caisse des Dépôts
Groupe Expansion
Séville 92
Musée des Arts décoratifs
Christofle

COMPANY PROFILE

Interior architecture and design, specializing in commercial and public spaces, and the design of cultural exhibits.

Agence d'architecture intérieure et designer spécialisée dans le traitement des espaces commerciaux, public, et la conception d'expositions à thèmes culturels.

Exposition "La mode, une industrie de pointe," Musée des Sciences et Techniques

Parc des Expositions, Paris

Nouvelles Galeries, Orléans

Centre Bourse, Nouvelles Galeries, Marseille

Zone accueil, Salle de Conférences, Paris

Self-service, Paris

Centre de Thalassothérapie

ATELIER JEAN-LUC CELEREAU

Jean-Luc Celereau

HEAD OFFICE

13-15, rue de la Verrerie
75004 Paris
☎ 1 40 29 95 05
Fax 1 40 29 00 96

CONTACT

Jean-Luc Celereau

SIZE OF COMPANY

Personnel: 30

AREAS OF SPECIALISATION

RECENT CLIENTS

Catena
Drugstore, Neuilly
Horeto, Paris
Ministère de la Défense
Société Française des Nouvelles
    Galeries Réunies
Office International des Epizooties
Parc des Expositions de la porte de
    Versailles
Société des Ciments Français
Union Internationale des Chemins de
Fer
Vetecom-Telecom
Thorntons "martial" "sunset"
Sovedi

COMPANY PROFILE

The studio is run by a team of highly motivated young architects, interior architects and designers, under the direction of J.L. Celereau. They carry out integrated missions of design conception and management in most fields. Their cardinal rule is to meet aesthetic requirements using new technology, and sticking to the basic criteria: i.e. cost, quality, deadlines, feasibility.

Environmental design: industrial architecture, trade architecture, work space, exhibition space, home and living space.

Communication design: corporate identity, signage/logos, packaging.

Industrial design: transportation, furnishings for public spaces.

L'Atelier est constitué d'une équipe de jeunes architectes, architectes d'intérieur, designers, animée par J.L. Celereau. Celui-ci prend en charge des missions complètes de conception et maîtrise d'œuvre, en alliant l'exigence esthétique à la technologie des années futures, et en s'attachant au respect des critères fondamentaux: coût, qualité, délais, faisabilité.

Design environment: architecture industrielle, architecture commerciale, espace de travail, exposition, stand, habitation et cadre de vie.

Design industriel: transport, mobilier urbain.

Design communication: identité de l'entreprise, conditionnement, signalétique.

ADDITIONAL INFORMATION

Atelier Jean-Luc Celereau is currently the exclusive Design Studio for the retail chain: Nouvelles Galeries.

A determining factor in our success has been the use of computer aided design in all stages of conception and management. The Atelier's high standard in this technology resulted in a partnership in an Apple Video, "Conception and Design on Macintosh."

Prize-winner UGAP for school furnishings.

Fusion, London, 1990

Fusion, London, 1990

Fusion, London, 1990

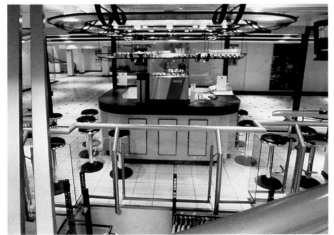

Fusion, London, 1990

BDFS GROUP
RETAIL & LEISURE Ltd

David Bromige   Stephen Barter

HEAD OFFICE

41-43 Mitchell Street
London EC1V 3QD
U.K.
☎ (0) 71 253 6172
Fax (0) 71 608 2155
Telex 21879 - 25247

CONTACT

David Bromige *Chairman*
Stephen Barter *Creative Director*

SIZE OF COMPANY

Personnel: 35

AREAS OF SPECIALISATION

RECENT CLIENTS

Ministry of Agriculture Fisheries
 & Food
Tower Centre, Blackpool
Walker Power
Fusion Retail
Brent Walker
Trusthouse Forte

COMPANY PROFILE

BDFS has behind it two decades of experience positioning products and services in the tough world of fast-moving consumer goods, creating brands and brand identities that have withstood the test of time.

Within BDFS, we have the research and visual auditing skills to ensure that we find and recognize the right opportunities, then the design and operational skills to help you realize them. It gives us the 360 degree vision that our retail and leisure clients need, and that our architecturally led competitors find difficult to match.

BDFS ha dietro di sè due decenni di esperienza nel piazzare beni e servizi sul mutevole e dinamico mercato dei beni di largo consumo, creando marchi e immagine che hanno resistito alla prova del tempo.

Abbiamo, nell'ambito della BDFS, i know-how di ricerca e di analisi visiva necessari per individuare e conoscere le migliori opportunità, nonchè le capacità grafiche ed operative in grado successivamente di realizzare quanto selezionato. Tutto questo ci garantisce la visione globale che sia i nostri clienti della distribuzione al dettaglio, sia quelli operanti nel tempo libero, necessitano e che i nostri concorrenti più orientati all'architettura hanno difficoltà a raggiungere.

BDFS kann auf zwei Jahrzehnte Erfahrung in der Positionierung von Produkten und Dienstleistungen zurückblicken – Positionierung in einer harten Welt schnellebiger und sich schnell umschlagender Verbrauchsgüter –, wobei BDFS Marken und Marken-identitäten kreiert hat, die sich dem Zahn der Zeit mit ERfolg widersetzt haben.

Unsere Firma, BDFS, verfügt über die notwendigen Forschungs- und visuellen Überprüfungsressourcen, um sicherzustellen, daß wir zunächst die richtigen Verwirklichung finden und erkennen; dann das Design, um dem Klienten alsdann mit operativem Talent bei der Möglichkeiten zur Seite zu stehen. So verschaffen wir uns jenen Rundblick um 360 Grad, den unsere Kundschaft im Einzelhandel und in der Freizeitbranche braucht, und an den unsere architektonisch geführten Wettbewerber nur schwer heranreichen können.

Adidas, conception and realization of an international chain store

NMPP, interior design and logotype for the French press leader

Concept, exterior façade, interior decor, logotype and brand identity.

Concept, interior view

Virgin Megastore, project management for the largest french record shop

Bull computer, design of a permanent showroom at Paris-La Défense

Opéra, interior decor for the offices of this advertising agency (meeting room)

Hotshop, interior decor for the offices of a packaging design agency (hall)

Bourjois an important P.O.S. design for one of the french cosmetics leaders

B.E.D.

Raymond Redon

Véronique Prieur-Laurent

Bertrand Verguin

HEAD OFFICE

50-54, rue de Silly
92513 Boulogne-Billancourt Cedex
☎ 49 09 75 75
Fax 49 09 73 79

CONTACT

Raymond Redon
Jérôme de la Grand'Rive

KEY PERSONNEL

Raymond Redon *Directeur Général*
Véronique Prieur-Laurent
Directrice Création
Bertrand Verguin *Directeur Production*

SIZE OF COMPANY

Personnel: 12

AREAS OF SPECIALISATION

 40%   40%  10% 10%

RECENT CLIENTS

Adidas, sport
Barbara Gould, cosmetics
Bourjois, cosmetics
Elancyl, cosmetics
Galenic, cosmetics
Bull, computers
Virgin Megastore, records
department store
NMPP, press chain stores
Concept, drugs and cosmetics
Comtesse du Barry, luxury food store
DMC Imagine, haberdashery
Etam, underwear
Descamps, linen chain store
Pingouin, wool chain store
Lacoste, sportswear
Ford, car industry
Finindice, bank
Grand-Bleu, advertising agency
Jardissimo, seedshops
La Fontaine au Chocolat,
luxury chocolat store
Lee Cooper, clothes
Silly-Bellevue Project, interior decor
for 24 societies

COMPANY PROFILE

Today, there are two major groups of players in our business: artistically oriented creators and designers who master the skills of marketing, research and consultancy, to create and organize a company's external image while respecting existing corporate identity.
We, at B.E.D., are designers, and as such contribute directly to our clients' success; over 6 000 productions have contributed to the accuracy of our statement.

ADDITIONAL INFORMATION

Member of ADC (Association Design Communication)
Prize-winner of the European competition for the Adidas Styles shops.

Character Hotels: Hotel & Country Club, Botley, 1990

Trusthouse Forte: Courtyard Restaurant, Kingston, 1986

Pier House Inns: Harvester Restaurant, Guildford, 1985

Character Hotels: Hotel & Country Club, Botley, 1990

THE BELL SLATER PARTNERSHIP

Alastair Bell
DA RIBA MCSD, Partner

David Slater
RIBA, Partner

HEAD OFFICE

287 Upper Richmond Road
Putney
London SW15 6SP
☎ (0) 81 785 30 30
Fax (0) 81 788 2934

CONTACT

Alastair Bell *DA RIBA MCSD, Partner*
David Slater RIBA, Partner

KEY PERSONNEL

Jim Hunt *Projects director*
Geoff Healey *Technical director*

SIZE OF COMPANY

Personnel : 16

AREAS OF SPECIALISATION

 20% 15% 65%

RECENT CLIENTS

Trusthouse Forte
Thistle Hotels
Character Hotels
Crest Hotels
Mecca Leisure
Young and Co Plc
Fuller Smith and Turner
Brands Hatch Leisure
Hotel Intercontinental
Quietwaters Club
Anchor Hotels
Baron Hotels and Leisure
Pier House Inns
Compass Healthcare Ltd
Barclays Bank Plc
Donovan Data Systems
International Thomson Publishing
Elemeta

COMPANY PROFILE

The Bell Slater Partnership is an experienced and uniquely qualified architectural and interior design practice offering a high standard of innovative and creative work. The practice has been built up to its present complement of 16 architectural and interior design staff since 1978 and is well regarded for its work in leisure, catering, hotel and office design. The partnership client list is testimony to its depth of experience in these and other fields.

Bell Slater understand a brief quickly and deliver a solution which addresses the entire problem, from concept to realisation, with close regard to programme constraints and cost controls. The client list testifies also to the success of the Bell Slater working philosophy – one that is refreshingly practical and devoid of pretension.

Trusthouse Forte: Clubhouse Restaurant, Farnborough, 1987

IGIN. Magasin prêt-à-porter, rue du Faubourg-Saint-Honoré, Paris

SCA Toyota Building. Création d'un siège social. 12000 m². Nagoya, Japon

BERBESSON RACINE ET ASSOCIÉS

APPLE COMPUTER. Création showroom. 400 m². Avenue de la Grande-Armée, Paris

COMMERZBANK. Siège social. 600 m². Place de l'Opéra, Paris

BEAUTIFUL. Agence de création graphique. Place du Panthéon, Paris

Gallery URBAN. Création musée privé. 3 000 m². Rond-point des Champs-Élysées Paris

HEAD OFFICE

1 villa Juge,
75015 Paris
☎ (1) 45 77 87 48
Fax (1) 45 77 78 34

CONTACT

Philippe Berbesson *Architecte DPLG -
Architecte d'intérieur*
Marie Racine
Architecte d'intérieur

KEY PERSONNEL

Daniel Le Pan *Chef d'agence*

AREAS OF SPECIALIZATION

SIZE OF COMPANY

Personnel : 8

RECENT CLIENTS

Aéroports de Paris
Apple Computer France
Babybotte/Beverly
Beautiful
Carrefour
Charles Jourdan
Commerzbank
Equipment
Euromercato
Gallery Urban
Groupama
Igin
Les Mercuriales
McKinsey
Magasin Vert
Pascal Morabito
Pryca
Société Générale
SCA Toyota Building
Young & Rubicam

COMPANY PROFILE

Interior design is a dynamic element of the firm's corporate identity programme, providing commercial identification as well as advertising image. Today, a client's commercial needs require interior design of exceptional quality if its marketing goals are to be attained.

Berbesson Racine et Associés are a team with varied experience and skills, able to assure a high level of expertise in :
• Architecture (building projects, administrative procedures, building permits)
• Interior design (design development, selection of colors and materials, graphics and signage)
• Furniture design (conceptual furniture design for specific programme requirements)
• Technical assistance (development of production methods, working drawings, cost control)
• Construction administration (construction supervision, schedule control)

Calzados Falgarona, Figueras (Girona)

Galeria Arte Lola Cerdan, Barcelona

Pass Difusion, Barcelona

Calzados Ferreres, Granollers

Modas Delta, Barcelona

Farmacia Maurici, Barcelona

BIAIX, S.A. - ARQUITECTURA INTERIOR

HEAD OFFICE

Rambla Cataluña n° 90
08008 Barcelona
☎ 3 215 89 67
Fax 3 487 28 10

CONTACT

Marta Reig Miró *Manager*

KEY PERSONNEL

Joan Antoni Mateo López
Design Manager
Antoni Tomás Bronchal
Artistic Manager
Carlos Mateo López
Design Manager

RECENT CLIENTS

Bambinos (childrens' fashion)
 Moda infantil
Choose-Me (haberdashery)
 Lenceria
Fabio Romano (mens fashion)
 Moda masculina
Forum (shoes)
 Calzados
Nuvol Dolç (confectionary)
 Golosinas
Planelles Donat (nougats)
 Turronería
Yacaré (shoes)
 Calzados

AREAS OF SPECIALISATION

COMPANY PROFILE

Biaix, S.A., ia a company consisting of professional people with more than 15 years of experience in interior design and implementation. The company was founded in 1986, and has already completed many projects in Catalonia.

We specialise in technical and commercial analysis, framing our recommendations within the context of the existing design.

Whilst meeting the demands of our local market we are very much aware of the new opportunities created by the imminent opening up of the European market.

BIAIX, S.A., es una empresa compuesta por profesionales con más de 15 años de experiencia en el diseño y montage de interiores, fundada en 1986, con numerosos trabajos realizados basicamente en el ámbito de Cataluña. Nuestra labor consiste principalmente en el asesoramiento técnico y comercial a nuestros clientes enmarcándolo en las tendencias actuales del diseño sin obviar las necesidades de nuestro mercado y la aproximación cada vez más inminente hacia una unidad Europea.

St Dupont Boutique, Paris. Shop front, with terrace in marble.

St Dupont Boutique, Paris Play of doors and mirrors in the changing rooms.

St Dupont Boutique, Paris. An element of the basic conception of the shop.

St Dupont Boutique, Paris. General view.

Château de la Grise. The atmosphere of the main drawing room.

Private house in the South of France. Detail.

Schroder Partenaires Paris. Director's office.

Schroder Partenaires Paris. Door detail.

Biennale des décorateurs: Grand Palais, 1988. Lauer's booth.

BRIGITTE DUMONT DE CHASSART SA

Brigitte Dumont de Chassart

HEAD OFFICE

108, rue Vieille-du-Temple
75003 Paris
☎ 42 77 06 50
Fax 42 77 65 70

CONTACT

Brigitte Dumont de Chassart

KEY PERSONNEL

Brigitte Dumont de Chassart

SIZE OF COMPANY

Personnel: 20

AREAS OF SPECIALISATION

 15% 15% 🎭 5% 🍷 55%
📖 10%

RECENT CLIENTS

Luxury service flats residences
  "Villa Corèse" Copra
  "Liberty" Kaufman et Broad
  "Orangerie" TAT Tours
  "Symphoniales" Capri
  "Espace Forbin" G.M.F.
Castle Hotels
  "Château de la Grise"
  Saumur, France
  "Château d'Ardrée" Tours, France
Shops
  "St Dupont Concept worldwide
  "Cèdre Rouge Conceptions"
Offices
  "B.A.I.I." place Vendôme, Paris
  "Schroder Partenaires"
  av. Franklin-Roosevelt, Paris
Private Houses
  Flat place des Vosges, Paris
  Properties in the south of France
  and the Loire Valley
Exhibition Stands
  Biennale of Design Editions
  Lelievre's show rooms

COMPANY PROFILE

For the past ten years the BDC Agency, with its talented team of about twenty designers, has defied all the odds. We have beaten hair raising deadlines and risen to impossible challenges in all the public and private sectors dealing with interior design, our overwhelming passion.

The Agency, with its well deserved reputation for luxury service flats, has now established as place of its own in numerous different fields such as castle hotels, luxury boutiques, offices, exhibition stands and renovations.

Our attractions are the use and colour of our materials (wood, fabrics and stone...), the density of our colours, and above all, our constant aim for perfection combined with respect for the project and its budget.

ADDITIONAL INFORMATION

Competitions won in 1988/1989:
• Worldwide concept of the new St Dupont "boutiques"
• A.G.F.: service flats residences "Les Symphoniales"
• Capri: service flats residences "Versailles Manèges"
• Axa: renovation of a building near the Champs-Elysées
• Pierre Invest: Club house of a residence in Belgium
• Adagio: shops in Paris and New York

Burger King (fast food), Centre Commercial, Bercy II

Burger King, Centre Commercial, Bercy

Haagen-Dazs (Glacier), place Victor-Hugo, Paris

Benlux (Duty free), rue de l'Échelle, Paris

Benlux (Duty free), rue de Rivoli, Paris

Benlux (Duty free), rue de Rivoli, Paris

Benlux (Duty free), rue de l'Échelle, Paris

Benlux (Duty free), rue de l'Échelle, Paris

Maison de l'Architecture, Conseil de l'Ordre des Architectes, Paris

Per Spook, Salon haute-couture, Paris

BUREAU D´ÉTUDES ARCHITECTURALES
BACHOUD-HECHT

B.E.A.

Jean-Louis Bachoud   Marc-Henri Hecht

HEAD OFFICE

6, bis rue Leconte-de-Lisle
75016 Paris, France
☎ 45 20 78 04
Fax 45 20 60 62
Telex 270 105 F

CONTACT

Marc-Henri Hecht
Jean Louis Bachoud

KEY PERSONNEL

Jean-Louis Bachoud
Ingénieur Arts et Métiers
Marc-Henri Hecht
Architecte d'Intérieur OPQAI
Jean-Marc Demoulin
Architecte DPLG
Dominique Deniau
Chef d'Agence

SIZE OF COMPANY

Personnel : 15

AREAS OF SPECIALISATION

RECENT CLIENTS

ORGANISMES PUBLICS
Villes de Franconville, Goussainville,
Nogent-sur-Marne, Poissy...
SERVICES
Chaînes Burger King, Haagen Dazs,
Léon de Bruxelles, Fimotel...
COUTURE - PRÊT-A-PORTER
Ted Lapidus, Louis Féraud, Per Spook,
Van Laack...
DUTY FREE
Benlux
RÉNOVATIONS IMMEUBLES HABITAT
et BUREAUX...
ARCHITECTURE
Immeubles à Nogent, Poissy, Paris...

COMPANY PROFILE

We aim to be partners to our clients. Their success has always meant expansion
for us. A shop, a shopping centre, an office block are places which lend themselves to special kinds of encounters by their very nature. Their design and construction must anticipate the client's evolving relationships with inhabitants and
passers-by. Because of this temporal dimension going beyond just architecture,
we have set ourselves a broader task: it starts with the conception of a design
and ends only when the result can be compared with the client's expectations.

Nous voulons être des partenaires pour nos clients. Leur réussite a toujours
entraîné notre expansion. Un magasin, un centre commercial, un immeuble d'activités, sont, par vocation, des lieux de communication privilégiés avec le public.
Leur conception et leur réalisation doivent intégrer l'évolution probable de leurs
relations avec le client, l'habitant, le passant. Nous avons pensé définir, en fonction de cette dimension temporelle où la seule architecture n'est plus suffisante,
une mission plus large qui commencerait à l'idée d'une création et s'achèverait à
la confrontation des résultats aux prévisions.

Agence Robert & Partners - Paris - © La Maison de Marie Claire - Dugied/Millet

Les Auditoriums de Joinville - © C.S.I.A.

Vidéo Day - Paris - © C.S.I.A.

Centre Culturel Français - Abidjan - © C.S.I.A.

C.S.I.A.
CHRISTOPHE SEGUIN INTERNATIONAL ART

Christophe Seguin

HEAD OFFICE

27 rue Buffault
75009 Paris
☎ 1 42 81 38 05

CONTACT

Christophe Seguin

AREAS OF SPECIALISATION

 40%   6%   15% 14%
25%

RECENT CLIENTS

Vidéo Day
Les Auditoriums de Joinville
Robert & Partners
French Connection
E.C.M. Joinville
Centre Culturel Français Abidjan
Real Bank
City Bank
Kiyi M'Bock Théâtre - Abidjan
Ministère de la Coopération et
   du Développement
Ministère des Affaires étrangères
M.N.H.N. Paris - Sahara/Sahel
Eurodisneyland

COMPANY PROFILE

C.S.I.A. creates comfortable and spacious areas tailored to each client, with a major emphasis on lighting and acoustics. Our attention to relevant decorative vocabulary renders spaces inviting and agreeable.

C.S.I.A. crée des milieux confortables et spacieux propres à chaque client, avec l'idée principale du confort lumineux et sonore. Le vocabulaire décoratif en découle naturellement et crée ainsi des espaces vivants et confortables.

ADDITIONAL INFORMATION

C.S.I.A. horizons and missions :
Architecture intérieure - Design - Scénographie - Stands - Expositions -
Conceptions graphiques.

Espace Rotonde - Cabinet immobilier Bignolais, Paris

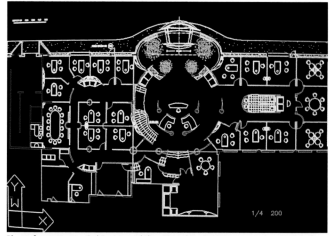

Plan informatique - Cabinet immobilier Bignolais, Paris

Sanitaires - Cabinet immobilier Bignolais, Paris

Détails escalier - Cabinet immobilier, Paris

Hall de distribution - Cabinet immobilier Bignolais, Paris

Palais des Congrès de Nice-Acropolis

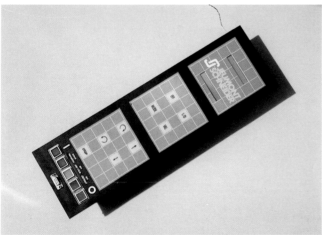

Design gamme mobilier Axos distribué par Viacom

Design clavier digital pour Jeumont-Schneider

CABINET AARKA / ÉRIK MORVAN

Willie Dobler, Pierre Caron, Érik Morvan,
Nathalie Brûlant, Anne-Henri Chombard de Lauwe

HEAD OFFICE

Agence Paris France
1, rue Théodule-Ribot
75017 Paris
☎ 1 47 66 33 64
Fax 1 48 88 93 05

Agence Nice France
Résidence Le Majestic
4, bd de Cimiez
06000 Nice
☎ 93 80 72 71

CONTACT

Érik Morvan
Anne-Henri Chombard de Lauwe
Sabine Bindschedler

KEY PERSONNEL

Pierre Caron
Assistant Responsable Informatique
Nathalie Brûlant
Assistante de Direction
Willie Dobler *Assistant*
Philippe Laillier *Conseil Financier*

AREAS OF SPECIALIZATION

RECENT CLIENTS

France Telecom
Aussedat Rey
Palais des Congrès de Paris
Palais des Congrès de Nice
AMF
Videosystem
Hauserman Clestra
Polyrey
Sommer
Jeumont Schneider
Design siège de spectacle
de la Géode ; Musée de la Science,
Cité de la Villette
Banque Internationale pour l'Afrique
occidentale : sièges internationaux
Afrique et États-Unis

COMPANY PROFILE

Cabinet : Design et architecture intérieure
1) Design
Recherche de nouveaux produits et étude formelle de tous objets.
Exemple : recherche matière et texture
– Designer de Polyrey Gamme Fréquence Grise et concept plafond Curva
   Oscar du SNAI 87 et lauréat concours innovation Bâtimat 89.
– Gamme Tecsom dalle moquette de chez Sommer.
– Clavier digital pour Jeumont Schneider.
2) Architecture intérieure
Recherche constante dans des espaces vécus en particulier pour le cadre de vie,
des loisirs, du travail ; étude d'ergonomie des espaces traités et définition de la
philosophie des fonctions traitées.

Cabinet : Product Design and Interiors
1) Design
New product research and analysis in all sectors.
eg: materials and textural research.
– Design of "Polyrey Gamme Fréquence Grise" and "Curva" ceiling concept.
– Tecsom carpet tile range for Sommer.
– Digital Keyboard for Jeumont Schneider.
2) Interior Design
Ongoing research into improving people's environment at work and at leisure.
We also undertake ergonomic analyses of design location, together with functional definition of each area.

ADDITIONAL INFORMATION

Dans le cadre de l'agence, traitement informatique des projets.
In-house computer-based analysis of each project.

Design concept faux-plafond Curva Polyrey (brevet)

Sheraton Princess Kaiulani Hotel, Waikiki

Hale Koa Dining Room, Waikiki

Penang Mutiara Beach Resort, Malaysia

Hawaiian Regent Hotel, Waikiki

Penang Mutiara Beach Resort, Malaysia

Alion at Kahala, Honolulu, Hawaii

Kula Bay Tropical Clothing, Honolulu, Hawaii

CONCEPT DESIGN GROUP, INC.

David K.Y. Chung
AIA

Clifford R. Tuttle
ASID

CONCEPT
DESIGN
GROUP

HEAD OFFICE

615 Piikoi Street, Suite 1406
Honolulu, Hawaii 96814
USA
☎ 808 523 7630
Fax 808 531 1706

INTERNATIONAL OFFICES

Concept Design Group(s) PTE Ltd.
Singapore
Fax 65 336 4306

CONTACT

Clifford R. Tuttle *ASID*,
Principal
David K.Y. Chung *AIA*,
Principal

KEY PERSONNEL

Oscar Gestoso *Associate*
Laura M. Atilano *Associate*

AREAS OF SPECIALISATION

🛍 10%   🎭 10%   🍷 80%

RECENT CLIENTS

Penang Mutiara Beach Resort,
   Malaysia
Mandarin Hotel, Singapore
Marina Mandarin Hotel, Singapore
Sheraton Hotels in the Pacific
Pernas OUE SDN BHD, Malaysia
HEMA OUE, Turkey
Emerald Hotel Corporation, Hawaii
Oliver Pacific Corporation, Hawaii

COMPANY PROFILE

CONCEPT DESIGN GROUP was started by David K.Y. Chung, AIA and Clifford R. Tuttle, ASID, formerly of the Gulstrom Kosko Group. David K.Y. Chung, AIA, formerly associated with Media Five Limited, serves as Vice-President and Managing Partner. Clifford R. Tuttle, ASID, formerly with Richard Crowell Associates, is President and Director of Design.

CONCEPT DESIGN GROUP is considered one of the top design firms in the state of Hawaii, with offices in Honolulu and Singapore. Offered are a full range of planning, architecture and interior design services specializing in the hospitality industry. We have been involved in a wide range of facilities including residences and small theme boutiques in commercial complexes. Above all, the CONCEPT DESIGN GROUP has developed a reputation for designing some of the most luxurious and exciting resort environments in the world.

CONCEPT DESIGN GROUP offers a diversified range of capabilities allowing us to communicate effectively with the varied professions involved in a project. Toward this end CONCEPT DESIGN GROUP's understanding of the hotel and resort industry offers unlimited options integrating interior architecture and design.

ADDITIONAL INFORMATION

1988 ASID Award of Merit
1989 ASID Award of Merit
1989 Designer's Circle Award
Lodging & Hospitality Magazine Best Hotel Lobby Renovation

Siège social Mutuelle, Paris

Agence de publicité, Paris

Agence de publicité, Paris

Musée, Paris

Show-room, Paris

Institut d'Études et de Sondages, Paris

CORAME

HEAD OFFICE

CORAME
5, boulevard Poissonnière
75002 Paris
☎ 1 42 36 19 91
Fax 1 42 36 28 28
Telex 215 056

CONTACT

Marc Brodin

KEY PERSONNEL

Marc Brodin
Gérant
Jean-Claude Avignon
Programmiste
Yves Bertaux
Architecte d'Intérieur
Mick Nicoll
Architecte d'intérieur
Geneviève Kouyoudjian
Responsable commerciale

AREAS OF SPECIALIZATION

COMPANY PROFILE

LE CONSEIL :
Concevoir un espace pour une entreprise, un magasin, un show-room, un salon, un musée, relève de la même démarche d'écoute, d'observation et de réflexion pour une meilleure stratégie immobilière.
Organiser un espace, c'est trouver l'équilibre entre l'utilisation fonctionnelle d'une surface et l'homme qui y évolue, optimiser un lieu en découvrant toutes ses potentialités.

ASSOCIÉS et PARTENAIRES : LE LERCEN
(Laboratoire d'Étude et de Recherche en Communication d'Entreprises) définit des concepts de communication en amont de la création.

OFFRES DE SERVICES :
Stratégie immobilière et programmation – Étude d'organisation d'espace – Étude mobilier et agencement spéciaux – Architecture intérieure et étude d'aménagement des espaces – Direction et coordination des travaux.

CONSULTANCY :
Conceptual design, whether for a company, a shop, a showroom, a gallery or a museum, involves the same process of listening, observation and creative thought to reach the best interior design strategy.
To organise a space is to find the balance between the functional use of a surface and the people who work there. It is to enhance a place while maximizing its potential.

ASSOCIATES and PARTNERS : LE LERCEN
LE LERCEN (our Corporate Communication Research and Analysis Group) specialises in conceptual analysis of communications needs as well as creative design. Our architects work closely with the rest of our team.

SERVICES :
Furnishing strategy and planning – Interior design – Specialist furnishing design – Project management and co-ordination.

ADDITIONAL INFORMATION

Specialities
– Museum design ; Company headquarters.
– Sectors : banking, petro-chemicals, advertising, food industries, tourism, financial institutions ; Trade Shows and exhibitions (travelling or permanent).
– Special events ; Show-rooms and shops.

Secteurs d'activités
– Muséologie ; Sièges sociaux d'entreprises. Secteurs : bancaire, pétrochimie, publicitaire, agro-alimentaire, tourisme, mutualiste.
– Salons et expositions (itinérants ou permanents) ; Stands.
– Événementiels ; Magasins et show-rooms d'exposition.

Western Developments Corp, and Donhoe Co's - Washington DC, 1987

Royal Life and Hardanger - Pride Hill Centre, Shrewsbury, 1988

Unisys Ltd, Unisys HQ, Uxbridge, 1989

Societe Generale - Gracechurch St, London, 1985

City of Charlotte, Mint Museum of Art, USA, 1984

S & W Berisford and LET Plc - Billingsgate, London, 1985

COVELL MATTHEWS WHEATLEY ARCHITECTS LIMITED

HEAD OFFICE

19 Bourdon Place
London W1X 9HZ
☎ (0) 71 409 2444
Fax (0) 71 493 8998

CONTACT

Peter Denner *Chairman*
Covell Matthews Wheatley

KEY PERSONNEL

CMWA
John Wheatley, *London*
Joanna Psaras, *London*

SIZE OF COMPANY

Personnel : 120

AREAS OF SPECIALISATION

RECENT CLIENTS

Arlington Securities Plc
British Aerospace
London & Edinburgh Trust
Marriott Corporation
British Telecom
Prudential Assurance of America
Saatchi & Saatchi
Tesco Stores Ltd
Unilever
Unisys

COMPANY PROFILE

Covell Matthews Wheatley provides an interior design and space planning service throughout western and eastern Europe in addition to the architectural and planning disciplines which form the company's historic base.

CMWA undertakes the design of corporate interiors and fit outs for high-technology and computer based uses, plus both new and refurbished retail, hotel and leisure complexes. These schemes accommodate the requirements for offices, banking and trading floors, seminar and conference facilities, research and development centres including pharmaceutical laboratories, shopping centres, art gallery and hotel complexes.

Together with its American associate Clark Tribble Harris and Li, CMW provides an experienced and fully resourced service to clients throughout Europe.

Covell Matthews Wheatley propose des services d'architecture d'intérieur et de conception pour l'aménagement et la reconversion de bâtiments et d'espaces à travers l'ensemble de l'Europe, de l'Est comme de l'Ouest, et ce, en complément des disciplines architecturales et urbanistiques qui constituent les fondements historiques de l'agence.

CMWA entreprend la conception d'espaces intérieurs pour des corporations et groupes de sociétés, pour l'aménagement de locaux destinés à des utilisateurs de haute technologie et d'informatique, ainsi que pour des réalisations nouvelles ou de reconversion de complexes commerciaux, hôteliers et de loisirs.

Ces programmes permettent de répondre aux besoins spécifiques requis par les aménagements de bureaux, de banques et salles de marché boursier, de lieux accueillant conférences et séminaires, de centres de recherche et de développement tels que des laboratoires pharmaceutiques, de même que des musées et galeries d'art.

CMWA peut offrir à ses clients européens un service basé sur une solide expérience et une équipe professionnelle hautement qualifiée, en association avec son partenaire américain Clark Tribble Harris & Li.

Covell Matthews Wheatley suministra un servicio de diseño interior, y renovación en toda Europa del este y del oeste además de disciplinas arquitectónicas y de planificación, lo que establecen la base histórica de la sociedad.

Covell Matthews Wheatley se encarga del diseño de los interiores de compañías; para tratamiento de alta tecnología y de base informática; tambien complejos nuevos o renovados de detalle, de hotel y de ocio. Esos planos proveen unos requisitos para oficinas, entidades bancarias o comerciales, facilidades de seminarios o de conferencias, centros de investigación y desarrollo, incluyendo laboratorios farmacéuticos, centros comerciales, complejos de hotel o de galerías de arte.

Junto con su socio americano Clark Tribble Harris & Li, Covell Matthews Wheatley suministra un servicio de amplios recursos y experiencia a sus clientes en toda Europa.

Jet corporate identity: UK 1990.

Arthurs quay shopping centre: Limerick, Ireland 1989.

F.I. group offices: Birmingham 1990.

The leading edge: London 1990.

Paco sweaters shop: London 1990.

CRABTREE HALL PROJECTS LIMITED

HEAD OFFICE

Crabtree Hall
70 Crabtree Lane
London SW6 6LT
☎ (0) 71 381 8755
Fax (0) 71 385 9575

INTERNATIONAL OFFICE

Crabtree Hall/Plan Créatif
10, rue Mercœur
75011 Paris
☎ 1 43 70 60 60
Fax 1 43 70 96 29

CONTACT

Linda C. Shoppee
Marketing Director

KEY PERSONNEL

Linda C. Shoppee *Marketing Director*
David S. Mackay *Managing Director*
Gerard Lecœur *Director*
Ian Lettice *Director*
David Lett *Director*

SIZE OF COMPANY

Personnel: 25

AREAS OF SPECIALISATION

RECENT CLIENTS

Casino Hypermarché
Conoco
South Western Electricity
Etam
Irish Airports
Speyhawk
Texaco
Quinnsworth
The Leading Edge
Madame Tussauds

COMPANY PROFILE

Crabtree Hall are a multi-disciplinary consultancy with experience in interiors, corporate identity and graphics. Our partnership with Paris – based at Plan Créatif – provides additional skills in product design and the ability to service organisations throughout Europe.

All our projects are supervised by highly experienced principals with a keen appreciation of our clients' objectives, markets and budgets.

Crabtree Hall est un groupe-conseil pluridisciplinaire en architecture commerciale et d'identité d'entreprise. Notre partenariat avec Plan Créatif à Paris, spécialiste en design de produit, permet d'offrir à nos clients une structure internationale capable d'aborder le marché européen.
Chacun de nos programmes est dirigé par un consultant hautement spécialisé qui guide son client en tenant compte de ses objectifs, de son budget et du marché en question.

Valentino Boutique, Barcelona, 1985

Valentino Boutique, Barcelona 1985

Scarpa Shoes, Barcelona 1988

Dyma Shoes, Tarrasa, 1990

Jewelry Mesara, Barcelona, 1988

Jewelry Mesara, Barcelona 1988

Majorica-Nobili-Lladro, Difusión, Barcelona, 1990

Grandor Shop, Barcelona, 1990

Grandor Shop, Barcelona, 1990

DECO STIL S.A.

Antonio Castello
Chairman

Albert Güell
Managing Director

HEAD OFFICE

Tomas Arcos *Manager*
c/o Santa Ana, 2
08002 Barcelona
☎ 3 301 02 48
　 3 301 02 90
　 3 301 00 05
Fax 3 412 33 38

KEY PERSONNEL

Concepcion Iglesias
Jose Mª Camps
Inma Rovira
Miguel Parra
Ney Vaz Haguiara
Ivan Castello, Jr.

SIZE OF COMPANY

Personnel: 15

AREAS OF SPECIALISATION

RECENT CLIENTS

T.I.S.A. S.A.
Calzados Reno S.A.
Green Bat
Persons S.A.
Carlos Feher
Optica Hispano
Rosalba Sport
Auto Layetana - Ford
Segura Viudas
Galeria Arte Surrealista

COMPANY PROFILE

We are specialists in interior design, and with 15 years of experience in the market, have gained the respect and friendship of all our clients.

Our existing business is in the Spanish market, but we are clearly focusing on European opportunities. To meet this objective we have a qualified and experienced team possessing all the technical skills necessary to plan and execute any kind of design project.

Somos especialistas del diseño de interiores, que a lo largo de 15 años de experiencia en el mercado, nos hemos granjeado la confianza y amistad de todos nuestros clientes.

Nuestras instalaciones son de ámbito nacional, con clara proyección europeísta. Para ello disponemos de un equipo técnico titulado que está capacitado y en posesión de las técnicas necesarias para proyectar y ejecutar cualquier tipo de diseño.

ADDITIONAL INFORMATION

Members of I.F.I.

Centre Commercial St-Martial, Limoges, 1989.

Galerie Rome St-Ferréol, Marseille, 1988

Galerie Rome St-Ferréol, Marseille, 1988

DESIGN ARCHITECTURAL

A. Daniel Poissonnet
Directeur Général

HEAD OFFICE

15 bis, rue du Général-de-Gaulle
94480 Ablon/Seine
☎ 1 45 97 43 41
Fax 1 45 97 27 52
Telex 264 918

CONTACT

M. Le Page
Directeur Création

KEY PERSONNEL

Daniel Poissonnet *Directeur Général*
Roger le Page *Directeur Création*
Jean-François Danet
Directeur Réalisation
Sebastiano Capodicasa *Responsable
de Programme*

SIZE OF COMPANY

Personnel : 35

AREAS OF SPECIALISATION

 30% 60% 10%

RECENT CLIENTS

Marks & Spencer
Norwich Union
Hammerson Group
Société des Centres Commerciaux
Segece
Espace Expansion
SDIF-Trema
Breguet Urbanisme Commercial
G3I
Soprec
Convergences
Urbanisme & Commerce
Commerce Expansion
Printemps
Rallye
Auchan

COMPANY PROFILE

DESIGN ARCHITECTURAL is a design office specialized in the design and realization of public places and especially, the commercial environment: chain
stores, hypermarkets, department stores, and shopping centres.

It is not by chance that our regular clients are amongst the "big names" in retail
and distribution. Our work on over 500,000 square metres during the last
12 years has enabled us to acquire a unique knowledge of commercial retail
requirements.

DESIGN ARCHITECTURAL est un bureau spécialisé dans la conception et la maîtrise d'œuvre des lieux ouverts au public, et principalement de l'environnement
commercial : chaîne de magasins, hypermarchés, grands magasins, centres
commerciaux.

Si nos clients fidèles sont les grands noms de la distribution ou de la promotion,
ce n'est pas un hasard. Grâce à plus de 500 000 m² réalisés en 12 ans, nous
avons acquis une expérience unique en matière d'implantation commerciale.

Magasin Printemps-Haussmann, Paris, 1987

Marks & Spencer, Villiers-en-Bière, 1990

Centre Commercial Rallye, Annecy, 1988

Vase, shop front for flower shop.

Vase, corporate graphics.

The Horniman at Hay's, exterior signage.

Ed's Easy Diner, 50s style American diner.

Ed's Easy Diner, counter position.

The Horniman at Hay's, pub exterior.

Midlands Electricity PLC, Power House out of town store.

Dulux paint merchandising for Habitat.

DESIGN HOUSE CONSULTANTS LIMITED

Tim May
Chairman

John Larkin
Managing Director

HEAD OFFICE

120 Parkway, Camden Town
London NW1 7AN
☎ (0) 71 482 2815
Fax (0) 71 267 7587

CONTACT

Jessica Stevens *Director*

AREAS OF SPECIALISATION

RECENT CLIENTS

Midlands Electricity PLC
The Victoria Wine Company
Whitbread
Rocket Restaurants
Portsmouth Building Society
Pedigree Petfoods
Boddingtons
Knickerbox
Mecca Leisure
Vase
Parasol Corporation

COMPANY PROFILE

Design House is an interdisciplinary consultancy with twenty years' experience in interiors, corporate identity and graphics. Our objective is to provide a flexible interiors consultancy capable of meeting a wide range of client requirements cost effectively. Our business and marketing awareness is matched by a commitment to creative excellence throughout all aspects of the design process.

We firmly believe that environments are brands too and that by establishing strong brand values our clients will be able to command premium prices, deter competitors and support efficient operations. Strong brands are built by creating a cohesive environment through careful use of both graphic and interior design skills.

Queens Quay Terminal, Toronton, 1982

The Forge, Glasgow, 1988

Jackson Brewery, New Orleans, 1982

The Borgata of Scottsdale, Scottsdale, 1980

Riverplace, Minneapolis, 1984

DESIGN INTERNATIONAL
D.I. DESIGN & DEVELOPMENT
CONSULTANTS (UK) LIMITED

Paul Mollé
Managing Director

HEAD OFFICE

12 Dryden Street
Covent Garden
London WC2E 9NA
☎ (0) 71 836 1853
Fax (0) 71 379 4727

INTERNATIONAL OFFICES

Offices in North America:

110 Bond Street
Toronto, Ontario
M5B 1X8
Canada
☎ 416 595 9598
Fax 416 595 0670
Colin Stephens *Chairman*

20 South Charles Street
Baltimore, Maryland
21201
U.S.A.
☎ 301 962 0505
Fax 301 783 0816
Roy Higgs *President*

KEY PERSONNEL

Linda D'Aguilar
Design Associate
John Timoney
Graphic Designer
Annabel Hallward
Research Consultant

SIZE OF COMPANY

Personnel: 150 (All offices)

AREAS OF SPECIALISATION

RECENT CLIENTS

UK:
Arlington Retail Developments Ltd
Asda
Burton Property Trust
Citygrove
Co-operative Wholesale Society
Ladbroke City & County Land Co Ltd
London & Edinburgh Trust
Marks & Spencer

Europe:
Carrefour (France)
Coopsette (Italy)
ECE (Germany)
Euromercato (Italy)
SCC (France/Spain/Italy)
SDIF/SOFIC (France/Italy)
SEGECE (France)
Skandia (Sweden)

COMPANY PROFILE

D.I. is an international design firm with over 25 years of experience, specialising in retail, leisure and mixed-use developments. Each project and client benefits from our unique multi-disciplinary approach to design and development, with each division (Design, Architecture, Research, Graphics and Interiors) working autonomously or together to create high profile, quality projects.

With our roots in both Europe and North America, we provide a special combination of local understanding and international expertise, resulting in innovative approaches and solutions to even the most challenging of situations.

The Littlewoods Organisation plc, Flagship Store, Oxford Street, London W1, 1989

Inkerman ltd, Offices, London W1, 1989

Guardian Royal Exchange, Speciality Shopping Centre, Princes Square, 1988

Henrys, Leather goods, fashion accessories and luggage shops, London W1, 1989

Henrys, Leather goods, fashion accessories and luggage shops, London W1, 1989

THE DESIGN SOLUTION

Peter Trickett   Robbie Gill

Littlewoods, Oxford Street, London W1, 1989

RESERVED

RESERVIERT

GERESERVEERD

RISERVATO

RESERVADO

RESERVERAD

RÉSERVÉ

Henrys, Leather goods, fashion accessories and luggage shops, London W1, 1989

HEAD OFFICE

20 Kingly Court
London W1R 5LE
England
☎ (0) 71 434 0887 / 0517
Fax (0) 71 434 0269

INTERNATIONAL OFFICES

Design Solution
65, rue Rambuteau
75004 Paris
☎ 1 42 77 03 63
Fax 1 42 72 93 11

CONTACT

Deirdre Morrow *Director*
Peter Trickett *Director*

KEY PERSONNEL

Peter Trickett
Robbie Gill

SIZE OF COMPANY

Personnel : 55

AREAS OF SPECIALISATION

RECENT CLIENTS

Caisse Nationale du Crédit Agricole
Carrefour France SA
BMW (GB) Ltd
Elf
Heron Property Corporation Ltd
Louis Vuitton
Ségécé
Stanley Gibbons
Villeroy & Boch
Volvo
W H Smith Ltd

COMPANY PROFILE

This advertisement introduces you to The Design Solution, one of Europe's leading design consultancies, which is responsible for the successful completion of projects in three specialist areas: graphic, interior and architectural design.

Some of the results we have achieved with our clients are illustrated on these pages and clearly demonstrate our belief in applying the highest creative standards to the commercial arena.

Our team of qualified designers and architects provides our international clientele with a totally committed service on programmes which range from corporate print, packaging and signage to retail, office, leisure and shopping centre design.

The Design Solution est l'une des agences de design-conseil les plus importantes d'Europe, et exerce son activité dans trois domaines spécialisés : le graphisme, l'architecture d'intérieur et l'architecture.

Une sélection de nos réalisations est présentée ici, et démontre concrètement la façon dont nous appliquons les standards de créativité les plus élevés à l'univers du commerce.

Notre équipe de cinquante spécialistes apporte sa compétence à notre clientèle internationale, dans le cadre de projets diversifiés touchant le packaging, l'édition, l'image de marque, la signalétique, l'aménagement de chaînes de distribution, de bureaux ou de centres commerciaux et de loisirs.

Nous souhaitons ajouter votre nom à la liste déjà prestigieuse de nos clients, et nous sommes prêts à répondre à toute demande d'information concernant vos projets futurs.

Lawyers' Office Babylon, Den Haag, photo : Otto de Feyter

World Trade Centre, Rotterdam, photo : Otto de Feyter

Technopolis, Twente University of Technology, photo : Marcel van Kerckhoven

Central Museum, Utrecht, photo : Gerhard Jaeger

Rotterdam Casino, photo : Otto de Feyter

EGM ARCHITECTEN BV

ir Gérard Gerritse

HEAD OFFICE

DORDRECHT
Laan der Verenigde Naties 9
Postbus 298
3300 AG Dordrecht
☎ (0) 78 330 660
Fax (0) 78 140 071

ROTTERDAM
Wijnhaven 14
Postbus 21301
3000 AH Rotterdam
☎ (0) 104 132 540
Fax (0) 104 048 491

UTRECHT
Geertestraat 2bis
3511 XE Utrecht
☎ (0) 30 322 352
Fax (0) 30 321 730

KEY PERSONNEL

ir J.P.T. Dekkers
R.B. van Erk AvB
ir G. Gerritse
A.C.L. de Krijger
J. van Middelkoop AvB
J. van Nes
Prof. M.A.A. van Schijndel
F.D.G. Prins
ir R. Willink

SIZE OF COMPANY

Personnel : 175

AREAS OF SPECIALISATION

COMPANY PROFILE

EGM architects is a firm of jointly operating architects, each of whom coope-rates in a team together with a building coordinator and several draughtsmen. In addition, EGM includes a number of supporting departments used by all the architects: cost control, building process control, production presentation and automation. The firm also boasts several self-supporting production depart-ments which operate independently of the architects: ACN design engineers, EGM engineering, EGM research and EGM housing. EGM came into being in 1974, as a result of a merger between the firms Eijkelenboom and Middelhoek in Rotterdam and Gerritse in Dordrecht. With a total of some 175 employees distributed over the branch offices in Dordrecht (130), Rotterdam (35) and Utrecht (10), EGM is one of the largest and most versatile architectural firms in the Netherlands.

University Teaching Hospital, Utrecht, photo : Arthur Blonk

House of Fraser, Headquarters Restaurant, London 1988.

Associated Newspapers, Boardroom, London 1989.

Daily Mail & General Trust Plc, Reception, London 1989.

Jackson Square, Shopping Centre, Bishops Stortford 1989.

De Groot Collis, Chartered Surveyors Office, London 1988.

Imprint Scanner, Packaging, EPR Design Graphics 1990.

EPR DESIGN LIMITED

S.R. Blundell FCSD
*Joint Managing
Director*

K.D. Smith FCSD
*Joint Managing
Director*

HEAD OFFICE

56/62 Wilton Road
London SW1V 1DE
☎ (0) 71 834 2299
Fax (0) 71 834 7524
Telex 917940 PRLON G

CONTACT

Stephen R. Blundell
Joint Managing Director
Kenneth D. Smith
Joint Managing Director

KEY PERSONNEL

Ken J. Clarke RIBA *Director*
Matthew Short DIP ARCH *Director*

SIZE OF COMPANY

Personnel: 40

AREAS OF SPECIALISATION

✏ 40%   📖 20%   🏛 15%   🎭 10%
🍷 10%   📕 5%

RECENT CLIENTS

Associated Newspapers
Colonial Mutual Group
Commercial Union Properties
De Groot Collis
Friends Provident Life Office
Heron Corporation Plc
House of Fraser Plc
National Westminster Bank Plc
Postel Property Services
MCA Artist (England) Ltd
Securicor Limited
Southend Property Holding Plc

COMPANY PROFILE

As a company, EPR Design has commitment and dedication to the achievement of design excellence related precisely to client need and purpose. Commitment comes from investment in design flair, technical skills and the most up to date technology, and dedication to the strongest principles of professional service which are the hallmark of the company.

EPR Design Graphics provide specialist communication skills in the area of corporate identity, brochures, packaging, all types of marketing material and signage projects. Creative design solutions are developed with the aid of the latest desk top publishing technology.

EPR Design, le concept d'architecture d'intérieur qui allie la créativité aux exigences de ses clients est garanti par la rigueur dans le respect des principes professionnels. Son image résulte de l'investissement humain – créativité et connaissance technique – ainsi que du matériel doté d'une technologie de pointe dans le domaine de la conception assistée par ordinateur.

EPR Design Graphics, le service de spécialistes dans le domaine de l'image de marque, de brochures, de l'emballage et autres matériels de marketing et de signalisation. Les solutions créatives s'appuient sur la technologie avancée du Desk Top Publishing.

ADDITIONAL INFORMATION

Bristish Council of Shopping Centre Award 1986
for refurbishment of the Queensmere Centre, Slough.
Royal Borough of Kensington and Chelsea Chamber of Commerce Award 1989
for Associated Newspapers Headquarters, London.

Banque Nationale de Paris, corporate headquarters, New York, 1988

Banque Nationale de Paris, regional headquarters, Limoges, 1989

Chubb Insurance, corporate headquarters, Paris, 1989

Banque Nationale de Paris, regional headquarters, Aix-en-Provence, 1989

Chubb Insurance, corporate headquarters, Paris, 1989

3Com France, French and European headquarters, Les Ulis, 1990

ÉRIC LIEURÉ
ARCHITECTURE INTÉRIEURE

HEAD OFFICE

89, rue du Faubourg-St-Antoine
75011 Paris
☎ 43 42 39 49
Fax 43 45 08 62

CONTACT

Eric Lieuré

INTERNATIONAL OFFICES

Eric Lieuré in association with Butler
Rogers Baskett
381, Park Avenue South
New York NY 10016
☎ 212.686.9677
Fax 212.213.2170
Contact : Jonathan Butler

KEY PERSONNEL

Eric Lieuré *Principal*
Patrice Ponticelli *Snr Project Mgr*
Jean-Pierre Richard *Snr Project Mgr*

SIZE OF COMPANY

Personnel: 22

AREAS OF SPECIALISATION

 60% ᵀ 30% 10%

RECENT CLIENTS

Apple Computer International Inc.
American Telephone & Telegraph
3Com France
Chubb Insurance
Banque Nationale de Paris
Conseil Général de la Corrèze
Morgan Stanley International

COMPANY PROFILE

Eric Lieuré's office has 25 years of experience and employs a team of designers and specialists providing complete interior design services from programming and conceptual studies to construction supervision. Eric Lieuré has considerable experience in the banking sector with many projects completed both in France and abroad. Eric Lieuré also has invaluable experience in planning and designing corporate space for American companies in Europe. Collaboration on a number of these projects with the New York firm of architects Butler Rogers Baskett has been extremely useful to the client.

Les 25 ans d'expérience d'Eric Lieuré et son équipe de concepteurs et de spécialistes lui permettent de proposer des prestations très complètes d'architecture intérieure. Eric Lieuré a une grande expérience d'aménagement d'espaces dans le secteur bancaire en France et à l'étranger. Notre groupe est également spécialisé dans la programmation et l'aménagement d'espaces pour des compagnies américaines en Europe. Certains de ces projets importants ont été réalisés en collaboration avec le cabinet d'architecte new-yorkais Butler Rogers Baskett.

ADDITIONAL INFORMATION

CAD equipped.

Equipé CAO.

Abbot Mead Vickers Office Headquarters, London 1988

Debenhams Department Store, Bristol, 1989

Fashion Dept for de Bijenkorf, Utrecht, 1989

Alexia Restaurant, Finland, 1989

Lee Carpets Showroom and Exhibition Design, Chicago, 1989

FITCH RS Plc

HEAD OFFICE

Porters South
4 Crinan Street
London N1 9UE
☎ (0) 71 278 7200
Fax (0) 71 833 1014

INTERNATIONAL OFFICES

Fitch RichardsonSmith
10350 Olentangy River Road
P.O. Box 360, Worthington
Ohio 43085
U.S.A.
☎ 614 885 3453
Fax 614 885 4289

Fitch RS
Am Seestern 24
4000 Düsseldorf 11
Germany
☎ 211 59 67 22/23/25
Fax 211 59 12 40

Fitch RS
Serrano 240 - 5°
Madrid 28016
Spain
☎ (9) 1 457 0781
Fax (9) 1 457 2079

KEY PERSONNEL

David Rivett
Group Development Director
Rune Gustafson
Client Services Director
Karl Ansorg
Germany
Claudine Baer
Spain

AREAS OF SPECIALISATION

RECENT CLIENTS

The Burton Group
ASDA
Midland Bank
Whitbread Plc
Kriegbaum, Germany
Ford Motor Company
MAB Group, Holland
The Pentos Group
Boots Plc
Expo 92 Spain
Lee Carpets, USA

COMPANY PROFILE

Fitch RS is one of the world's leading design consultancies, with offices in London, Newark, Ohio, Boston, Düsseldorf and Madrid. It employs 500 people world-wide and is committed to a multidisciplinary approach to design embracing architecture, corporate identity, retail and product design.

At Fitch RS interdisciplinary project teams, including architects, designers, marketing experts, researchers, strategists and project managers - work to develop a creative process which embraces strategic analysis through to design development and implementation.

Our design plus approach tackles real business problems head on and brings tangible results for our clients.

Porsche Cars Great Britain, Millbrook II event, Bedfordshire, 1990

British Telecom, Network Management Centre, London, 1988

Royal Northumberland Fusiliers, Regimental Museum, Alnwick, 1990

Porsche Cars Great Britain. Millbrook I Graphics package, 1989

John Furneaux and
Laurie Stewart

FURNEAUX STEWART

HEAD OFFICE

24 Beaumont Mews
London W1N 3LN
☎ (0) 71 935 5724
Fax (0) 71 486 0304

CONTACT

Clare Nash
Project coordinator

KEY PERSONNEL

John Furneaux
Managing Director
Laurie Stewart
Director

SIZE OF COMPANY

Personnel: 10

AREAS OF SPECIALISATION

RECENT CLIENTS

British Telecom
BET
City of Westminster
Davis Langdon & Everest
English Heritage
Natural History Museum
Nuclear Electric
Porsche
STC plc
Sultanate of Oman

COMPANY PROFILE

Design is clearly one of the most useful tools business and industry can employ. We see ourselves playing an important role in this growing and vital partnership.

Our field of activity includes exhibitions, product launches and conferences, commercial interiors and special events as well as leisure and heritage sites and museum design. We are involved in the fusion of design skills and the technologies of video, audiovisual, theatre lighting and special effects to create unique environments.

We are able to draw upon our graphics capability, highly effective in all areas of corporate communications, to undertake your event identity, packaging or product launch material, thereby offering a total solution.

Our philosophy? We believe in creativity. We analyse and interpret client briefs rather than merely answer them. Strategy is important too – we like to be in at the foundation of a project rather than being reactive to a problem. We believe in attention to detail.

And that brings us to the last point.

Enjoyment. We enjoy the design process. We like the challenge of new clients and new projects.

Porsche Cars Great Britain Image Wall Point of Sale System, 1988

St Enoch's Shopping Centre, Glasgow

Shell-Mex Restaurant, London

BOC World Headquarters, Windlesham Surrey

Banque Belge, London

Shell-Mex Servery, London

Shell-Mex Entrance, London

Barings Investment Services Ltd, London

Shell-Mex Board Room, London

GMW PARTNERSHIP

John Bevan
Partner

HEAD OFFICE

GMW Partnership
Chartered Architects and
Interior Designers
PO Box 1613
239 Kensington High Street
London W8 6SL
☎ 071 937 8020
Fax 071 937 5815

INTERNATIONAL OFFICE

Associated office in Brussels

KEY PERSONNEL

John Bevan
Partner
Gordon Cobban
Senior Associate
Sarah Jane James
Senior Associate
Marilyn Cattle
Senior Associate

SIZE OF COMPANY

Personnel: 300

AREAS OF SPECIALISATION

RECENT CLIENTS

British Telecom
Shell UK
Barings Investment Services Ltd
Banque Belge
P & O Cruises
Royal Opera House
Barclays Bank
Mobil
BOC
Property Services Agency
Prudential Portfolio Managers
King Saud University, Riyadh

COMPANY PROFILE

For over 40 years GMW has maintained a consistent record of high quality design while meeting the needs of developers, corporate clients, institutions and public sector bodies alike. Our (innovative) design approach is characterised by a commitment to client involvement and team work.

The 25 strong Interior Design team work independently or in association with architects according to project needs. The size of the practice ensures a wealth of knowledge and experience supported by ancillary services such as computer aided design, model making and graphic design.

Pendant plus de 40 ans, GMW a maintenu un très haut niveau de prestation professionnelle tout en répondant aussi bien aux exigences des promoteurs et organismes privés qu'à celles du secteur public. Notre approche innovatrice en conception est caractérisée par la place importante que nous donnons au travail d'équipe et à l'implication même du client.

La section d'architecture d'intérieur comprend 25 membres travaillant indépendamment ou en collaboration avec des architectes selon les besoins du projet.

L'importance de notre entreprise assure une richesse tant en connaissances qu'en expérience et permet des auxiliaires tels que la conception assistée par ordinateur, la conception des maquettes et des arts graphiques.

Immeuble La Mondiale Assurance, Hall d'entrée

Immeuble groupe de communication Hersan/La Cinq TV

Accueil

Détails Horloge

Ascenseurs accès

Détails colonne lumineuse

AGENCE HART-LABORDE

Groupe Hart-Laborde
**Agence Hart-Laborde
Architecture d'intérieur**
**Halabama, Société civile
d'Architecture**
**Plus Design Sarl, création et
distribution pour l'habitat**

Patrice Hart
André Laborde

HEAD OFFICE

174, av Charles-de-Gaulle
92200 Neuilly-sur-Seine
France
☎ 1 46 24 76 89
Fax 1 47 45 50 42
Telex Hartlab 620 049 F

CONTACT

André Laborde

INTERNAITONAL OFFICES

Ruwi/Muscat
Sultanat d'Oman

KEY PERSONNEL

Patrice Hart
Architecte d'intérieur OPQAI/SNAI
André Laborde
Architecte d'intérieur OPQAI/SNAI
Noël Forgeot
Chef d'Agence OPQAI/SNAI
Christian Berger
Directeur Financier

SIZE OF COMPANY

Personnel : 15

AREAS OF SPECIALISATION

30 %   10 %   10 %   30 %
20 %

RECENT CLIENTS

Commerces :
Forum des Halles, Paris
TEAM 05
Cartier
Flo Prestige Traiteur

Loisirs :
Ken Club
Vitatop
Aqualand, Gif-sur-Yvette

Restauration :
Le Bœuf sur le Toit
Casino de Boulogne
La Rotonde de la Muette
Casino de Forges-les-Eaux

Hôtellerie :
Hôtel Baumann/Kammerzel,
Strasbourg
Hôtel des Maréchaux, Mulhouse
Résidence du Marché, Genève

Bureaux :
Tour Dunlop, La Défense
Passy Kennedy La Mondiale
Passy Kennedy Snecma
Crédit Foncier, Nancy
Mairie de Gif-sur-Yvette

Expositions :
Montreal, Paris, Ryad, Abu Dhabi,
Hong Kong

COMPANY PROFILE

Advice, studies, creation, design guidance. On-site supervision and implementation of projects. Our team of interior designers, decorators and stylists can give
assistance at every stage from design to turnkey conclusion.

ADDITIONAL INFORMATION

Le groupe Hart-Laborde est constitué de 3 entités indépendantes :
Agence Hart-Laborde Architecture d'Intérieur
Halabama, Société civile d'Architecture
Plus Design Sarl, création et distribution de produit pour l'habitat
Bourse de la vocation
IFI AWARD SAD/85
Expositions SAD Paris 85-87-90

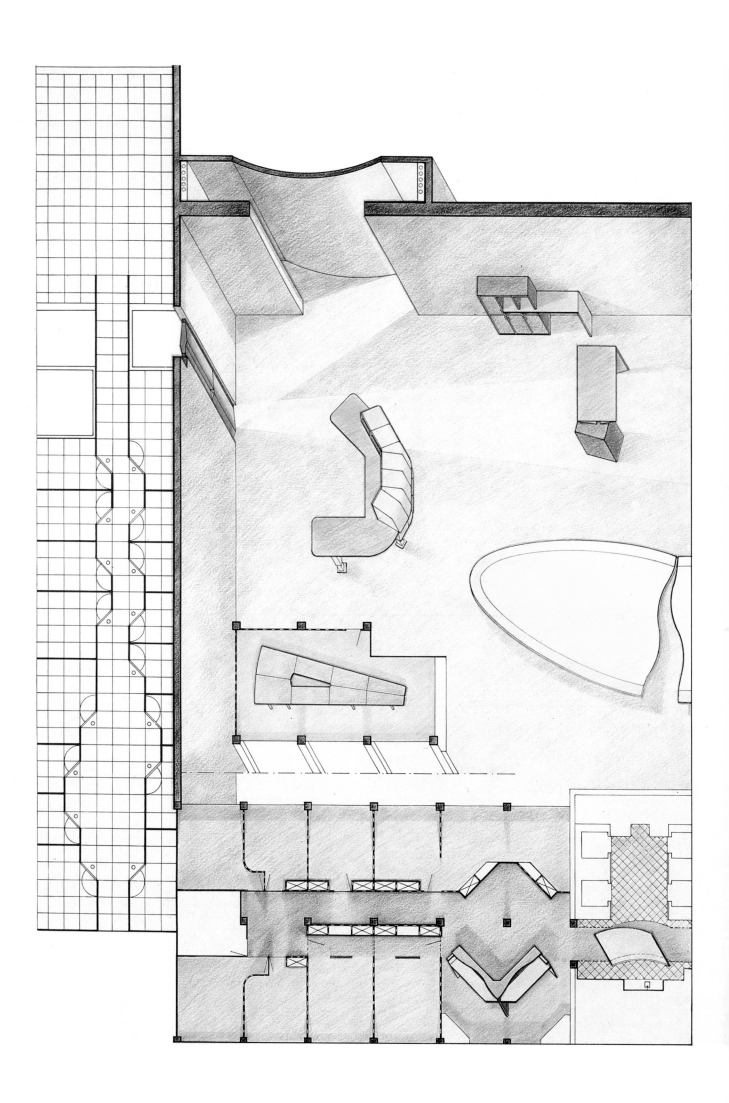

HIDDE CONSULTANTS

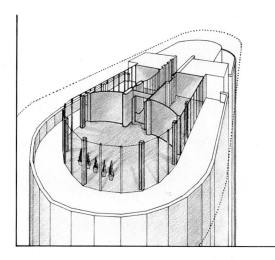

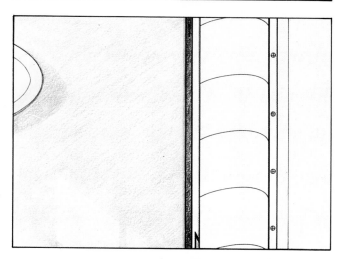

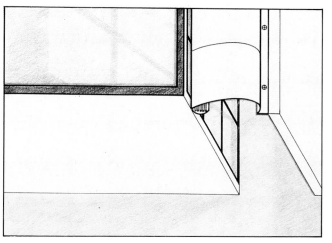

Herengracht 162
1016 BP Amsterdam
The Netherlands
☎ 20 38 21 37
Fax 20 38 21 38

CONTACT

Roeland H. van der Hidde M. Sc, Bni
Director

KEY PERSONNEL

Paul Kavelaars, BNI *Designer*
Jan Hein Marcus *Designer*
Wendi Bakker *Designer*
Karin de Vaal, KIO *Industrial Designer*

SIZE OF COMPANY

Personnel : 8

AREAS OF SPECIALISATION

RECENT CLIENTS

Dutch National Gas Board,
 Groningen
Royal Dutch Exhibition Center, Utrecht
FGH Mortgage Bank, Utrecht
IGF Engineering, Maastricht
Fugro McClelland, Groningen
Fugro McClelland, Hemel Hempstead,
 U.K.
Holland Chemical International,
 Amsterdam
Hatéma Contract Carpeting, Helmond

COMPANY PROFILE

Hidde Consultants offers a group of multi-talented young designers under the management of an internationally trained and experienced designer.

Ideas, concept, design and implementation are developed within this team to produce the final solution to any given problem. Skills in all related design fields are practiced, both separately, and as a multidisciplinary service. Interior design for the building trade as well as industrial design for industrial products. Design for organisations as well as organisation for design!

ADDITIONAL INFORMATION

Roeland van der Hidde is president of BNI, the official organisation of professional interior designers in the Netherlands. Most of the firm's designers, are also members of the professional organisations appropriate to their fields of specialization.

Established according to the BNI regulations, Hidde Consultants is a full-service design bureau which operates independently of any commercial or trade enterprises.

Hidde Consultants frequently cooperates in team efforts with a broad range of other consultants. Permanent relationships have been established with Hans Wolff & Partners Theatre and Lighting Consultants, Amsterdam, and Castelet Interior Designers, Paris.

Post Office Counters, National Crown Office Redesign, 1987

Photo : P.K. Childs.

British Rail Network SouthEast, Station Product and Identity Redesign, 1989

Photo : P.K. Childs.

British Rail Network SouthEast, Station Product and Identity Redesign, 1989

HODGE ASSOCIATES LIMITED

Post Office Counters, National Crown Office Redesign, 1987

Head Post Office, Listed Building Refurbishment, 1987

British Gas, Dealing Room, 1987

HEAD OFFICE

3 Lambton Place
London W11 2SH
☎ (0) 71 727 8600
Fax (0) 71 727 6195

CONTACT

David Hodge
Managing Director

AREAS OF SPECIALISATION

 30%   70%

KEY PERSONNEL

David Hodge
Managing Director
Malcolm Wright
Design Manager

COMPANY PROFILE

Hodge Associates is an established design consultancy with more than 12 years experience in interior/public environment design. Our expertise in interiors, graphics, architecture and product design allow us to offer a complete service in a wide variety of projects.

Our working philosophy is based on both a clear understanding of our clients' business needs and a close working relationship with them. Matching our design expertise to clients' business objectives, and taking projects from concept to completion, has enabled us to produce many original and cost-effective solutions. Solutions which have received a number of design awards. If you would like to find out more about Hodge Associates, please write for our brochure.

Our clients include British Rail, Post Office Counters Limited, British Gas and Photo-Me International.

ADDITIONAL INFORMATION

Two Design Council Awards
British Steel Design Award

Prudential Shopping Centre, Hong Kong, 1979

No 1 London Bridge : Commercial Offices, London, 1987

GOIC Headquarters Building, Doha, 1984

Green End Park Hotel, Hertfordshire, 1985

UNESCO Headquarters Refurbishment, Paris, 1980

Salters Hall, London, 1975

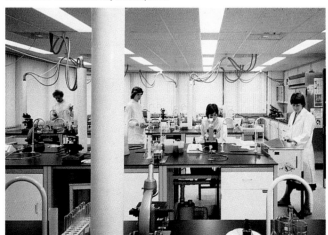

UAC House Refurbishment, London, 1985

Sunderland Polytechnic Life, Sciences Building, 1980

INTERIOR CONSULTANCY SERVICES LIMITED

HEAD OFFICE

Tyttenhanger House
St-Albans Herts, England
☎ (0) 727 23633
Fax (0) 727 26488
Telex 299169 JAYBEE G

AREAS OF SPECIALISATION

30%   5%   25%   10%

25%   5%

RECENT CLIENTS

Saga Holidays Plc
Merieux (UK)
The Bank of Cyprus
Help the Aged
Black Arrow Plc
Servier Laboratories (UK) Ltd
Doha Zoological Gardens

CONTACT

Norman Allanson
DesRCA, FCSD
Managing Director

KEY PERSONNEL

Ian Graham, Dip Arch RIBA
Director
Anthony Sully, DesRCA
Senior Designer
Godfrey Smeaton, AIAC, NDD
Senior Designer
Graham Stretton, FCSD, FRSA
Senior Designer

COMPANY PROFILE

Interior Consultancy Services Ltd has developed it's expertise over the past 30 years having been involved in many varied projects both in the United Kingdom and abroad.

Design work includes the complete fitting out and furnishing of universities, polytechnics, offices, banks, libraries, shopping centres, showrooms, hotels, restaurants, banqueting halls, golf and leisure centres, conference halls, theatres, military camps, laboratories and religious buildings.

In addition to complete interiors for both existing and new buildings the group has developed designs for office and laboratory furniture for commercial production and architectural graphic programme for zoos, commercial developments, hotels and golf clubs.

Interior Consultancy Service a développé son savoir durant les trente dernières années en accomplissant de nombreux et divers projets aussi bien au Royaume-Uni qu'à l'étranger.

Son travail de création englobe l'aménagement d'ensemble et l'équipement d'universités, de collèges, de bureaux, de banques, de bibliothèques, de centres commerciaux, de salles d'exposition. d'hôtels, de restaurants, de salles de réception, de terrains de golf, de salles de conférences, de théâtres, de laboratoires, de centres militaires et religieux.

En plus de ces installations complètes de bâtiments existants ou nouveaux la société a également conçu du mobilier de bureaux et de laboratoires en vue de leur production commerciale ainsi que des éléments d'art graphique pour des parcs zoologiques, des centres commerciaux, des hôtels et des clubs de golf.

ADDITIONAL INFORMATION

Interior Consultancy Services forms part of the John S Bonnington Partnership, Consultant Architects and Services Engineers, together with other companies offering services in Computer Aided Design, Landscape Architecture and Quantity Surveying. In addition, as a result of long-standing working relationships with a number of established Civil & Structural Engineers, the Group is able to provide a complete consultancy service to clients.

The Partnership has worked in over 20 countries, including Europe, Cyprus, the Middle East, Hong Kong, Singapore, Indonesia, Japan and the Pacific Basin.

Four Seasons Hotel, Los Angeles, Ca. 1987-1988

Four Seasons Hotel, Los Angeles, Ca. 1987-1988

Four Seasons Hotel, Los Angeles, Ca. 1987-1988

Vista Marquette, Minneapolis, Mn. 1989

by Mary E. Nichols

Century Plaza Tower, Los Angeles, Ca. 1985-1988

by Klein & Wilson

Le Meridien at Coronado, San Diego, Ca. 1988

INTRADESIGN Inc.

Richard Mayhew	Cynthia Forchielli	Richard Callen
Design Director	*Design Partner*	*Managing Director*

HEAD OFFICE

910 North La Cienega Boulevard
Los Angeles, California 90069
☎ 213 652 6114
Fax 213 652 6945
Telex 317 779

CONTACT

Richard Callen
Managing Director
Richard Mayhew
Director of Design
Darlene de Monfreid
Director of Operations
Elaine Proby
C.F.O.

INTERNATIONAL OFFICES

Intradesign Inc.
c/o Robinson Conn Partnership
68 Alma Road Windsor, Berkshire
☎ 075 383 0055
Fax 075 385 0913

KEY PERSONNEL

Richard Mayhew
Design Director
Cynthia Forchielli
Design Partner, London
David Hyun
Design Partner

SIZE OF COMPANY

Personnel : 40

AREAS OF SPECIALISATION

 5%   5%   90%

RECENT CLIENTS

Hilton International, London
Conrad International, Los Angeles
Four Seasons Hotels, Toronto, Ontario
Hyatt Corporation, Chicago, Illinois
ANA Entreprises, Tokyo, Japan
JMB Properties, Chicago, Illinois
Meridien Hotels, Inc., New York,
    Paris
Princess Hotels, Inc., New York City
Sherwood Plaza Ltd., Taipei, Taiwan
Hanil Leisure Dev. Co., Seoul, Korea
Nichiei, USA, Honolulu, Hawaii
Beaufort Hotels International,
    Singapore
Fairmont Hotel Corp., San Francisco

COMPANY PROFILE

INTRADESIGN Inc., established in 1976, is known internationally for the refined luxury of its interior design of hotels, commercial spaces and fine residences.

The company follows the atelier concept wherein junior staff members and apprentices learn directly from senior designers experienced at integrating residential design concepts into hotels and other commercial developments.

The Intradesign team thoroughly researches an area's culture, history and art, incorporating indigenous traditions into the design. The firm is noted for its discriminating selection of fine art and antiques, resulting in art acquisitions both integral to the design scheme and valuable corporate investments for clients. Intradesign offers expertise in interior architecture, space planning, textiles, furnishings and art, lighting design, and project management, including coordination of graphic design and landscaping.

The firm also offers clients sophisticated, cost-effective renovation and refurbishing services through a system of phased programs tailored to a hotel's in-house requirements.

Several recent resort projects have contributed to the diversity of the corporate portfolio. Intradesign is uniquely prepared to meet the current challenges of international hospitality, commercial and residential design.

"Sears Cafe," Metro Centre, 1986

Marks and Spencers "Garden Restaurant," Metro Centre, 1986

"Gas Works," Out-of-Town Unit Thurrock, 1989

"Le Chef" Kitchen Shop, 1989

"Laces Shoe Shop", London, 1989

"Wine Shop", Selfridges, 1988

"Gas Works", Out-of-Town Unit Thurrock, 1989

JOHN HERBERT PARTNERSHIP LTD

John Herbert
Principal

HEAD OFFICE

8, Berkeley Road
Primrose Hill
London NW1 8YR
☎ (0) 71 722 3932
Fax (0) 71 586 7048

CONTACT

John Herbert *Principal*
Patricia Herbert *Director*

KEY PERSONNEL

Stephen Collis
Trevor Long
Raj Wilkinson

SIZE OF COMPANY

Personnel: 25

AREAS OF SPECIALISATION

RECENT CLIENTS

British Airports Authority
British Shoe Corporation
British Gas
British Rail
Capital & Counties
Coventry Building Society
Harrods
Mappin & Webb
Marks & Spencers
National Trust
Sears Holdings
Selfridges

COMPANY PROFILE

The John Herbert Partnership has been at the forefront of innovative design throughout the 1980's. It is a multi-disciplinary consultancy of interior, graphic and product designers specialising in retail, restaurant and office design.
Our imaginative conceptual work is related to extensive experience of the market potential and in the implementation of our projects we are committed to professionalism and cost control.

Die John Herbert Partnership ist seit Beginn der 80er Jahre führend auf dem Gebiet fortschrittlicher Innenarchitektur.
Es ist eine vielseitige Designagentur und beschäftigt Innenarchitekten, Grafiker und Produktdesigner, die sich insbesondere auf Ladenbau, Restaurants und Bürodesign spezialisieren.
Unsere ideenreiche Entwurfe sind das Ergebnis unserer Erfahrung in den verschiedenen Marktbereichen – in der Durchführung unserer Projekte achten wir insbesondere auf Qualität und Kostenkontrolle.

L'association "John Herbert" fut à travers les années "1980" à l'avant-garde du monde du design.
C'est une société-conseil multidisciplinaire dans les domaines de la décoration d'intérieur, du graphisme et de la conception d'objets industriels, particulièrement spécialisée dans les magasins, la restauration et les bureaux. La créativité de notre démarche est due à une riche expérience dans le potentiel du marché et dans l'exécution de nos projets grâce auxquels nous pouvons nous engager à un professionnalisme et à une bonne maîtrise des coûts.

ADDITIONAL INFORMATION

Awards:
Sears Store at the Metro Centre, Gateshead - Best Retail Scheme of 1987; National Association of Shopfitters & Design Council.

Coventry Building Society – Design Effectiveness award for 1989; Design Business Association in association with Confederation of British Industry.

"Gasworks" – Retail Design Award for 1989; Expo Shop.

Anna Bassett's Claire Pearone, Troy, Michigan, USA

Winkelman's (Division Petrie Stores), National, USA

Henry's, Wichita, Kansas, USA

Kositchek's, Lansing, Michigan, USA

Lerner New York (Division The Limited Inc), National, USA

Fendi, Short Hills, New Jersey, USA

JON GREENBERG & ASSOCIATES Inc

Kenneth E. Nisch
President

Michael D. Crosson
Executive Vice President

HEAD OFFICE

2338 Coolidge Highway
Berkley, Michigan 47072
USA
☎ 313 548 8080
Fax 313 548 4640

CONTACT

Robert Berlin
Director Client Services
Tony Camilletti
Director Visual Communications

KEY PERSONNEL

Mark J. Carlini *Project Supervisor*
Jerry M. Gaudet *Project Supervisor*
Max Zanoni *Project Manager*
Gordon Eason *Project Manager*

SIZE OF COMPANY

Personnel : 65

AREAS OF SPECIALISATION

🛍 80%   🎭 5%   🍷 5%   ♉ 5%
📖 5%

RECENT CLIENTS

Sears USA & Canada
K Mart Corporation
The Limited Inc
Abercrombie & Fitch
Lerner Woman
Mercantile Stores Corp
Ringling Bros & Barnum & Bailey
    Retail
General Nutrition Corporation
Major League Baseball Clubhouse
    Stores
Konica Corporation / Fotomat
Petrie Stores Corporation
Charming Shoppes Inc
Melville Stores

COMPANY PROFILE

Founded in 1971, Jon Greenberg & Associates, Inc., is a leading retail design
and architectural firm committed to providing the most innovative and consumer
responsive design required to compete in today's global marketplace.

JGA's clients come from a variety of retail and consumer marketing businesses.
Most of JGA's clients savor an entrepreneurial spirit and are sensitive to the
impact of a strategically positioned, three-dimensional image.

JGA offers a myriad of design and procurement services to clients. They include
conceptual and protopye development, schematic layout and floorplans, architectural and construction documents and elemental planning of integral compo-
nents of lighting, fixturing, graphic design, visual presentation, materials and
finishes.

The design and imaging services provided by JGA are insightful to our clients'
businesses and visionary to their growth into the future.

ADDITIONAL INFORMATION

JGA projects have been the recipients of more than 100 awards for Design
Excellence. JGA also maintains membership and involvement with industry associations such as the National Retail Federation, National Association of Display
Industries, Institute of Store Planners, International Council of Shopping Centers
and several specific associations for stores merchandising furniture, stationary,
gifts, books and art supplies.

Lobby in the Rittenhouse Hotel, Philadelphia, PA

Guestrooms in the Rittenhouse Hotel, Philadelphia, PA

Mary Cassatt Tea Room, Rittenhouse Hotel, Philadelphia, PA

"210" Fine Dining Restaurant, Rittenhouse Hotel Philadelphia, PA

Treetops Cafe, Rittenhouse Hotel, Philadelphia, PA

Lobby, Frenchman's Reef Hotel, St-Thomas, U.S.V.I.

Lobby Atrium, Marriott at Sawgrass, Jacksonville, Florida

LYNN WILSON ASSOCIATES INC.

Lynn Wilson
President

HEAD OFFICE

East Coast
111 Majorca Avenue
Coral Gables
Florida 33134
☎ 305 442 4041
Fax 305 443 4276

West Coast
8500 Melrose Avenue, Suite 201
Los Angeles, Ca. 90069
☎ 213 854 1141
Fax 213 854 1149

INTERNATIONAL OFFICES

Lynn Wilson Assoc, Paris, France
☎ 331 40 49 02 34
Fax 331 40 49 02 73

McColl/Wilson London, England
☎ 4471 935 4788
Fax 4471 224 3424

CONTACT

Danette Brockhouse *Marketing*
Joyce Hicks *Executive Secretary*

KEY PERSONNEL

Jerry Szwed
Vice-president
B. Brockhouse
Director of Interior Architecture
Cheryl Romano
Director of Design, East Coast
Terry Ruiz de Castilla
Director of Design, West Coast
Andrea Korn
Director of international Purchasing

SIZE OF COMPANY

Personnel : 64

AREAS OF SPECIALISATION

 100 %

RECENT CLIENTS

Hotel du Pont, Delaware
Stouffer's Vinoy Hotel, Florida
Hyatt Regency International
    Airport, Orlando, Florida
Marriott Cozumel, Mexico
Walt Disney World
Tui Fuerteventura Palace,
    Canary Islands
Mannegon Hills Resorts, Guan

COMPANY PROFILE

Lynn Wilson Associates, Inc. has since 1970 earned an enviable, wide-ranging reputation as international, hotel-hospitality interior design specialists. The firm's offices in Miami, Los Angeles, Paris, London and Tokyo give it the ability to accommodate it's international clientele, while allowing its staff to remain well-informed about the latest in product development and trends in the industry.

The time-tested disciplines of the firm include development of every aspect, from market research and space planning to interior architectural drawings and specifications. Our skills are supplemented by state of the art computer systems including CAD, computer specifications, budgets and custom control systems that assure aesthetic quality with predetermined budget perimeters. If sought, the firm is available to fulfill, expediently and authoritatively, its client's ultimate assurance of any environment of exceptional quality. Further, the firm's complimentary associates afford related auxiliary consultations. Its award-winning forte - the Hospitality Industry - has merited the continuing respect of the media and also its peers. Lynn Wilson Associates approaches every installation as a challenge. The firm is proud to be recognized in its achievements in Europe and throughout the U.S.

ADDITIONAL INFORMATION

Gold Key Award - Excellence in Design Finalist for the Hyatt Key West Resort Luxury Suites, 1989. 1st Place Lodging Hospitality - Restaurant Renovation of the Biltmore Hotel, 1988. 2nd Place Lodging Hospitality -Lobby of the Hilton Hotel in Ocala Florida, 1988. Gold Key Award - Excellence in Design Winner Restaurant at the Palm Beach Polo & Country Club in Palm Beach, FL.

Sala de Actos de la Camara de la Propriedad Urbana de Barcelona

Sala de Actos de la Camara de la Propriedad Urbana de Barcelona

Sala de Actos de la Camara de la Propriedad Urbana de Barcelona

Sala de Actos de la Camara de la Propriedad Urbana de Barcelona

Sala de Actos de la Camara de la Propriedad Urbana de Barcelona

Sala de Actos de la Camara de la Propriedad Urbana de Barcelona

MANBAR, S.L.

Emili Bargalló i Ferrer   Jaume Bargalló i Ferrer   Enric Bargalló i Ferrer

HEAD OFFICE

MANBAR, S.L.
Via Augusta, 61
08006 Barcelona
☎ 93 218 64 50
Fax 93 217 34 37

KEY PERSONNEL

Emili Bargalló i Ferrer
Jaume Bargalló i Ferrer
Enric Bargalló i Ferrer

SIZE OF COMPANY

Personnel : 36

AREAS OF SPECIALISATION

⌀ 85 %   ▥ 10 %

RECENT CLIENTS

Cresa Aseguradora Iberica, S.A.
Fiatc Mutua de Seguros
Viajes Norda, S.A.
Banco Hispano Americano
Camara Oficial de la Propiedad
   Urbana de Barcelona
Camara Oficial de Comercio Industria
   y Navegación de Barcelona
Bufete Cuatrecasas S.C.P.
Arthur Andersen Auditores, S.A.
Danone, S.A.
Lotus Development European
   Corporation, S.A.
La Vanguardia
Agfa Gevaert, S.A.
Winterthur Sdad, Suiza de Seguros
BASF Española, S.A.
Televisio de Catalunya, S.A.
Seat Sociedad Española
Sun Alliance, S.A.

COMPANY PROFILE

Manbar was set up in 1953. At Nr. 61 Via Augusta in Barcelona, we have a 1500 sq. m. exhibition of business furnishings. We specialise in the complete installation of all aspects of projects, particularly for offices, on a "turnkey" basis. Our Barcelona showroom incorporates the best items of office furniture from the leading international designers. Our nearly 40 years of existence confirm the high quality and value of our furniture, and the excellent level of service we provide. Our company is part of the M GRUP, whose network of member companies covers almost the whole of Spain, ensuring that we can carry out projects throughout the country.

Nuestra empresa, MANBAR, fue fundada en el año 1953. En la barcelonesa calle de la Vía Augusta, en el nº 61, tenemos ubicada una exposición de casi 1500 m,^{2} dedicada en su totalidad, para el mueble de empresa. Nuestra especialidad, radica, en la instalación integral de todo tipo de obras, sobre todo relacionadas con el mundo de la oficina, realizando las obras, "llave en mano." En nuestro show room de Barcelona, están representados los muebles de oficina de las mejores firmas internacionales, realizados por los diseñadores más prestigiosos dentro del sector, con un alto valor de calidad en los muebles y con un gran cuidado en nuestro servicio que avalamos con los casi 40 años de existencia de MANBAR.

Nuestra sociedad está integrada en el M GRUP, selección de diseño, cuya red de establecimientos miembros, abarca la práctica totalidad de España, siendo una garantia de ejecución de obras en todo el territorio español.

ADDITIONAL INFORMATION

In our studio, we have assembled a group of technical specialists, who can undertake a comprehensive project analysis incorporating interior design and architecture, as well as planning the project implementation.

En nuestra plantilla, se encuentran un grupo de profesionales técnicos, que pueden realizar el estudio completo, de cualquier tipo de obra, tanto a nivel de interiorismo, como a nivel arquitectónico, resolviendo, posteriormente, la ejecución de la misma.

Kings Walk Shopping Centre, Chelsea, London 1988

Kings Walk Shopping Centre, Chelsea, London 1988

Eagle Star Head Office, St. Mary Axe, London 1989

Eagle Star Head Office, St. Mary Axe, London 1989

Mary Quant, Neal Street, London 1988

Mary Quant, Neal Street, London 1988

Mobil Oil, Corporate Communication Pack, UK 1989

MFI, Weston Supermare, 1987

McCOLL GROUP INTERNATIONAL

HEAD OFFICE

64 Wigmore Street
London W1H 9DJ
☎ (0) 71 935 4788
Fax (0) 71 935 0865

INTERNATIONAL OFFICES

Marques de Riscal No 6
28010 Madrid
☎ 341 308 2764

111 Majorca Avenue*
Coral Gables
Florida USA
☎ 305 442 4041

320 West 13th Street*
New York NY 10014
☎ 212 206 0444

* Associates Offices

BRITISH OFFICES

61 Queen Square
Bristol BS1 4JZ
☎ (0) 272 255444
Fax (0) 272 255077

124/125 Princes Street
Edinburgh EH2 4AD
☎ (0) 31 220 3322
Fax (0) 31 220 4454

Ashley House
181/195 West George Street
Glasgow G2 2PN
☎ (0) 41 221 5566
Fax (0) 41 221 5661

Astley House
Quay Street
Manchester M3 4AH
☎ (0) 61 834 6655
Fax (0) 61 834 0705

CONTACT

Stefan Zachary
Managing Director

KEY PERSONNEL

Chris Chanin *Creative Director
interiors*
Clive Newman *Director, graphics*
Tom Ball *Chief Architect*
Gordon Watson *New Business
Development Director*

SIZE OF COMPANY

Personnel : 300

AREAS OF SPECIALISATION

RECENT CLIENTS

Allders
BUPA
Burton Group
Church Commissioners
Halifax Building Society
J Sainsbury
Leeds Building Society
Nabisco Group
National Power
Olympia & York
Prudential
Sears

COMPANY PROFILE

McColl Group International is a multi-disciplinary design consultancy committed to creating commercially successful, cost effective solutions.

Already established as one of Europe's leading shopping centre and retail design specialist, the McColl Group offers clients a complete range of design services from architecture through interior, product and graphic design. Clients also benefit from the consultancy's joint ventures with top design specialists in the hotel/hospitality (Lynn Wilson Associates) and watersport and leisure (S & P) sectors.

The company is already consultant on 60 shopping centre developments and refurbishments throughout Europe.

McColl's reputation is based not only on its understanding of design as a strategic tool for consolidating market share in today's increasingly competitive markets, but also on an ability to interpret the individual needs of our clients, believing that the success of a design solution can only come from informed and effective teamwork between client and designer.

Each of our areas of expertise can be commissioned separately or as a multi-disciplined service, managed through a single line of communication resulting in innovative creative solutions.

Established in 1974, McColl Group International plc employs more than 300 people and is part of the worldwide marketing services group, WPP Group plc. Based in central London, the group has regional offices in Bristol, Cardiff, Manchester, Edinburgh and Glasgow, international offices in Madrid, New York, Miami, Los Angeles, Atlantic City, Paris and Tokyo.

Sweet Factory, development of a new concept in "self-select" confectionery retailing.

ATS; new identity and graphics system for a car service specialist.

Nicolas, Wine Merchant; "flagship" store in Place de la Madeleine, Paris, France.

Country Casuals; identity and interior refurbishment for ladies fashion chain.

Club Méditerranée; design and refurbishment of the Central London Sales Office.

MICHAEL PETERS GROUP
RETAIL ARCHITECTURE AND INTERIORS

Business Design Centre; Exhibition and Trade Centre.

Citibank; design and refurbishment within the European Corporate Headquarters.

Les Arcs; design of a travel office for a unique French ski resort.

HEAD OFFICE

3 Olaf Street
Holland Park
London W11 4BE
☎ (0) 71 229 3424
Fax (0) 71 221 7720

INTERNATIONAL OFFICES

AMSTERDAM
Koningslaan 54
1075 AE Amsterdam
☎ (0) 20 758 551

COPENHAGEN
Gl Lundtoftevej 1A
DK-2800 Lyngby/Copenhagen
☎ (0) 42 888 555

DÜSSELDORF
Bilker Strasse 32
4000 Düsseldorf
☎ (0) 211 13 35 91

MADRID
Velázquez 24, 5° D
28001 Madrid
☎ 91 575 3964

MILAN
Via Dante 4
20121 Milano
☎ (0) 2 7202 0181

KEY PERSONNEL

Rob Davie
Managing Director
Anne Bacon
Marketing Director
Alan Bishop
Design Services Director
John Greensword
Business Development Director

AREAS OF SPECIALISATION

RECENT CLIENTS

Alfa Romeo
Barclays Bank
British Airways
Bruno Magli
Burton Group
Club Méditerranée
Co-op Schweiz
Dixons Group
Eurohub - Birmingham Airport
Gruppo Rinascente
Harvey Nichols
Liberty
Nicolas
Norwich Winterthur
Olympia & York
Phildar
Shell

COMPANY PROFILE

The Michael Peters Group was founded in 1970 and provides an international design and communications consultancy service through offices and studios in Europe, North America and Japan. We combine considerable international design experience with a real understanding of local market conditions.

Our Retail Architecture & Interiors division specialises in the design of commercial environments with particular experience in retail, offices, public spaces and the leisure industry. Our skills include large scale planning and space management, all aspects of interior and retail design and the development of new identities, environmental graphics and signage systems.

Our aim is to optimise the effectiveness of a company's physical resources by turning commercial environments into valuable marketing assets.

Working closely with our clients to understand their specific requirements and establish clear business and design objectives we combine careful analysis and a strategic approach to problem-solving, with a determination to create forward thinking and innovative design.

Our commitment to creative excellence and to finding the right solution is matched by rigorous attention to detail and an ability in practical terms to deliver what we promise.

In September 1990 this company was reorganized
New company's name : **XMPR**
151 Freston Road, London W10 6TH
Tel.: **(0) 71 229 1010** - Fax: **(0) 71 792 9462**

Exchange Travel, Finchley, London

Granada TV & Video Retail Enhancement Newcastle Upon Tyne

Boots Stationary Department, Nottingham

BMW (GB) Ltd. Showroom Display concept, Huntingdon

Parker Pen Department, Selfridges, London

THE PD DESIGN COMPANY LIMITED

Kevin Ryan, Malcolm Tebbatt, John Soppet, Brian Searson, Paul Carr,
David Tilley, Ian Payne, Mike Dolman

HEAD OFFICE

The Grange
Wigston
Leicester LE8 1NN
☎ (0) 533 810 018
Fax (0) 533 813 010

KEY PERSONNEL

John Soppet
Group Chief Executive
Kevin V Ryan
Group Client Services Director
Ian K Payne
Group Marketing Director
Christopher Croyden-Naylor
Sales and Marketing Director –
Display Division
Barry Dorbyshire
Business Development Director –
Interiors Division
Soheila Clarke
Business Development Manager –
Graphics Division
Brian Soarson
Divisional Managing Director –
Manufacturing Services

SIZE OF COMPANY

Personnel: 190

AREAS OF SPECIALISATION

RECENT CLIENTS

BMW (GB) Ltd
Boots Co
British Rail
Calor
Alfred Dunhill Limited
Exchange Travel
Granada TV and Video
Omnix (I.T.) Ltd
Parker Pen Co
Samuel
The Royal Bank of Scotland
The Post Office

COMPANY PROFILE

A truly creative and professional design company, devoted to a fundamental
belief in the design contribution to the business environment.

Our purpose is to help our client's businesses succeed, through the application
of a full range of skills that we can provide in the areas of graphic design, corporate and brand identity, packaging design, design for print, interior design
and display and merchandising.

We recognise our success is dependant upon providing originality in design, fitness for implementation, value for money and design solutions that are commercially effective.

HM Customs & Excise, Staff Restaurant, London, 1990

HM Customs & Excise, Staff Restaurant, London, 1990

OY Stockmann AB, Helsinki store, Finland, 1989

OY Stockmann AB, Helsinki store, Finland, 1989

Alliance & Leicester Building Society, London, 1988

Stuart Trust, New House, Hampstead, (N London), 1987

John Lewis Partnership, Store Restaurant, Edinburgh, 1989

PENNINGTON ROBSON LTD

Jonathan Pennington
MDes RCA, FCSD

Dennis E Robson MA
MA(RCA), FCSD

HEAD OFFICE

Tea Warehouse,
10a Lant Street
London, SE1 1QR
☎ (0) 71 378 0671
Fax (0) 71 378 0531

CONTACT

Jonathan Pennington
Dennis Robson

INTERNATIONAL OFFICES

PRJ Group SL
Plaza Sta Eulalia, 7-6°
07001 Palma de Mallorca, Spain
☎ 34-71 72 07 44
Fax 34-71 72 04 41

Rupert Gardner AB
Sibyllegatan 53
S-114 43 Stockholm, Sweden
☎ 46-8 665 19 10
Fax 46-8 662 70 26

KEY PERSONNEL

Angel Juncosa *Spain*
Rupert Gardner *Sweden*

SIZE OF COMPANY

Personnel : 20

AREAS OF SPECIALISATION

 20% 30% 20% 10%
20%

RECENT CLIENTS

Alliance & Leicester Building Society
Ahlens City (Sweden)
English & Overseas Properties
HM Customs & Excise
ICI
International Wool Secretariat
IRPC (Willis Faber)
John Lewis Partnership
Johnson Wax
Mastercard
Sedgwick Group
Standard Chartered Bank
OY Stockmann AB

COMPANY PROFILE

OUR SPECIALITIES : • Retail • Offices • Refurbishments • Restaurants

WE ESTABLISH : • Realistic budget and programme • Effective project organisation • Clear statement of the brief • Understanding of our clients' business objectives

WE OFFER : • Thorough and rapid problem solving • Solutions responsive to our clients' needs • Rigorous analysis leading to imaginative design • Quality and integrity • Appropriate schemes on time and to budget

NOS SPECIALITES : • Magasins • Bureaux • Rénovations • Restaurants

NOUS ETABLISSONS : • Des programmes et des budgets réalistes • Une organisation efficace du projet • Un exposé clair des missions • Une compréhension des objectifs commerciaux de nos clients

NOUS OFFRONS : • Une réponse rapide et intégrale aux problèmes • Des solutions adaptées aux besoins de nos clients • Une analyse rigoureuse aboutissant à un projet créatif • Qualité et intégrité • Des programmes adaptés, dans les délais et dans les limites budgétaires.

ADDITIONAL INFORMATION

A third of our jobs over the past three years have been in Europe. Our joint venture in Spain and our associates in Sweden offer architecture, interior design and complete fitting-out services. The principals are all graduates of the Royal College of Art.

Current European projects include : • A second department store for OY Stockmann AB (Finland) • Restaurants for a new ship (Scandinavia) • Hotel and commercial interiors (Spain).

Eckes Anuga, Köln, 1989

Eckes Anuga, Köln, 1989

Schneekoppe Anuga, Köln, 1989

Schneekoppe Anuga, Köln, 1989

Canon Cebit, 1990, Hannover

"Frank Rudolph" men's underwear, Hamburg, 1989

Jacobs Suchard ISM, Köln, 1987

Canon Cebit, 1990, Hannover

PETER SCHMIDT VEIT MAHLMANN DESIGN
UND BORN & STRUKAMP MESSEBAU GmbH

Peter Schmidt und Veit Mahlmann

Detlev Strukamp und Jürgen Born

HEAD OFFICE

Peter Schmidt Veit Mahlmann Design
Badestraße 19
D-2000 Hamburg 13
☎ 040 - 44 38 67 und 41 76 00
Fax 040 - 44 68 30

Born & Strukamp Messebau GmbH
Großenbaumer Weg 9
4000 Düsseldorf 30
☎ 0211 - 41 10 25
Fax 0211 - 42 40 53

CONTACT

Gaby Röbber *Contact Director*
Jürgen Born *Associate Director*

KEY PERSONNEL

Detlev Strukamp *Associate Director*
Veit Mahlmann *Design Director*

SIZE OF COMPANY

Personnel PSVM : 16
B & S : 21

AREAS OF SPECIALISATION

RECENT CLIENTS

Toyota
Canon Copylux
Pringle of Scotland
Estee Lauder
Betrix
Blenday
Herlitz
Gilette
Granini
Beiersdorf
Juvena
Jil Sander

COMPANY PROFILE

For twenty years now, Born and Strukamp have been designing and constructing exhibition stands for an international circle of clients: SKF, Uhde Engineering, Erco, Battenfeld industries, Helit.

Peter Schmidt Veit Mahlmann Design work in the area of product, shop and exhibition stand design: Joopl, Davidoff, Lancaster, Schwarzkopf, Schlips & Co, Wella, Bahlsen.

Both companies co-operate freely to produce individually designed exhibition stands which underline our clients' corporate identity, providing the perfect backdrop against which to present their products.

Rowenta, Stand d'exposition Salon des Arts Ménagers, 1989

Bosch, Stand d'exposition Salon Sicob, 1989

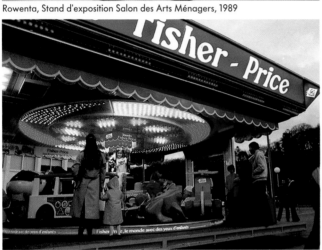

Fisher Price, Manège itinérant

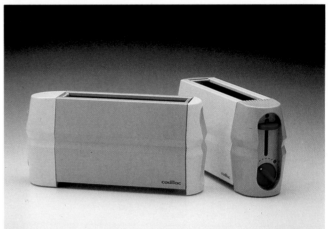

Rowenta-Cadillac, Grille-pain

Groupe Corpus, Bureaux Paris, 1989

Rowenta, Agence commerciale, Paris, 1988

U.C.B., Décor de film studios de "LA 5", Paris, 1987

Friedrich Grohe, Stand d'exposition Salon Bâtimat, 1989

PPH VOLUME

PPH VOLUME

HEAD OFFICE

10, rue Duvergier
75019 Paris
France
☎ 1 40 35 43 45
Fax 1 40 35 43 47

CONTACT

Philippe de Saint-Rémy

KEY PERSONNEL

Philippe de Saint-Rémy *Directeur*
Éric Grisard *Gérant*
Maryse Duret *Assistante Production*
Valéry Taillebois *Bureau d'études*

SIZE OF COMPANY

Personnel : 6

AREAS OF SPECIALISATION

 30 % 20 % 50 %

COMPANY PROFILE

How can a company communicate ?
– A company's headquarters and other working premises reflect its own corporate image, can provide an incentive for corporate consensus and a means of public communication.
– PPH VOLUME can furnish and outfit all headquarters and retail outlets (commercial architecture).
– PPH VOLUME can provide design, packaging and advertising services.
– PPH VOLUME can design and equip your exhibition stands, your space at major events, and your audio-visual presentations.

L'entreprise communique par :
– Le cadre permanent ou occasionnel de son activité ; image d'elle-même, facteur de cohésion à l'intérieur et instrument de promotion à l'extérieur. PPH VOLUME conçoit l'aménagement de sièges sociaux et de locaux commerciaux (architecture commerciale).
– Ses produits, PPH VOLUME les habille (design, P.L.V.).
– Ses manifestations extérieures, PPH VOLUME plante le décor (stands, événements, scénographie).

Holiday Inn, Hamburg

Holiday Inn, Hamburg'

The Dorchester, London

Barbizon Palace, Amsterdam

Le Soufflé Restaurant, Inn on the Park Hotel, London

Oak Room Restaurant, Piccadilly Hotel, London

RICHMOND INSTON

Noel Pierce   Philip Kitchingman

HEAD OFFICE

52-70 Shorts Gardens
London WC2H 9AB
☎ (0) 71 379 6556
Fax (0) 71 240 1915

CONTACT

Elizabeth Purvis
Marketing Strategist
Emma Davies
Marketing Assistant

KEY PERSONNEL

Noel Pierce
Joint Managing Director
Philip Kitchingman
Joint Managing Director
Robert Lush
Chairman

SIZE OF COMPANY

Personnel: 100

AREAS OF SPECIALISATION

100 %

RECENT CLIENTS

Holiday Inns
Inter-Continental Hotels
Hyatt International
Marriot Corporation
Hilton International
Mount Charlotte Hotels
Thistle Hotels
Metropole Hotels
Embassy Hotels
Copthorne Hotels
De Vere Hotels
Ladbroke Hotels
Crest Hotels
Sultan of Brunei
Brent Walker
B.A.A. Hotels
Norfolk Capital Hotels
Voyager Hotels
Swallow Hotels
Gleneagles Hotels
Grand Met Hotels
Golden Tulip Hotels
Forum Hotels
Mecca Leisure
Hanson Trust
Hong Kong Resorts
Pemberton Resort Hotels
International Resort Holdings
Biltimore Hotels

COMPANY PROFILE

Richmond Inston is the largest European based interior design and architecture practice which is fully dedicated to servicing hotel clients around the globe.

The group brings together over fifty years of experience from its origins as The Richmond Design Group and The Peter Inston Design Company. Unmatched technical, commercial and creative resources enable Richmond Inston to act quickly and efficiently anywhere in the world and to complete every project on time and within budget.

Offering clients a choice between a full range of services including architecture, planning, interior design, graphics and purchasing, Richmond Inston provides Hotel groups with additional advantages of cost-effectiveness and coordination.

Every Richmond Inston activity is motivated by a single belief which ensures a fresh approach to every project. The group states:

"A good design is measured by its success in fulfilling our clients objectives. There is no doubt that we produce architectural and interior design solutions which enhance our clients profitability by increased sales, repeat visits and a focussed image within the marketplace."

The Gap, Bath, 1988

Charrington Fuel's HQ, London, 1974

Austin Reed Limited, London, 1976–1981

The Gap - Glasgow, 1989

The Gap - Market Place, Cambridge, 1989

Bathroom interior - Pilkington HQ, St James' London, 1988-1990

Main staircase detail - house, London, 1980

Private house rebuilding, London, 1980

The Gap - Eldon Square, Newcastle, 1988

ROBERT BYRON ARCHITECTS

HEAD OFFICE

78 Fentiman Road
London SW8 1LA
☎ (0) 71 735 0648
Fax (0) 71 735 1843

CONTACT

Robert Byron
Senior Partner
Ann Webb
Partner

SIZE OF COMPANY

Personnel: 6

AREAS OF SPECIALISATION

RECENT CLIENTS

The Gap, Inc. (US retail chain
900 shops)
Austin Reed Limited
J. Rothschilds Limited
Olympus Sports
Charrington Fuel
Goulandris Brothers Shippers
Global Asset Management Limited
Pilkington Glass Limited
Constantine Holdings Limited
Zervudachi & Kuelderli Limited

COMPANY PROFILE

We are an architect based interior design practice with 18 years experience in rebuilding and refurbishment works. Our skills extend from new building design to project management. We specialise in retail shopfitting and have completed 20 stores for The Gap (USA) in the UK and Europe in the last 2 years. Value £8 million. In the past we were responsible for fitting out the Austin Reed "Flagship" in Regent Street, London and have just completed the refurbishment of Pilkington Glass' Headquarters in St James'.

We have chosen to remain a small firm with all design work done by the principal. The emphasis is on a personal service to discerning clients and the provision of unique design work. We are not fashion prone and our interiors have often lasted well over a decade without dating.

Robert Byron est d'origine québecoise et travaille à Londres depuis 25 ans. Il a offert ses services à plusieurs clients d'Europe continentale et conçu des propositions de décoration d'intérieur pour des projets particulièrement complexes. Nous envisageons d'entamer en 1990 un programme continu de développement de locaux commerciaux pour "The Gap USA" en Allemagne, en France et en Italie.

ADDITIONAL INFORMATION

Design Awards. We won the first annual UK wide NAS Interior Design Competition sponsored by the National Associaiton of Shopfitters, the Royal Institute of British Architects and The Design Council.

Cardiff Castle Tourist Centre Architectural Competition Winner, 1990.

Reception, Country Club Hotels

Boardroom, Country Club Hotels

Pool, Country Club Hotels

Bedroom, Intercontinental Hotel

Bathroom, Intercontinental Hotel

THE RPW DESIGN PARTNERSHIP

Patrick Reardon   Jan Wilson   Susan Webster

HEAD OFFICE

77 Weston Street
London SE1 3RS
☎ 071 378 8001
Fax 071 403 6386

CONTACT

Patrick Reardon

KEY PERSONNEL

Karina Knight
Associate
Richard Morton
Associate

SIZE OF COMPANY

Personnel : 14

AREAS OF SPECIALISATION

  20% 80%

RECENT CLIENTS

Country Club Hotels,
Whitbread Retail Division
Norfolk Capital Group Plc
Thistle Hotels Ltd
Metropole Hotels Ltd
Inter-Continental Hotels
Anton Mosimman
The Ritz Hotel, Paris

COMPANY PROFILE

The RPW Design Partnership was established in January 1988 specifically to serve the hotel and leisure industry. Both Patrick Reardon and Jan Wilson jointly have had more than 25 years experience in that field.

The Partnership is dedicated to producing highly creative lasting design solutions which maintain the sense of theatre essential to a hotel's attraction but are not based on fashionable whim or fancy. These solutions are created upon sound operational planning knowledge and a highly developed commercial under-standing of hotel operation. RPW possesses unrivalled expertise in the field of hotel planning and on many occasions we have been brought in to advise and guide the project architect in this critical area.

We pride ourselves on the quality and technical competence of our drawing and specifications documentation. We also have a highly efficient purchasing section which provides a full administrative service dealing on the client's behalf with the ordering, delivery and installation of loose FF&E.

RPW is currently responsible for interiors projects with a value in excess of £12 million sited both in UK and Europe.

Sonia Rykiel, Paris

Aéroport de Gatwick, Londres

Christian Dior, Paris

Habitat, Barcelone (Espagne)

Conran Shop, Londres

RSCG SOPHA DESIGN

Roland De Leu
Creative Director

Jean-Marc Piaton
Chief Executive

Pascal Mathieux
Business Manager

HEAD OFFICE

8, rue Rouget-de-Lisle
92130 Issy-les-Moulineaux
☎ 40 93 93 94
Fax 46 62 60 72
Telex 631 262

INTERNATIONAL OFFICES

RSCG SOPHA DESIGN Tokyo
(c/o H & A)
☎ (813) 499 52 37
Fax (813) 498 42 34

RSCG DESIGN GROUP :
RSCG CONRAN DESIGN/Londres
☎ 071 631 0102
Fax 071 255 2049
Telex 265 490

RSCG CONRAN DESIGN PACIFIC/
Hong Kong
☎ 852 58 68 26 63
Fax 852 58 68 46 58

CONTACT

Pascal Mathieux

KEY PERSONNEL

Roland De Leu (President)
Creative Director
Jean-Marc Piaton *Chief Executive*
Jean-Michel Hieaux
Strategy and Development Manager
Pascal Mathieux *Business Manager*

SIZE OF COMPANY

Personnel : 80

AREAS OF SPECIALISATION

 10%   40%   30%   10%

10%

COMPANY PROFILE

RSCG SOPHA DESIGN, launched in 1979, is the French partner of the RSCG DESIGN GROUP. RSCG SOPHA DESIGN is now the leading design group in France and aims within 5 years to be in the top 5 design groups worldwide.

What sets RSCG SOPHA DESIGN apart and of course RSCG CONRAN DESIGN, is our exceptional breadth of expertise. In Paris, London and Hong Kong, our specialists and support teams are divided into three groups : interior design, graphic design and product design. Our Tokyo office specializes specifically in architecture and interior design services.

RSCG SOPHA DESIGN, créée en 1979, est aujourd'hui leader en France sur son marché et partenaire en France de RSCG DESIGN GROUP qui a pour objectif de se situer dans les 5 plus importants design groupes mondiaux avant 1995.

RSCG SOPHA DESIGN, comme RSCG CONRAN DESIGN, se distingue par l'enseigne exceptionnelle de ses capacités créatives. Notre compétence de spécialistes et nos équipes sont réparties à Paris comme à Londres et Hong Kong en trois divisions : l'architecture intérieure, le design graphique et le design de produit. Seules l'architecture et l'architecture d'intérieur sont aujourd'hui développées par notre bureau de Toyko.

ADDITIONAL INFORMATION

Prix 1989 : Grand prix des inventions de Genève (Ikari, allumeur à flamme rigide), Industriform Hanover (Ikari, allumeur à flamme rigide), Janus de l'industrie (Ikari, allumeur à flamme rigide), Grand prix Stratégies de la publicité (Rapport annuel 1988 Matra).

Nos références à Paris : Assistance Publique - Bouchara - Crédit Agricole d'Ile-de-France - Christian Dior - Céline - Club Méditerranée - Citroën - Caisse des Dépôts et Consignations - La Chemise Lacoste - Décathlon - FNAC - Gervais-Danone - Gan - Givenchy - Habitat - Isabel Canovas - Ville de Nîmes - Nina Ricci - O.J. Perrin - Pari Mutuel Urbain - Panséa - Société des vins de France - Sélection du Reader's Digest - Sophia Antipolis - Société Générale - Procter & Gamble - Whitehall.
A Londres : Aéroport de Londres Gatwick - Conran Shop - Hachette - Pizza Hut.

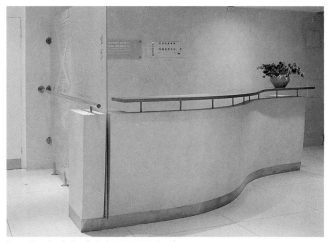

Reception Desk, Trade Indemnity PLC, London

Atrium Finishes, TSB (Scotland) PLC, Edinburgh

Food Court, The Kyle Centre, Ayr

Terraced Water Garden, Triton Court, London

Reception Desk, Matthews Goodman, London

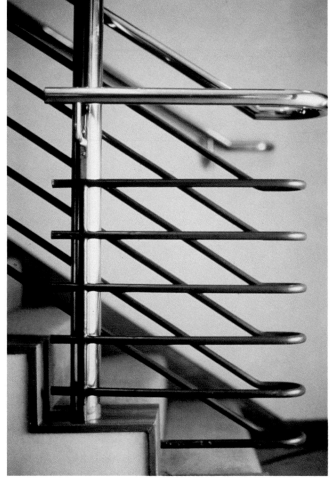

Staircase detail, Harbour Exchange, London

Rouxl Britannia Restaurant, London

Stairwell, Brunel University

Interior Finishes, Dun & Bradstreet International Headquarters, High Wycombe

SHEPPARD ROBSON

HEAD OFFICE

77 Parkway
Camden Town
London NW1 7PU
☎ (0) 71 485 4161
Fax (0) 71 267 3861
Telex 22157

CONTACT

William Dickson *Partner*
Martyn May *Associate*
Robert Malcolm *Senior Designer*
David Siverson *Senior Designer*

KEY PERSONNEL

Amanda Culpin *Interior Designer*
Katerina Giebel *Interior Designer*
Morag Morrison *Interior Designer*

SIZE OF COMPANY

Personnel: 210

AREAS OF SPECIALISATION

RECENT CLIENTS

Dun & Bradstreet International
TSB (Scotland) PLC
American Airlines
Roux Restaurants
Skanska AB
Merck Sharpe & Dohme
Glaxo Group Research Ltd
Sun Alliance Group Properties Ltd
The Royal London Mutual Insurance
   Society Ltd
Trade Indemnity PLC
U.S.A.A.
Westminster & Chelsea Hospital
London & Caltrust Properties

COMPANY PROFILE

Sheppard Robson is an established design practice which offers comprehensive services to its clients. We are architects, interior designers and planners, and our objective is to apply creative thinking and control to the full spectrum of design. We regard Interior Design both as a specialist expertise and as an integral part of the total activity of designing buildings. Our interior design team blends I.D. and architectural skills. It handles specialist interior projects of all descriptions as well as the comprehensive design and implementation of the interiors of major buildings won by the practice.

We believe in a close interaction with our clients to whom we offer creativity and motivation combined with a disciplined design method, and the capacity to manage each project on schedule and to budget.

Basin Alape / tiles Agrob / carpet Gebhan / furniture Duravit

Table lamp BIRD GKS

Garden Hotels, Hamburg

Garden Hotels, Hamburg

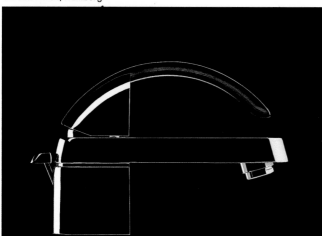

Fitting FINO Dornbracht

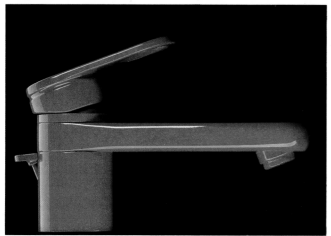

Fitting DOMANI Dornbracht

SIEGER DESIGN

SIEGER DESIGN

HEAD OFFICE

Dieter Sieger
Schloss Harkotten
4414 Sassenberg 2
☎ (0 54 26) 27 96 + 28 16
Fax (0 54 26) 38 75

KEY PERSONNEL

Dieter Sieger *Managing Director*
Christian Sieger *Marketing Director*
Michael Sieger *Design Director*
Benedikt Sauerland *Associate Director*

SIZE OF COMPANY

Personnel : 14

RECENT CLIENTS

Agrob
Alape
Alliance Enamelsteel
DAL
Dornbracht
Duravit
Gebhan
GKS
Hoesch
Hüppe
Peill + Putzler
Stiebel Eltron
Twick + Lehrke
WMF

AREAS OF SPECIALISATION

COMPANY PROFILE

Sieger Design is a full service design consultancy with an architectural background, founded in 1965.

Besides product design, our main area of activity, we can also offer our clients a total concept approach. This might start with the formulation of a company philosophy for our client and can end with the PR support of the final hardware.

International awards and worldwide press releases underline our cross-cultural experience and activity.

Sieger Design ist ein "Full Service" Design Büro, welches sich nach seiner Gründung in 1965 vorrangig mit hochwertiger Architektur befaßte.

Parallel zu unserem Haupttätigkeitsfed, dem Produkt Design, bieten wir unseren Kunden die komplette Konzeption. Diese kann neben der Formulierung einer Firmenphilosophie auch die PR-Betreuung des Endproduktes beinhalten.

Internationale Auszcichnungen und weltweite Veröffentlichungen unterstreichen unsere kulturübergreifende Erfahrung und Aktivität.

ADDITIONAL INFORMATION

Services :
Development of CI
Graphic Design
Product Design
Exhibition Stands
Public Relations
Design Management

The Billen House: Hasselt

The Billen House: Hasselt

The Billen House: Hasselt

Café Hemelryk: Hasselt

The Calliano Apartement: Hasselt

Vittorio Simoni
Manager

N.V. SIMONI INTERIEUR

HEAD OFFICE

Hentjenslaan 9A
3511 Kuringen-Hasselt
Belgium
☎ 011/25 35 02
Fax 011/87 21 00

KEY PERSONNEL

Vittorio Simoni *General Manager*
Patrick Kwanten *Design Manager*
Hilde Thierie *Assistant Manager*

SIZE OF COMPANY

Personnel: 5

AREAS OF SPECIALISATION

RECENT CLIENTS

Saatchi & Saatchi: Brussels
Bell telephone Company: Antwerp
Philips industries: Hasselt
Centurion Communications
　International: Hasselt
Mayor's office: Hasselt
City Museum: Hasselt

COMPANY PROFILE

During twelve years of experience in all fields of interior design, NV Simoni Interieur has developed a distinctive style notable for its manipulation of the architectural aspects of space, rather than application of straightforward decorative solutions. NV Simoni Interieur is especially concerned to select and work with materials of a timeless quality, a timelessness which is transferred to the interiors the firm has designed.

Hairstylist Buzzi: Hasselt

Chicago Board Options Exchange, Trading Complex, Chicago

Chicago Mercantile Exchange, Offices CME Tower

Sydney Futures Exchange, New Trading Floor, Sydney, Australia

Sanwa Business Credit Corporation

Chicago Mercantile Exchange, Committee Room Reception Area

National Futures Association

Chicago Board of Trade, New Trading Floor Complex, Chicago

Ernst & Young

SPACE/MANAGEMENT PROGRAMS Inc.

HEAD OFFICE

230 North Michigan Ave.
Chicago, Illinois 60601
☎ 312 263 2995
Fax 312 263 1236

CONTACT

Charles R. Kinsey *C.E.O.*
James B. Duke *President*
Robert T. Noonan *Business Development*

KEY PERSONNEL

Charles R. Kinsey *C.E.O.*
James B. Duke *President*
Robert A. Geddis *V.P.*
Steven C. Meier *V.P.*
Catherine J. Ritz *V.P.*
Curtis Yoshizumi *V.P.*

AREAS OF SPECIALISATION

🖉 75%   🏛 15%

RECENT CLIENTS

Pacific Stock-Exchange
Sydney Futures Exchange Ltd
National Association of Securities
    Dealers (NASD)
Continental Illinois National Bank
Sanwa Business Credit Corporation
Rich, Inc.
Kemper Financial Services
J. Walter Thompson
Crédit Agricole, C.N.C.A.
London Intl. Futures Exchange
Chicago Board Options Exchange
Sloan Valve Company

COMPANY PROFILE

Space/Management Programs Incorporated is a space planning, architectural interior design and systems consulting firm. The majority of our assignments involve multiple aspects of space planning, interior architecture, and industrial design.

Our premise is that design is problem solving. Our philosophy embodies a team approach involving the client and ourselves, augmented by other consulting professionals as required. We approach our work in such a way that the client is not faced with last minute "surprises." We believe that our design work is only successful when it is on time, on budget, and both functionally and aesthetically appropriate.

We have no branch offices. Centralized senior staff, accessible to one another, allow us to provide cohesive design and project management to both domestic and international clients.

Our approach to environmental design is expressed by our role as problem solvers. We base our planning on the anticipation, accommodation, and management of change. Most importantly, we believe good design must be based on the needs of the end users.

ADDITIONAL INFORMATION

Since 1973, when the firm was founded by Charles R. Kinsey, Space/Management Programs Inc. has grown to become one of Chicago's Largest Design firms.

Space/Management Programs received Industrial Design Excellence awards in 1982 and 1985 for the design of trading complexes for the Chicago Board of Trade and the Chicago Board Options Exchange.

Space/Management Programs, as a firm, has produced almost 500,000 S.F. of trading floors during the past ten years and over 1,000,000 S.F. of trading related support facilities.

Rescalli S.r.L. via Belfiore 11, Milano, 1987

Rescalli S.r.L. via Belfiore 11, Milano, 1987

La Giada Verde, Abbiategrasso (MI), 1987

La Giada Verde

Show-room Paone Muscella, Milano, 1988

EWT SA, Lugano, 1989

Gioielleria Martimucci, Milano, 1987

Bar Ideal, Magenta (MI), 1988

Show-room Paone Muscella, Milano, 1988

STUDIO 2A S.A.S.

HEAD OFFICE

Via Novara 13
20013 Magenta, Milan, Italy
☎ (0) 2 9793177
Fax (0) 2 9794276

INTERNATIONAL OFFICES

c/o Blu Consult
Holzstrasse 11
8000 Munich Germany
☎ (0) 89 260 7799
Fax (0) 89 260 7586

CONTACT

Mainini Roberta
Arico' Laura

KEY PERSONNEL

Bettoncelli Fausto
Passerini Luigi
Mainini Roberta

AREAS OF SPECIALISATION

15% 60% 20% 5%

COMPANY PROFILE

Since 1975, we have been finding solutions to the problems of successfully designing and installing shops, restaurants and business premises. We bring together a wide range of skills in interior architecture, but above all, in decorations, colours, materials and finishings.

We adapt modern, highly specialised materials in response to the needs of specific projects. We are particularly noted for the original yet practical way in which we combine materials, such as iron and steel linked with wood and glass.

We carefully consider the aesthetic and functional requirements of each development we undertake, to be certain that the end result adequately meets the needs of the market-place, and those of our clients.

Abbiamo sviluppato, già dal 1975, una ricerca diretta alla soluzione di ogni problema legato alla progettazione e alla realizzazione di negozi, ristoranti e locali pubblici. Applichiamo una scelta diversificata nel campo del design ma soprattutto delle decorazioni, dei colori, dei materiali e delle finiture.

Adeguiamo alle nostre soluzioni materiali moderni e altamente specializzati per soddisfare una produzione articolata. La nostra peculiarità é basata sul particolare accostamento dei materiali quali il ferro e l'acciaio abbinato al legno, vetro, ecc.

Osserviamo attentamente l'evoluzione delle esigenze estetiche e funzionali per capirle e trasformarle in un prodotto adeguato alle richieste del mercato.

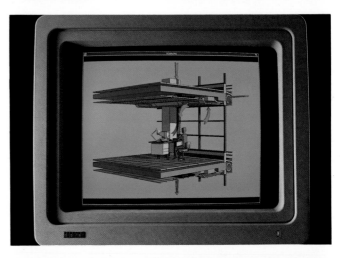

ttsp

HEAD OFFICE

90-98 Goswell Road
London EC1V 7DB
☎ (0) 71 490 8899
Fax (0) 71 490 5845

56 Queen Square
Bristol BS1 4LF
☎ (0) 272 252 207
Fax (0) 272 252 208

CONTACT

Albert V Hayden *FCSD Partner*

INTERNATIONAL OFFICE

Wilhelm-Leuschner - Strasse 7
6000 Frankfurt am Main 1
Germany
☎ 49 69 25 33 08
Fax 49 69 25 33 84

KEY PERSONNEL

John Cossins *ARIBA FCSD (Managing)*
Derek Joiner *FCSD (Managing)*
Albert V Hayden *FCSD*
Derek Amos *DiplArch*
Michael Carter
Anthony Buchanan *NDD*
Paul W Frostick
William Harrison *B Arch RIBA*
A S H Keep *RIBA*
Keith Warner

SIZE OF COMPANY

Personnel: 170

AREAS OF SPECIALISATION

RECENT CLIENTS

Credit Lyonnais Capital Markets plc
British Aerospace plc
Cameron Markby Hewitt
The Chase Manhattan Bank NA
Clifford Chance
Dow Chemical Company Ltd
MEPC Group of Companies
Mercury Asset Management
Norwich Union Life Insurance Society
Peat Marwick McLintock
Price Waterhouse
Prudential Corporation plc
Shearson Lehman Hutton
S G Warburg & Co.
The Wellcome Foundation
Westpac Banking Corporation

COMPANY PROFILE

Founded in 1961, ttsp has consciously evolved a policy of developing a "multi faceted" Practice with contemporary skills and services.

ttsp has extensive experience in designing and fitting-out buildings throughout the U.K., Middle East and in France.

Die Firma ttsp, die im Jahr 1961 gegründet wurde, arbeitet in der Praxis bewußt nach dem Prinzip, das vielseitig ist und durch fachkundige Kenntnisse und Betreuung den Anforderungen der Zeit entspricht.

Die Firma ttsp hat umfassende Kenntnisse im Entwurf und in der Ausstattung von Gebäuden in England, im Nahen Osten und in Frankreich.

ADDITIONAL INFORMATION

ttsp employs the most advanced computer aided design and draughting technology to assist both the design and draughting process and the analysis of complex data.

The CADD system is integrated into all working groups within the Practice and provides a versatile facility for evaluating space and building forms, producing detailed drawings, solid modelling and 3-dimensional visualisations and design concepts in colour.

Benefits to the client include a faster more efficient service, an ability to provide alternative solutions for client consideration, improved cost control and more efficient time management and enhanced expertise.

Mecca Leisure, ritzy discotheque, Derby, 1989

Alexandra Theatre, cafe bar, Birmingham, 1989

First Leisure Corporation, superbowl, Derby, 1988

Drummonds, cafe bar, Glasgow, 1989

Fuller, Smith & Turner, restaurant, Docklands, London, 1989

First Leisure Corporation, amusement arcade, Blackpool, 1989

Bass, disco-bar, Birmingham, 1988

Grand Metropolitan, mature bar, Newbury, 1988

TIBBATTS & CO DESIGN GROUP LIMITED

Neil Tibbatts

HEAD OFFICE

1 St. Paul's Square
Birmingham B3 1QU
☎ (0) 21 233 2871
Fax (0) 21 236 8705
Telex 336947 TIBCO G

CONTACT

Peter Detre
Group Marketing Director
Alison Gilbert
Managing Director - Interiors
Stephen Larcombe
Managing Director - Turnkey Projects
James Bundred
Managing Director - Architecture

KEY PERSONNEL

Arnold Hurley
Business Development Exec.
John Sabell
Business Development Exec.
Pat Jones
Marketing Manager

SIZE OF COMPANY

Personnel: 90

AREAS OF SPECIALISATION

RECENT CLIENTS

First Leisure Corporation
The Rank Organisation
Granada Leisure Ltd.
Whitbread
Fuller, Smith & Turner, Plc
Grand Metropolitan Retailing Ltd.
Pier House Inns Ltd.
Fownes Hotels
Bass Leisure Ltd.
Hilton
Toby Restaurants
Leading Leisure Plc
Mecca Leisure Ltd.

COMPANY PROFILE

Tibbatts & Co. is one of the UK's leading design groups, specialising in commercial leisure and hospitality design and offering a chartered architecture, interior design and turnkey service.

The company has extensive experience gained over a decade in working with major hospitality, leisure and hotel companies in the U.K. and Western Europe, in addition to Canada and North America. Tibbatts & Co. prides itself on the use of creative design and architecture, along with an understanding and knowledge of the leisure and hospitality market, and the influences upon that market, to produce successful operations for its clients. The group's ability to create and implement creative environments on time and on budget has enabled it to establish longstanding working relationships with all its clients.

IBM UK, Customer Centre, Croydon, 1989

IBM UK, Customer Centre, Croydon, 1989

Suits You, Menswear Shop, London, 1988

Lloyds Bank, Swansea, 1987

Whittard, tea & coffee retailers, Oxford, 1989

TILNEY LUMSDEN SHANE LIMITED

Kathy Tilney   Marvin Shane   Callum Lumsden

HEAD OFFICE

5 Heathmans Road
London SW6 4TJ
☎ (0) 71 731 6946
Fax (0) 71 736 3356

CONTACT

Heather Shane *Financial Director*

KEY PERSONNEL

Kathy Tilney *Director*
Marvin Shane *Director*
Callum Lumsden *Director*
Judi Shaw *Senior Associate*

AREAS OF SPECIALISATION

RECENT CLIENTS

Austin Reed Group plc
BMG/RCA Records Limited
British Airways plc
British Rail
FBK Group plc
IBM UK Limited
Lex Service plc
London Underground Limited
Norsk Hydro Limited
Ogilvy & Mather plc

COMPANY PROFILE

Established in 1980, Tilney Lumsden Shane have design expertise in corporate identity, retail, leisure and commercial interiors for a wide range of European clients.

Our design solutions are based upon an in-depth understanding of each client's marketing and operational strategies. We have a reputation for creativity with high standards in project management and production of information for manufacture.

Établi en 1980, Tilney Lumsden Shane s'est spécialisé en conception pour une grande diversité de clients européens, dans le champ d'image corporative, de même que le détail, les loisirs et les intérieurs commerciaux.

Nos conceptions sont fondées sur une compréhension profonde de la stratégie de marketing et d'opération de chaque client. Nous avons une réputation pour les solutions créatives liées aux normes les plus élevées dans la conduite des projets et la préparation de l'information pour les fabricants.

Desde 1980, Tilney Lumsden Shane evoca en una gran variedad de clientes europeos la experiencia en el diseño, tanto de la imagen corporativa como del de interiores comerciales, tiendas y la industria del ocio.

Nuestros diseños se basan en un profundo entendimiento de la estrategia operativa y de mercado de nuestros clientes. Nuestra reputación se fundamenta en la creatividad aunada a las más altas normas al gestionar proyectos y producir información para las fabricantes.

Financial & General Bank, London, 1989

Christmas exhib., Natl. Gallery, London

Doulton Story, Victoria & Albert Museum

London Brick exhibition, Interbuild, Birmingham

Collins Publishers at Frankfurt Bookfair

Reception for Redland Plasterboard, Reigate

TRICKETT ASSOCIATES/TRICKETT & WEBB

Lynn Trickett   Brian Webb   Terry Trickett

HEAD OFFICE

The Factory
84 Marchmont Street
London WC1N 1HE
☎ (0) 71-388 6586
Fax (0) 71-387 4287

CONTACT

Terry Trickett *Director*
Brian Webb *Director*
Lynn Trickett *Director*

INTERNATIONAL OFFICES

Russell/Trickett & Webb
584 Broadway
New York, NY 10012
☎ 212 431 8770
Fax 212 431 8771

KEY PERSONNEL

Andrew Thomas
Alexandra Prescott

SIZE OF COMPANY

Personnel: 20

AREAS OF SPECIALISATION

RECENT CLIENTS

British Telecom
Canon Research Centre Europe
Collins Publishers
European Science Foundation
Financial Times
London Brick
NCR
Nicholas Angell (France)
Price Waterhouse
Redland

COMPANY PROFILE

Set up in 1972, Trickett Associates (architects and interior designers) and Trickett & Webb (graphic designers) together produce exhibitions which communicate effectively and are visually exciting. Our work ranges far and wide geographically (from world-wide travelling shows to one-off events in Birmingham, London, Frankfurt, Los Angeles, etc.) and serves an extensive range of purposes including museum displays, trade events and long-term showroom installations.

A brochure illustrating successful solutions for Signs and Exhibitions is available.

Fondés en 1972, les bureaux d'études de Trickett Associates (architectes et architectes d'intérieurs) et Trickett & Webb (compositions graphiques) produisent conjointement des expositions à la fois efficaces sur le plan de la communication et d'un fort attrait visuel. La gamme de nos réalisations est très étendue sur le plan géographique et va des expositions itinérantes, couvrant le monde entier, aux manifestations uniques (qu'elles aient lieu à Birmingham, à Londres, à Francfort ou à Los Angeles). Elle répond à une grande variété de besoins, qu'il s'agisse d'installation de musées, de manifestations commerciales ou d'aménagement de salles d'expositions permanentes.

Une brochure illustrant certaines de nos réalisations en matière de signalétique et d'expositions est disponible.

ADDITIONAL INFORMATION

Award winning work includes : D & AD Silvers for corporate identity, direct mail & book design ; Design Week Gold award for calendar design : Donside Paper Gold for financial literature ; International Package Design Gold, New York ; a medal in the first Poster Trienniale at the Museum of Modern Art in Toyama, Japan ; National Business Calendar Awards ; & Exhibition Design Awards at Interbuild. Our work has been exhibited extensively in the UK and throughout the World.

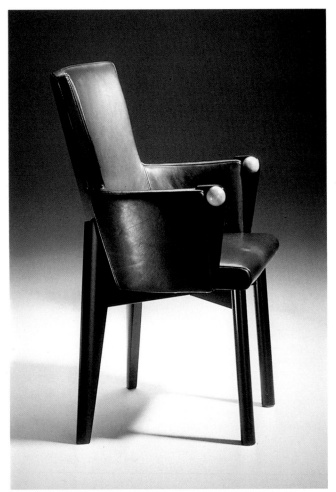

Chair Napoleon, 1989

Mölnlycke Library and cultural building

IHM. Business School. Göteborg, 1988

WHITE DESIGN

Elisabeth Rosenlund

Hans Gunnarsson

Olle Anderson

IBM. Göteborg, 1989

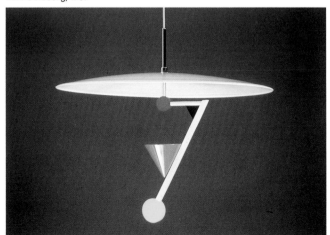

Lighting Halo There, 1983

Hotel Gothia. Göteborg, 1986

HEAD OFFICE

Box 2502
S 40317 Göteborg
☎ 46 31 173460
Fax 46 31 114642

INTERNATIONAL OFFICES

White & Partners
Avenue L Gribaumont, 1
B-11500 Brussels
Belgium
☎ 32-02-7724310
Fax 32-02-7724308

KEY PERSONNEL

Elisabeth Rosenlund *Chief Designer*
Hans Gunnarsson *Chief Designer*
Olle Anderson *Professor at the
University of Design and Craft in
Göteborg. Managing Director*

SIZE OF COMPANY

Personnel: 25

AREAS OF SPECIALISATION

RECENT CLIENTS

IBM
Volvo
SAS Servicepartner
Ericson
Skanska
PK Banken
City of Göteborg
SARA Hotels
Mc Donalds
IHM Business School

COMPANY PROFILE

White Design is an independent division of White Arkitekter, one of the leading
architectural practices in Sweden, with 35 years of experience in all fields of
architecture and design.
Total number of personnel : 300

The Design Group works with all kinds of interiors but also provides industrial
design for the most demanding and famous furniture and lighting companies in
Sweden. Through the interdisciplinary approach and close cooperation with the
architectural practice, the team has developed a deep understanding of all
aspects of the design field. The group has received many awards for interior
and industrial design.

Hyatt Regency Coolum, Australia

The Grand Floridian Beach Resort, Orlando, Florida

The Grand Floridian Beach Resort, Walt Disney World, Orlando, Florida

The Ritz-Carlton, Laguna Niguel, California

Sheraton Hobart Hotel, Tasmania

Shangri-La Hotel, Singapore

WIMBERLY ALLISON TONG & GOO

HAWAII / FAR EAST
Sidney C.L. Char *Managing Director*
J. Patrick Lawrence, *Director*
2222 Kalakaua Avenue
Honolulu, Hawaii 96815
USA
☎ (808) 922 12 53
Fax (808) 923 63 46

INTERNATIONAL OFFICES

LONDON / EUROPE
George Berean *Managing Director*
Ronald D. Van Pelt *Director*
Waldron House
57 Old Church St. London SW3 5BS
England

CALIFORNIA / NORTH AMERICA
Michael M.S. Chun *Managing Director*
Gerald L. Allison *Director*
140 Newport Center Drive
Newport Beach, California 92660
USA
☎ (714) 759 89 23
Fax (714) 759 34 73

SIZE OF COMPANY

Personnel : 300

AREAS OF SPECIALISATION

 5% 15%  80%

RECENT CLIENTS

Anheuser-Busch Companies
Costain Homes, Ltd
Euro Disneyland
Four Seasons Hotels
Hilton Hotels Corporation
Hyatt International Corporation
Kajima Corporation
Kumagai Gumi Company, Ltd
Maltauro Group
Marriott Corporation
Orient-Express Hotels, Inc
Ritz-Carlton Hotel Company
Royale Resorts international
Serena Hotels
Sheraton Corporation
Shimizu Corporation
Takenaka Corporation
Westin Hotels

COMPANY PROFILE

Wimberly Allison Tong & Goo is recognised as one of the world's leading architectural firms specialising in the field of hotel and resort planning and design.
Since its founding in 1945, the firm has completed work in over 50 countries,
with projects throughout Europe, the Pacific Rim, Hawaii, across the U.S. Main-
land, Mexico, South America, the Caribbean, Africa and the Middle East.

WAT&G's expertise centres around the planning, design and renovation of
urban and resort hotels, mixed-use projects, retail centres, restaurants, theatres,
clubs and recreational facilities.

WAT&G has over 25,000 new hotel rooms to its credit in projects that have
been widely acclaimed with prestigious design awards and featured in over
150 publications worldwide. The firm has been recognised for its ability to
design outstanding facilities which respect the environment and cultural heritage
of each host community. This sense of place has become an important feature
of WAT&G projects around the world.

Midland Bank, Corporate Banking Centre, Croydon, 1987

Q8, Station, Madrid, 1988

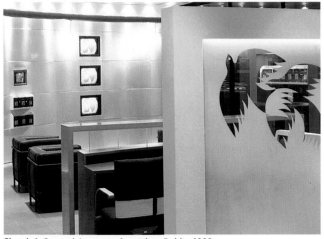

Church & General, Insurance Specialists, Dublin, 1988

Repsol, Station, Madrid, 1988

Butano, Showroom, Barcelona, 1989

Regus Business Centre, London, 1989

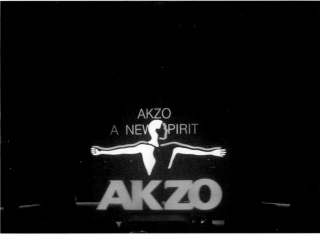

Regus Conference Centre, London, 1989

AKZO launch, Belgium, 1987

Maybox Cinema, Slough, 1985

WOLFF OLINS/HAMILTON

Steve Lightbody,
Managing Director

Doug Hamilton,
Creative Director

HEAD OFFICE

22 Dukes Road,
London WC1H 9AB
☎ (0) 71 387 0891
Fax (0) 71 388 2460
Telex (0) 71 261 438

AREAS OF SPECIALISATION

30%   20%   20%   20%

10%

INTERNATIONAL OFFICES

Wolff Olins
72, rue du Faubourg Saint-Honoré
75008 Paris
☎ (1) 40 07 86 06
Fax (1) 40 07 80 40

KEY PERSONNEL

Roger Adams *Director*
Cathy O'Reilly *Director*
Julie Barker *Director*

RECENT CLIENTS

Allied Irish Banks
British Telecom International
Heidrick & Struggles
Prudential
Sun Alliance
3i
Toshiba
Toyota
Unilever
Vauxhall
Welcome Biotech

COMPANY PROFILE

WOLFF OLINS/HAMILTON is the three dimensional design division of WOLFF OLINS involved in architecture, interior and exhibition design. Established in 1985, Wolff Olins/Hamilton seeks to provide its clients with effective design solutions providing them with competitive advantage in their markets.

ADDITIONAL INFORMATION

WOLFF OLINS has viewed Europe as its home market since the late 60s and has a reputation for producing both pioneering and durable work. "The management of change through the strategic use of design" summarises the business philosophy of a design group incorporating corporate identity, literature, behaviour and communications as well as three dimensional design. The group employs a total of 170 people and with offices in London and Paris is able to service clients in Continental Europe.

Midland Bank

Minster Court, CAD drawing

Berwin Leighton legal practice

Mitsubishi Trust International

Octopus Publishing Group, Michelin Building

Water sculpture, North Terminal, London Gatwick Airport

RAC Motorway Control Centre

YRM INTERIORS

YRM INTERIORS

YRM Interiors Divisional Directors

HEAD OFFICE

YRM Interiors
24 Britton Street
London EC1M 5NQ
☎ (0) 71 253 4311
Fax (0) 71 250 1688
Telex 21692 YRM G

CONTACT

Garry Griffiths *FCSD*
Managing Director
John Holt *BA*
Associate

KEY PERSONNEL

Michael Hart *FCSD*
Roland Gibbard *Des RCA FCSD*
Sevil Gence *FCSD*

SIZE OF COMPANY

Personnel:
YRM Interiors: 35
YRM Partnership: 550

AREAS OF SPECIALISATION

RECENT CLIENTS

Allied Dunbar
Arthur Andersen
BAA (Airports and Hotels)
British Airways
C & A
Chemical Bank
Glaxo
Goldman Sachs
Hilton
IBM
Oxford University
J P Morgan
Midland Bank
Reckitt + Colman
Standard Chartered Bank Hong Kong

COMPANY PROFILE

YRM Interiors is concerned with all aspects of the interior environment, from overall spatial concept through design and contract management, to specification of furniture, furnishings, graphics and artwork. Its leading position in the design industry is maintained through a commitment to dynamic project management with strong emphasis on Computer Aided Design and space planning.

YRM Interiors accepts major commissions in its own right, specialising in both fit-out and refurbishment from 2,000 to 100,000 m². As part of YRM Partnership Ltd. with 550 professional staff, it can also draw on the resources of the Architectural, Engineering and International divisions to provide a genuine multi-disciplinary service to any client.

YRM Interiors is arguably Britain's foremost corporate office design practice, and an international brand leader in the financial and professional services sector, but our broader experience includes interiors of airports, offices, hotels, hospitals, universities, civic and residential buildings. Projects are located in the UK, Europe and worldwide.

YRM Interiors' professional staff speak English, Finnish, French, German, Irish Gaelic, Spanish and Turkish.

ADDITIONAL INFORMATION

YRM Partnership's many commendations include RIBA Architecture Awards, Civic Trust Awards, Structural Steel Design Awards, Financial Times Industrial Architecture Commendations, and Office of the Year award.

INTERIOR DESIGNER (O.P.Q.A.I.)
A QUALIFICATION RECOGNIZED THROUGHOUT EUROPE

The professional interior designer is someone who, having become qualified through the teaching he has received and through his experience and talent,
1) identifies, analyses and solves in a creative way problems which are specific to the quality and the function of an interior environment;
2) deals with the services which relate to the interior spaces, such as analysing the project, planning the space, making aesthetic decisions and managing the site, using his particular expertise in the techniques of the secondary stage of architectural work, in construction systems and building regulations, and in fittings materials and furnishings;
3) prepares drawings, plans and documents relating to the conception of the interior spaces,
... all in order to bring out the quality of life, and protect the health, the security and the well-being of the public.
This definition was adopted by the I.F.I. General Assembly which took place in Hamburg (Germany) on 25 May 1983.
In France the title of "Architecte d'Intérieur" (Interior Designer) is recognized by the Professional Office for the Qualification of Interior Designers (O.P.Q.A.I.).
O.P.Q.A.I. comprises two founder members: the Order of Architects and the National Union of Interior Designers. Its goal is to guarantee to public or private customers the professional competence of interior designers who have qualified with O.P.Q.A.I.
The following are the criteria for these professional qualifications:
THE CERTIFICATE of QUALIFICATION is awarded to professionals with at least 5 years of professional work behind them, upon submission of a dossier of work (3 complete projects) and of references which testify to ten years of work on the level of project manager, and which provide proof of work practices and a respect for the rules of ethics such as these are defined by the code of professional duties of interior designers.
THE CERTIFICATE of COMPETENCE is awarded to young professionals who have had at least 3 years of experience, and who hold a diploma in interior design recognized by the O.P.Q.A.I. and awarded through the following schools:
École Nationale des Arts Décoratifs; École Nationale Supérieure des Arts Appliqués et des Métiers d'Art; École Boule; École Comondo; École Supérieure d'Arts Graphiques et d'Architecture d'Intérieur; École Nationale Supérieure des Beaux-Arts de Toulouse.
This certificate is valid for 3 years. At the end of this period the holder must apply for a Certificate of Qualification or an extension for a limited period of 2 years.
This Qualification is awarded on the advice of a commission made up of interior designers, architects and outside individuals who are known for their competence in the realm of architecture and the plastic arts.
The O.P.Q.A.I. qualification allows the holder to use the title Interior Designer, the right to carry out interior design commissions and access to the State sector market.
At present 750 professionals have set out to obtain, or have already obtained, this qualification. Their ever growing numbers will allow the S.N.A.I. to prepare in the best possible conditions the setting up of a procedure for validating equivalent qualifications in time for the opening of the greater European market in 1992.

André LABORDE
President of the S.N.A.I.

ARCHITECTE D'INTÉRIEUR OPQAI
UNE COMPÉTENCE RECONNUE POUR L'EUROPE

L'architecte d'intérieur professionnel est une personne qui, qualifiée par l'enseignement reçu, l'expérience et des talents reconnus,
1) identifie, analyse et résout de façon créative les problèmes spécifiques à la qualité et à la fonction de l'environnement intérieur ;
2) traite des services relatifs aux espaces intérieurs tels que : définition du programme, analyse du projet, planification d'espace, choix esthétique et direction du chantier, en utilisant ses connaissances particulières des techniques du second œuvre, des systèmes de construction, des réglementations du bâtiment, des équipements, des matériaux et de l'ameublement ;
3) prépare dessins, plans et documents ayant trait à la conception des espaces intérieurs,
... afin de mettre en valeur la qualité de la vie, de protéger la santé, la sécurité et le bien-être du public.
Cette définition fut adoptée par l'Assemblée Générale de l'IFI qui eut lieu à Hambourg, R.F.A., le 25 mai 1983.
En France, le port du titre d'Architecte d'Intérieur est reconnu par l'Office Professionnel de Qualification des Architectes d'Intérieur O.P.Q.A.I.
O.P.Q.A.I. se compose de 2 membres fondateurs : l'Ordre des Architectes et le Syndicat National des Architectes d'Intérieur.
Son objectif est de garantir aux utilisateurs publics ou privés la compétence professionnelle des architectes d'intérieur qualifiés par l'O.P.Q.A.I.

Les critères de qualification professionnelle sont les suivants :
LE CERTIFICAT DE QUALIFICATION est délivré aux professionnels ayant au moins 5 ans d'activité professionnelle sur présentation d'un dossier de réalisation (3 projets complets) et de références

justifiant d'une assurance décennale de maître-d'œuvre et apportant la preuve d'un mode d'exercice et de respect des règles déontologiques telles qu'elles sont définies dans le code des devoirs professionnels des architectes d'intérieur.
LE CERTIFICAT DE CAPACITÉ délivré aux jeunes professionnels ayant moins de 3 ans d'exercice, titulaires d'un diplôme en architecture intérieure reconnu par l'O.P.Q.A.I. est délivré par les écoles suivantes :
École Nationale des Arts Décoratifs ; École Nationale Supérieure des Arts Appliqués et des Métiers d'Art ; École Boule ; École Comondo ; École Supérieure d'Arts Graphiques et d'Architecture d'Intérieur ; École Nationale Supérieure des Beaux-Arts de Toulouse.
Ce certificat est valable 3 ans. A l'issue de cette période, le titulaire doit demander un certificat de qualification ou une prolongation pour une durée limitée de 2 ans.
Cette qualification est accordée après avis d'une commission composée d'architectes d'intérieur, d'architectes et de personnalités extérieures connues pour leurs compétences dans le domaine architectural et plastique.
La qualification O.P.Q.A.I. permet le port du titre d'Architecte d'Intérieur, le droit à l'exercice des missions d'architecture d'intérieure ainsi que l'accès au marché public d'état.
Aujourd'hui 750 professionnels ont entrepris ou obtenu leur qualification. Ce nombre toujours plus grand permettra au S.N.A.I. de préparer, dans les meilleures conditions, la mise en place d'une procédure d'équivalence pour l'ouverture du grand marché européen de 1992.

André LABORDE
Président du S.N.A.I.

L'ARCHITECTURE INTERIEURE DANS LES ANNEES 90

PAR JEREMY MYERSON ET WENDY SMITH

C'est la combinaison de divers facteurs économiques, culturels et technologiques de l'évolution qui a mis sur le devant de la scène internationale le designer de l'environnement et l'architecte d'intérieur.
La tendance culturelle à réhabiliter les constructions anciennes, dans le souci de conserver un héritage, explique sans aucun doute la place importante faite aux designers d'intérieur dans les commissions de rénovation.
L'impulsion technologique que les techniques de conception assistée par ordinateur ont apportée au cabinet de design, permettant une grande productivité sur de vastes projets, et une approche plus scientifique et plus rationnelle dans la discipline, est un autre facteur-clé dans l'émergence de l'audit du design intérieur en tant que force capitale au sein des milieux des affaires et du bâtiment.
Mais toute l'activité que nous avons vue en Europe, en Amérique du Nord et dans le Pacifique a été stimulée par la direction des courants économiques sous-jacents. Les baromètres économiques pointaient tous une direction apte à soutenir le niveau de croissance.

ECONOMIE

Le marché mondial du design et de l'architecture a grimpé à des niveaux impressionnantes. Des estimations industrielles fiables situent le niveau des rentrées provenant du design et de l'architecture – rentrées qui ont été séparées des budgets de la construction et de la documentation – à 12 milliards de dollars dans le monde. L'Amérique du Nord est le plus gros marché, comptant environ 6 milliards de dollars de rentrées. L'Europe en compte 4 milliards et on lui prévoit la croissance la plus rapide grâce à la future harmonisation du marché en 1993. Quant à l'Extrême-Orient, il compte 2 milliards de dollars et représente un potentiel énorme, étant donné les récentes initiatives politiques et commerciales.
Si l'on divise les 12 milliards de dollars selon les catégories, la part du lion revient à l'architecture commerciale (4,1 milliards de dollars) et au design intérieur comprenant le commerce de détail (2 milliards de dollars). Le design graphique et de produits finis représente un peu moins de 2 milliards.
Le designer d'environnement et l'architecte d'intérieur travaillent maintenant dans un marché de plus de 10 milliards de dollars qui ne cesse de croître et manient des budgets de construction et de rénovation pouvant être estimés à plus de 100 milliards de dollars.
Pourquoi ce niveau d'activité ? L'explication la plus simple réside dans la prospérité grandissante des nations – il y a plus de richesses à consacrer à l'amélioration de l'environnement, des conditions de vie, de travail et de loisirs. On peut avoir un simple aperçu de ce processus en mesurant les poussées prononcées du PNB (produit national brut) dans les pays comme l'Allemagne de l'Ouest, l'Espagne, la Grande-Bretagne et le Japon.
L'accroissement de la prospérité a donné suffisamment confiance aux sociétés du monde entier – tant grands magasins, chaînes d'hôtel que promoteurs – pour qu'ils investissent dans un design intérieur plus sophistiqué. Il y a aussi eu une poussée de la part de l'usager. Car les gens sont mieux éduqués, voyagent plus et sont plus demandeurs que jamais.

LES INNOVATEURS

Cependant, même si les baromètres économiques sont bien orientés, il faut du courage et de la conviction de la part des innovateurs et de leurs équipes de design pour créer un design intérieur qui brise les carcans.
Un bref survol des innovations récentes révèle qu'on trouve une évolution importante dans trois principaux marchés du design intérieur. Où est le secteur de pointe dans l'architecture intérieure japonaise ? "Le commerce de détail et l'hôtellerie" selon Ken Walker, le président du Walker Group/CNI américain de designers, qui a un bureau à Tokyo.
"Les Japonais sont friands des nouvelles idées internationales et ils traitent les nouvelles idées comme des objets. Tout est construit en contraste par rapport au reste. Tokyo n'a absolument aucun sens du design contextuel. Les Japonais vont prendre quelque chose de Waldter, de Nigel Coates, de Frank Gehry ou de Philippe Starck, et ils vont construire une succession de nouveautés qui vont rivaliser."
Ces nouveautés sont aussi de courte durée.
L'architecte anglais Nigel Coates, qui a beaucoup travaillé au Japon sur des plans d'intérieur tels que le Caffe Bongo et l'Hôtel Otaru Marritimo, raconte avec découragement comment les clients commencent à faire de gros dégâts avant même que le designer ait pris le chemin de l'aéroport.
Pourtant, Ken Walker dit que des sociétés comme Sony ou Nissan sont de véritables créatifs. "En particulier les constructeurs automobiles, qui ont fait de leurs magasins des centres d'idées," souligne-t-il.
Les compagnies japonaises ont aussi fait leurs preuves à Hong Kong, selon Patrick Bruce, P.-D.G. de RSCG Conran Design Pacific. Néanmoins, pour Bruce, le meilleur plan intérieur d'Extrême-Orient n'est pas un magasin ou un hôtel. C'est le Changi Airport de Singapour, qu'il vante pour "l'excellence de son design et son ambiance appropriée." Les designers étaient Chaix et Johnson, une société américaine ayant un bureau à Singapour.
Si nous en revenons aux Etats-Unis, un courant innovateur a aussi émergé dans un aéroport. Les essais de lumière, d'espace et de sculpture de Murphy/Jahn au United Airlines Terminal de l'aéroport O'Hare de Chicago sont un bonheur pour les voyageurs qui y passent. Mais c'est dans les hôtels et les loisirs que les efforts sont actuellement le plus concentrés aux USA.
Etant donné la situation précaire de l'économie américaine, Ken Walker prévoit que les opportunités du design intérieur américain pour les années 1990 résideront "plus dans le gain de part de marchés que dans une croissance du marché."
Mais il n'y a pas besoin d'aller si loin pour voir à l'évidence l'extraordinaire éclosion du design intérieur européen. C'est probablement en France et en Espagne qu'elle a été le plus spectaculaire, sans oublier, bien entendu, la Grande-Bretagne.
Les Français ont bénéficié d'un avantage particulier, d'une sorte de soutien éclairé de l'Etat dont seuls les

designers peuvent rêver. Mais les designers d'intérieur et d'ameublement en France ont su capitaliser les opportunités qu'ont constitué les grands projets initiés par François Mitterrand et Jack Lang pendant les années 80.

La mane gouvernementale s'est répandue dans une série de projets de constructions publiques considérés comme exercices pour amorcer la pompe qui fera de Paris un leader mondial de l'art, de l'architecture et du design, et pour donner un exemple au reste du pays. Les Français ont maintenant émergé sur la scène internationale en qualité de sérieux leaders, développement illustré par l'acquisition récente de Conran Design Group, le plus grand nom du design intérieur, par le groupe RSCG.

Les designers espagnols n'ont sans doute pas encore la maîtrise des affaires internationales de leurs équivalents français, mais assurément l'Espagne a été le lieu d'importantes innovations créatives dans les espaces intérieurs ; quantité d'entre elles sont rassemblées à Barcelone et s'inspirent des traditions culturelles, illustrant l'âme catalane. Salvador Ballarin, chez McColl Spain, fait remarquer que le travail d'avant-garde s'est fait dans "les bars et les restaurants en vue, les médias et les sociétés financières."

L'Espagne ne sortira sans doute pas de la scène internationale, du fait des jeux olympiques de Barcelone et de l'Exposition Universelle de Séville, même si, au grand dam des Espagnols, on introduit de plus en plus d'architectes internationaux sur les projets de design associés à ces événements. Les compagnies italiennes se mettent, elles aussi, à demander un design intérieur haut de gamme, notamment Olivetti et le géant de la mode GFT. L'approche latine du design se veut un contraste au modèle anglo-saxon le plus terre-à-terre et le plus empirique, le boum anglais, par exemple, ne s'est pas fait grâce à une science visuelle infuse des clients. Il est bien plutôt dû à l'émergence d'une nouvelle génération de managers de projets travaillant dans de grosses sociétés ou dans le public : le soutien des designers de l'environnement par des gens comme Jane Priestman à British Rail, Dick Petersen à BAA (direction des aéroports), Tony Key à British Rail Telecom et Jeremy Rewge-Davies au London Transport, a donné naissance à de nombreuses commissions d'innovations.

Cependant que le designer allemand Dieter Sieger Design cite le fabricant de cuisines Bulthaup et la firme d'éclairage Erco comme exemples de sociétés allemandes ayant une excellente philosophie du design scandinave : la foi en la qualité, en l'intemporalité et en la prise en considération de l'environnement.

PROCESSUS

La façon dont le travail de design intérieur est commandé et réalisé varie d'un pays à l'autre, et se situe de toute façon dans un cycle de constants changements. Pourtant, il y a un certain nombre de tendances qui se font jour et valent d'être débattues. Le Dr Frank Duffy du DEGW d'architectes et de designers britanniques fait la distinction entre l'approche du design intérieur américain et européen. Le modèle américain partage la responsabilité entre le designer de la carcasse du bâtiment et le designer de l'intérieur. Cela se traduit, explique-t-il, par le fait qu'un bâtiment robuste peut être utilisé plusieurs fois

dans son existence, décoré de diverses manières par divers designers d'intérieur. Mais c'est une idée qui répugne à nombre d'architectes allemands et scandinaves commis au design d'un bâtiment et qui en prévoient jusqu'au plus infime détail. Cette approche européenne ira jusqu'à inclure le design de l'ameublement et des accessoires à l'intérieur du bâtiment.

Le conflit entre la vision d'ensemble de l'architecte et l'art plus spécialisé du designer d'intérieur a été le trait saillant du design de l'environnement de ces trente dernières années.

L'initiative va et vient entre les designers et les architectes selon les circonstances économiques et technologiques. Dans les années 80, par exemple, les architectes britanniques étaient engagés dans tant de projets de constructions nouvelles que les designers d'intérieur firent de grandes incursions dans le commerce de détail, les loisirs et les bureaux. Depuis que la récession frappe l'industrie de la construction au Royaume-Uni, les architectes se battent pour reconquérir la rénovation et l'architecture d'intérieur. Pendant ce temps, l'Espagne et l'Italie se préoccupent de repousser les limites du design – une approche plus souple, renaissante, du design intérieur soumise à de nombreuses influences culturelles. En Extrême-Orient, le processus est encore différent, particulièrement au Japon où, explique Ken Walker, "les sociétés de design et construction feront gratuitement le design intérieur pour avoir le contrat de construction d'un magasin. Cela peut rendre très difficile le travail qui consiste pour un indépendant à vendre le projet de design d'un magasin."

Le degré grandissant de spécialisation des équipes multidisciplinaires de design du bâtiment est une caractéristique commune au monde entier. Les spécialités de l'hôtellerie sont une force en expansion, tout comme les consultants en éclairage et les acousticiens.

AVENIR

Les designers de l'éclairage sont assurés d'avoir à l'avenir un rôle beaucoup plus important parce que les thèmes de l'économie d'énergie et de la protection de l'environnement seront au premier plan dans les années 90. En Europe, déjà, les architectes et les designers d'intérieur s'attaquent aux problèmes de conservation de l'énergie et des matériaux, mais les thèmes concernés sont terriblement complexes. Ceux qui arrivent à voir dans les boules de cristal prédisent que le design intérieur va prendre une quantité de directions différentes, reflétant l'éclatement du marché global des années 70 et 80 en une quantité de secteurs. L'impératif de l'aspect homogène lancé par les multinationales qui étendent leurs activités dans le monde entier sera contrebalancé par la poussée croissante des styles traditionnels locaux.

S'il est un thème central pour les tendances à venir, c'est bien "l'échelle humaine" : en Allemagne, par exemple, Dieter Sieger parle de donner une âme et une atmosphère à la géométrie de base du modernisme, et d'axer davantage le design sur l'homme.

Mais les plus grands changements dans le design intérieur sont liés aux événements économiques et politiques. L'Europe d'après 1992 va créer un marché unique de 320 millions d'habitants, 200 millions d'entre eux étant à moins de trois heures de voyage les uns des autres. Leur pouvoir d'achat sera plus grand que l'économie de l'Amérique toute entière, et les opportunités de design intérieur dans la création d'une nouvelle infrastructure dans le commerce de détail, les transports et la finance sont immenses. Pas étonnant que tant d'ateliers d'architectes et de designers américains aient des bureaux à Londres. Il ne faut pas non plus oublier de prendre en considération la libération des économies de l'Europe de l'Est. Cela procurera inévitablement plus d'activité quand les questions de devises fortes seront résolues. Un certain nombre de centres d'affaires internationaux sont actuellement en construction en Extrême-Orient. Ils seront l'occasion d'un travail-exposition dans les quatre ans. Où que l'on se tourne, le design intérieur est en mouvement. C'est de bon augure pour les années 1990.

INNENDESIGN IN DEN NEUNZIGER JAHREN
JEREMY MYERSON UND WENDY SMITH

Das Zusammenspiel verschiedener wirtschaftlicher, kultureller und technologischer Entwicklungstendenzen hat die Innenarchitekten und Ambiente-Designer plötzlich ins internationale Rampenlicht gestellt.

Der kulturelle Trend, alte Gebäude praktisch per "Recycling" einer neuen Verwendung zuzuführen, wobei auf die Erhaltung des Überlieferten wieder viel mehr Acht gegeben wird, hat fraglos dazu beigetragen, daß Innendesignern größte Renovierungsprojekte übertragen werden. Ein weiterer Faktor, der dazu führte, daß sich Berater für Innenarchitektur und Design als bedeutende Kraft des allgemeinen Geschäftssektors und natürlich speziell der Baubranche weltweit etablieren konnten, war die technologisch getriebene Einführung modernster, computergestützter Designtechniken ins Entwurfsstudio. Die Konsequenz dieser Entwicklung: Mehr Produktivität auch bei Großprojekten und ein rationelleres, mehr auf Wissenschaft basierendes Vorgehen in der Design-Disziplin.

Aber dennoch waren es die ökonomischen Trends, die den in Europa, Nordamerika und im pazifischen Raum zu beobachtenden Innendesignaktivitäten als entscheidendes Moment zugrundeliegen. Alle Wirtschaftsbarometer haben in die richtige Richtung gewiesen, und diese Richtung heißt Wachstumserhalt.

ÖKONOMISCHE ASPEKTE

Weltweit kann der Markt für Dienstleister im Architektur- und Designbereich auf eine beeindruckende Wachstumsrate verweisen. Nach zuverlässigen Branchenschätzungen läßt sich die Gesamtsumme aller für Design- und Architekturleistungen gezahlten Honorare – aus den Bau- und Corporate Identity-Etats säuberlich ausgesondert –, auf weltweit rund sechs Milliarden Pfund Sterling beziffern. Mit einem Honoraraufkommen von circa drei Milliarden Pfund stellt Nordamerika den größten Einzelmarkt; auf Europa entfallen etwa zwei Milliarden Pfund, und diesem Markt wird im Hinblick auf die bis 1992 zu realisierende Markt- und Handelsharmonisierung das rasanteste Wachstum vorausgesagt. Auf den Fernen Osten entfallen unterdessen rund eine Milliarde Pfund an Honoraraufkommen, und auch hier haben wir es angesichts jüngster politischer und wirtschaftlicher Initiativen mit einer Region zu tun, die ein ganz enormes Potential in sich birgt.

Teilt man diese sechs Milliarden Pfund auf die verschiedenen Fachdisziplinen auf, entfällt der Löwenanteil auf den Sektor gewerblicher Architekturleistungen (4,1 Milliarden) und auf das Innendesign, Einzelhandelssektor eingeschlossen (mit einer Milliarde Pfund). Produkt- und graphisches Design bringen es zusammen auf knapp eine Milliarde Pfund Honorareinkommen. Somit arbeiten der Umfeld-Designer und der Innenarchitekt heute in einem Marktgefüge, das durch ein Honoraraufkommen von mehr als fünf Milliarden Pfund und durch kontinuierliches Weiterwachstum gekennzeichnet ist. Die in ihrer Betreuung liegenden Bau- und Renovierungsetats lassen sich insgesamt auf ein Volumen von mehr als 50 Milliarden Pfund schätzen.

Wie ist es zu dieser gewaltigen Aktivitätenentfaltung gekommen? Die simpelste Antwort liegt in der wachsenden Wohlhabenheit der einzelnen Länder: es sind einfach sehr viel größere Geldmittel vorhanden, um das Bauumland auf ein höheres, besseres Niveau zu stellen, um in bessere Wohnungen, bessere Arbeitsräume und bessere Freizeiteinrichtungen zu investieren. Am augenfälligsten wird dieser Punkt durch eine einfache Einsichtnahme in die Relation zwischen einer mehr oder weniger konstant bleibenden Bevölkerungszuwachsrate und dem im Vergleich dazu sehr viel stärker anwachsenden Bruttosozialprodukt, wie es in Ländern wie Deutschland, Spanien, Großbritannien und Japan der Fall ist.

Wachsende Wohlhabenheit hat auch den Firmen weltweit – ob es sich um Kaufhäuser, Hotelketten oder Errichter von Bürokomplexen handelt –, die Zuversicht vermittelt, mehr Geld in verfeinertes, ausgefeiltes Innendesign zu investieren. Und kräftig an demselben Strang mitgezogen hat letztlich auch der Endverbraucher selbst: Schließlich und endlich ist es doch so, daß Menschen überall ein höheres Bildungsniveau erlangt haben, weiter gereist sind und höhere Ansprüche stellen als je zuvor.

TRENDSETTER

Doch selbst wenn mit dem Konjunkturbarometer alles stimmt, braucht es immer noch Mut und Überzeugung seitens der trendmachenden Firmen und deren Designteams, um zu Innendesign-Konzeptionen vorzustoßen, die alte Gußformen sprengen.

Ein kurzer Blick auf die Innovationen der jüngsten Zeit enthüllt bedeutsame Entwicklungen auf allen drei Hauptmärkten des Innendesigns. Wo hat das japanische Innendesign die Nase vorn? "Einzelhandel und Hotels," so die Antwort von Ken Walker, dem Chef der amerikanischen Designfirma Walker Group/ CNI, die in Tokio ein Büro unterhält. "Die Japaner," erläutert Walker weiter, "sind vor allem auf internationale Ideen aus, und neue Ideen werden von ihnen wie Objekte behandelt. Was gebaut wird, stößt sich an allem anderen. Tokio hat absolut keinen Sinn für kontextuelles Design. Die Japaner nehmen irgend etwas von Walker oder Nigel Coates oder Frank Gehry oder Philippe Strack und errichten ganz einfach eine Aufeinanderfolge neuester Baukonzepte, die miteinander im Wettstreit liegen." Solchen Baunovitäten ist nur eine kurze Lebensdauer beschieden. Nigel Coates, der englische Architekt, der ausgiebig an Innenprojekten wie für Caffe Bongo und Hotel Otaru Marritimo gearbeitet hat, berichtet reumütig, wie Klienten bereits zu wesentlichen Planänderungen greifen, noch bevor der Designer den Rückweg zum Flughafen angetreten hat. Ken Walker indes lobt Unternehmen wie Sony und Nissan als die wahren Trendsetter. "Vor allem sind es die japanischen Automobilhersteller," meint er, "die ihre Ausstellungsräume zu wahrhaften Ideen-Centern umgewandelt haben."

Japanische Firmen haben ihre Spuren auch in Hongkong hinterlassen, wie Patrick Bruce, leitender Direktor von RSCG Conran Design Pacific zu berichten weiß. Für Bruce ist das herausragendste Innendesignprojekt des Fernen Ostens jedoch weder ein Kaufhaus noch ein Hotel, sondern der Changi Airport von Singapur, den er wegen seines "exzellenten Designs und seiner relevanten Ambiente" hervorhebt. Für das Design zeichneten Chaix & Johnson verantwortlich, eine amerikanische Architekturfirma mit einer Niederlassung in Singapur.

Zurück zu den Trendsettern in Amerika: Richtungsweisende Kreationen zeigen sich mehr und mehr in den Terminals der Flughäfen. Zum Beispiel der United Airlines Terminal im Chicagoer O'Hare Airport, eine Komposition aus Licht, Raum und Skulptur, mit der sich die Designer von Murphy/Jahn's den Reisenden empfehlen, die das Glück haben, dieses Bauwerk selbst erleben zu können. Am konzentriertesten zeigen sich Design-Anstrengungen in den USA derzeit jedoch auf dem Hotel- und Freizeitsektor.

Stellt man freilich die prekäre US—Konjunkturlage in Rechnung, so könnte die Eroberung von Marktanteilen für Innendesignfirmen in den neunziger Jahren chancenreicher sein als die Erwartung weiteren Marktwachstums, wie Ken Walker warnend anmerkt.

Um auf Beweise für die außerordentliche Blüte des Innendesigns in Europa zu stoßen, braucht man nicht weit und lange zu suchen. Während Frankreich und Spanien wohl mit den spektakulärsten Entwicklungen aufzuwarten haben, ist Großbritannien fraglos auch im Mittelpunkt des Geschehens geblieben. Den Franzosen kam dabei eine Art aufgeklärter staatlicher Schirmherrschaft zugute, von der Designer im allgemeinen nur träumen können. Doch bewiesen die französischen Innenarchitekten und Möbeldesigner zumindest auch das nötige Talent, um aus den großen Möglichkeiten Kapital zu schlagen, die sich durch die von Mitterand und dessen Kultusminister Jack Lang in den achtziger Jahren in Gang gesetzten "Pracht-Projekte" ergaben. Staatliche Gelder ergossen sich in eine ganze Reihe von ehrgeizigen öffentlichen Bauprojekten, denen eine Sogwirkung zukommen sollte, um Paris zur Weltstadt Nummer Eins in Sachen Kunst, Design und Architektonik werden zu lassen, die dem restlichen Frankreich ein Beispiel geben würde. Auf der Weltbühne sind die Franzosen jetzt dabei, als ernstzunehmende Führungsmacht des Designsektors zunehmend in Erscheinung zu treten – eine Entwicklung, für die auch die unlängst erfolgte

Übernahme der Conran Design Group – bestbekannter Markenname in Innendesign – durch den französischen Kommunikationsgiganten RSCG kennzeichnend ist.

Den spanischen Designern mag der internationale Geschäftstrieb ihrer französischen Kollegen heute noch fehlen, daß Spanien aber auch zum Schauplatz vieler künstlerischer Innovationen im Innendesign geworden ist, steht außer Zweifel. Vieles dreht sich dabei um Barcelona und schöpft dabei sicher auch aus der katalanischen Tradition und dem für den katalanischen Geist typisch optimistischen Ausblick. Salvador Ballarin von McColl/Spanien bezeichnet die "im Trend liegenden Bars und Restaurants und die Interieurs von Media- und Bankgebäuden" als Beispiele für führende spanische Designarbeit. Die Olympischen Sommerspiele 1992 in Barcelona und die Weltausstellung in Sevilla werden mit dafür sorgen, daß Spanien weiterhin im Mittelpunkt des globalen Blickfeldes bleiben wird, auch wenn – sehr zum Ärgernis einheimischer Firmen – mehr und mehr internationale Architekten mit Designaufgaben betraut werden, die mit diesen Großereignissen zu tun haben. Auch in Italien bleiben bekannte Firmen, wie etwa Olivetti oder der Modegigant GFT bei ihrer Devise, Innendesignprojekte höchstens Standards zu vergeben.

Die Art, wie man sich in den romanischen Ländern des Designs annimmt, steht im Kontrast zum angelsächsischen Modell, das eher nüchtern, geschäftsmännisch und empirisch ist. Der Interieur-Boom in Großbritannien geht zum Beispiel nicht auf angeborene visuelle Kenntnis der Kundschaft zurück, sondern hat mit dem Aufstieg einer neuen Generation von Design-Managern zu tun, die in Großfirmen und öffentlichen Instituten tätig sind: Daß sich so namhafte Persönlichkeiten wie Jane Priestman von den britischen Eisenbahnen (British Rail), Dick Petersen von der Flughafenbehörde BAA, Tony Key von British Telecom und Jeremy Rewse-Davies vom Londoner Verkehrsverbund (London Transport) zur Schirmherrschaft über Umwelt-Design aufgeschwungen haben, hat zum Beispiel zur Vergabe vieler Projekte geführt, mit denen designerisches Neuland betreten wurde.

In Deutschland ist es der Designfachmann Dieter Sieger von Sieger Design, der den Küchenhersteller Bulthaup und den Hersteller von Beleuchtungselementen Erco als beispielhafte deutsche Firmen heraushebt, deren Design-Philosophie als exzellent zu bezeichnen ist. In mancherlei Hinsicht hat das charakteristische deutsche Design mit dem der skandinavischen Länder vieles gemeinsam: Glaube an Qualität, in die Zeit passende Konzepte und Rechenschaft gegenüber der Umwelt.

PROCEDERE

Wie Innenarchitekturaufträge vergeben und ausgeführt werden, ist von Land zu Land unterschiedlich – und ohnehin dem Zyklus des professionellen Wandels unterworfen. Es zeichnen sich jedoch einige Allgemeintrends ab, auf die näher eingegangen werden sollte. Dr. Frank Duffy vom britischen Architekten- und Designer-Verband DEGW unterscheidet beim innenarchitektonischen Vorgehen zwischen typisch europäischen und nordamerikanischen Verfahrensmodalitäten. Beim nordamerikanischen Modell wird die Verantwortung zwischen dem für die Gebäudeschale verantwortlichen Architekten und dem Innendesigner geteilt. Auf diese Weise, so erläutert Duffy, kann ein gutes, solides Gebäude zu Zeiten seiner Lebensdauer verwendet und mehrfach wiederverwendet werden – im Innenbereich von verschiedenen Innenarchitekten jedesmal unterschiedlich ausgestaltet. Vielen deutschen und skandinavischen Architekten widerstrebt dieser Gedanke: Ihnen wird ein Bauauftrag in die Hand gegeben, und sie sind darauf erpicht, diesen in eigener Regie bis zum kleinsten Detail und bis zum Schluß durchzuführen. Das europäische Auftragsmodell schließt vielfach auch maßgeschneidertes Mobiliar- und Innenausstattungsdesign mit ein.

Der Konflikt zwischen der allesumfassenden Vision des Architekten und der mehr aufs Spezielle ausgerichteten Kunst des Innendesigners ist kennzeichnend für das Umfeld- Design der letzten 30 Jahre. Von wem die Initiative ausgeht, Innendesigner oder Gebäudearchitekten, verhält sich wie Ebbe und Flut, je nach den ökonomischen und technologischen Umständen. In den achtziger Jahren waren die Architekten in Großbritannien etwa mit Neubauprojekten derart vollbeschäftigt, daß den Kollegen vom Innendesign- Bereich bedeutende Vorstöße in die Terrains des Einzelhandels, der Bürogestaltung und der Freizeiteinrichtungen gelangen. Heute jedoch, wo die britische Bauwirtschaft die Rezession zu spüren bekommt, sind die Architekten zum Kampf angetreten, um verlorengegangenes Renovierungs- und Interieurterrain zurückzugewinnen.

In Italien und Spanien ist das Überqueren von Designgrenzen mittlerweile zu einem Hauptanliegen geworden : fließenderes, mehr an die Renaissance erinnerndes designerisches Vorgehen, bei dem viele unterschiedliche kulturelle Einflüsse zum Tragen kommen. Im Fernen Osten verfährt man wiederum auf ganz andere Weise, vor allem in Japan, wo - wie Ken Walker ausführt -, "Design-und-Bau-Firmen die Innenarchitektur- Leistungen gratis mit hineinwerfen, nur um den Bauauftrag etwa für ein Ladengeschäft zu erhalten." Diese Praxis kann die Aufgabe, Innendesign auf Einzelhandelsebene zu verkaufen, zu einem harten Job machen.

Ein bedeutendes, überall auf der Welt anzutreffendes Merkmal ist das wachsende Ausmaß der Spezialisierung in Verbindung mit einem multidisziplinären Bau/Design-Team. Hotelspezialisten entwickeln sich zu einer immer stärker werdenden Kraft, wie auch die Fachberater für Beleuchtung und Akustik.

AUSBLICK

Beleuchtungsdesigner werden in Zukunft garantiert eine weitaus größere Rolle spielen, denn Energieeinsparung und Umweltfragen werden im Interessenmittelpunkt der neunziger Jahre stehen. In Europa ringen Architekten und Innendesigner schon heute um Mittel und Wege der Energie- und Baumaterialieneinsparung - die dabei mitspielenden Probleme sind jedoch von einer horrenden Komplexität.

Was die Stilistik anbetrifft, so prophezeien die Kristallkugelgucker dem Innendesign die Hereinnahme unterschiedlicher Gestaltungsrichtungen ins Entwurfsportfolio, was die Aufsplitterung des Massenmarktes der siebziger und achtziger Jahre in eine größere Anzahl kleinerer Marktnischen reflektiert. Die waschsende Sogkraft ortstypischer Stilistik wird sich zu einem Gegengewicht zum Imperativ des homogenen Looks entwickeln, wie ihn die weltweit agierenden Multis initiiert haben.

Gibt es ein den sich abzeichnenden Trends zugrundeliegendes Zentralthema, dann das des "humanen Maßstabs". In Deutschland spricht Dieter Sieger zum Beispiel davon, daß der fundamentalen Geometrie der Moderne etwas Seele und Atmosphäre beigegeben werden muß, daß der Mensch stärker in den Mittelpunkt des Designerischen zu bringen ist.

Die größten Veränderungen jedoch, die es im Bereich des Innendesigns geben wird, sind mit den ökonomischen und politischen Ereignissen verknüpft. Ab 1992 wird das Europa des Gemeinsamen Binnenmarktes ein Marktgefüge mit 320 Millionen Menschen darstellen - 200 Millionen davon nur drei Reisestunden voneinander entfernt. Ihre Kaufkraft wird größer sein als die der gesamten US-Wirtschaft - und die Chancen, die sich dem Innendesigner bei der Schaffung neuer Infrastrukturen für Einkauf, Transport und Finanzwesen bieten, sind enorm. Kein Wunder also, daß sich schon viele amerikanische Architektur- und Designfirmen mit ihren Niederlassungen in London etabliert haben.

Hinzu kommt die wirtschaftliche Liberalisierung in den Ländern Osteuropas - ein Faktor von beträchtlichem Ausmaß. Mit der Einführung harter, konvertierbarer Währungen wird es auch in diesen Ländern für Innenarchitekten künftig viel zu tun geben.

An einer ganzen Reihe von Welthandels-Centern wird gegenwärtig im Fernen Osten gebaut. Für die nächsten vier Jahre bedeutet das einen ganzen Schub von Aufträgen im Ausstellungsbereich. Egal, wo man auch hinschaut : Das Geschäft des Innendesigns ist in Fahrt. Gute Vorzeichen für die neunziger Jahre !

EL INTERIORISMO EN LOS 90
POR JEREMY MYERSON AND WENDY SMITH

Diversas ramas del desarrollo económico, cultural y tecnológico se han combinado de tal manera que han convertido a los diseñadores y a los arquitectos interioristas en un punto de mira internacional.

El impuslso tecnológico que han aportado las computadoras en las técnicas del diseño, ofreciendo una mayor productividad en los grandes proyectos y un acercamiento más, científico y racional hacia esta disciplina, es otro de los factores clave en la aparición de los estudios de los interioristas, considerados como una baza de importancia tanto en el mundo de los negocios como en el de la construcción. La tendencia cultural de restaurar edificios antiguos, prestando más atención a la tradición y a la conservación, ha jugado una parte indudable en los numerosos encargos de restauración que han recibido los interioristas.

Sin embargo, la actividad interiorista que hemos observado en Europa, América del Norte y en el Pacífico, ha estado estimulada por la dirección. Los barómetros económicos han apuntando todos en la dirección de mantener el nivel de desarrollo.

ECONOMIA

El mercado mundial de los servicios para el diseño y la arquitectura se ha desarrollado de una manera impresionante.

Las estimaciones actuáles de industrias fiables sitúan el nivel de las retibuciones obtenidas por trabajos de arquitectura y diseño – retribuciones que han sido desgajadas de la construcción y nivelado en los presupuestos –, en 6 billones de mundiales. América del Norte es el mercado más importante si tenemos en cuenta los 3 billones aproximados pagados en honorarios o retribuciones. Europa nos da unos 2 billones estando abocada a mayor crecimiento debido a la tendencia futura de armonización prevista para 1992, entre tanto, el lejano Oriente contabiliza 1 billón, siendo una zona con un potencial tremendo si tenemos en cuenta las íniciativas recientes tanto en lo político como en la comercial. Si dividimos los 6 billones en diversas disciplinas, la parte del león corresponde a la arquitectura comercial (4,1 corresponde a la arquitectura comercial (4,1 billones) y el diseño de interior, incluyendo los detallistas, (1 billón). La producción y el diseño gráfico contabilizan justo por debajo de 1 billón en ingresos por honorarios. El interiorista y el arquitecto de interiores trabajan en la actualidad sobre los 5 billones para unas retribuciones que crecen sin parar, y manejando presupuestos para construir y para restaurar que pueden estimarse por encima de los 50 billones de & (Libras).

¿Por qué ha aparecido este nivel de actividad? La explicación más sencilla puede encontrarse en la reciente abundancia de paises con buena salud económica que invierten en mejorar la calidad de vida, el trabajo y las posibilidades del ocio. Se puede obtener una idea aproximada de este proceso, midiendo el aumento de la población pasiva frente al crecimiento pronunciado del Product Nacional Bruto PNB en países como Alemania Occidental, España, Grand Bretãna y Japón.

El crecimiento de la abundancia ha dado lugar a la aparición de sociedades en todo el mundo, bien como grandes almacenes, cadenas hoteleras o despachos, reveladoras en todo caso de la confianza en invertir en un diseño de interior más sofisticados. También ha habido un empujón fundamental. La gente, se diga lo que se diga, se está educando, viaja más y es más exigente que antes.

TENDENCIAS EN ALZA

Sin embargo, aun cuando los barómetros apuntan todos en la bueno dirección, se requiere valor y convicción por parte de los creadores de las nuevas tendencias y de sus equipos de diseño para romper moldes en interiorismo.

Une breve estudio de las recientes innovaciones nos descubre que en los tres grandes mercados en relación con el interiorismo, existen importanrtes evoluciones. ¿Dónde se encuentra el punto álgido del interiorismo japonés? "En el comercio y hoteles" dice Ken Walker, presidente de los diseñadores Walker Group7CNI de USA, el cual tiene un despacho en Tokyo.

Los japoneses tienen nuevas ideas internacionales y tratan a las nuevas ideas como si fuesen objetos. Todo se construye para chocar contra todo lo demás. Tokyo no tiene el menor sentido en lo que se refiere a diseño. Los japones toman ideas de Walker Starck y construyen simplemente una sucesión de novedades competitivas.

Estas novedades tienen un ciclo de vida corto. El arquitecto inglés Nigel Coates quién trabajó en el Japón en proyectos como el Caffe Bongo y el Hotel Otaru maritimo se lamentó de como los clientes efectúan cambios importantes incluso antes que el diseñador haya llegado al europuerto.

Por otro lado, Ken Walker, alabó a las compañias Sony y Nissan como verdaderos innovadores. Los fabricantes japoneses, expecialmente los de coches, han convertido sus salas de exhibición en centros de ideas, observa.

Las compañias japonesas también muestran sus realizaciones en Hong Kong según Patrick Bruce, Director Gerente de la R.S.C.G., Conran Design Pacific. Los proyectos de interiorismo más sobresalientes del lejano Oriente para Bruce, no son los grandes almacenes ni los hoteles. Es el Aeropuerto Changi de Singapur, al cual alaba por su "excelente diseño y selecto ambiente." Sus diseñadores fueron Chaix y Johnson una firma americana con oficina en Singapur.

En América, el trabajo de innovación aparece también en la terminal del Aeropuerto. Las propuestas de luces, espacios y esculturas que configuran lo que es la Terminal de United Airlines del Aeropuerto O'Hare de Chicago, obra de Murphy y Jahn, son alabadas por todos aquellos afortunados pasajeros que tienen la suerte de atravesarlo.

Pero los esfuerzos más importantes en diseño en USA se concentrari en general en hoteles y lugares de esparcimiento.

Sin embargo, dado la precaria situación de la economía de USA, Ken Walker nos advierte que las posibilidades de l diseño en USA en los próximos 1990 serán "ganancias en mercados compartidos más que ganancias por crecimiento de mercado."

No hay que esforzarse mucho para darse cuenta del extraordinario florecimiento del diseño de interior europeo. Es en Francia y en España donde este fenómeno ha sido más espectacular, aunque Gran Bretaña también es un foco de atención importante. Los franceses han gozado de una ventaja especial, por la protección de una plataforma cultural que los demás diseñadores sólo podrían imaginarse en sueños. En cuanto a los diseñadores de interior y mobiliario franceses han tenido el talento de capitalizar las oportunidades que se les han presentado con los grandes proyectos iniciados en 1980 por Mitterand y su Ministro de Cultura Jack Lang. El dinero del Gobierno fue gastado pródigamente en una serie de ambiciosos proyectos de edificios públicos y ello como una especie de ejercicio del gasto público para hacer de París un líder en arte, arquitectura y diseño. Los franceses han empezado a emerger en el escenario mundial como unos serios líderes del diseño comercial, desarrollo que se refleja en la reciente adquisición del Conran Desing Group, la firma comercial en diseño interior más conocida, por las telecomunicaciones francesas R.G.S.C.

Los diseñadores españoles quizás no hayan alcanzado todavía el liderazgo comercial internacional de sus vecinos franceses, pero sin duda, España ha sido escenario de muchas innovaciones artísticas en interiorismo – la mayor parte de ellas en Barcelona y que derivan de las tradiciones culturales y de la manera específica de ser de los catalanes. Salvador Ballarin de McColl Spain, dice que los trabajos más importantes realizados han sido "bares modernos y restaurantes, para realizar proyectos derivados de estos acontecimientos."

El acercamiento latino al diseño contrasta con el modelo más empírico y comercial anglo-sajón, por ejemplo, el "boom" de los interioristas en Gran Bretaña no ha tenido lugar debido a un instinto innato de los clientes. Más bien ha sido la consecuencia de la aparición de unas nuevas generaciones de managers del diseño que trabajan en grandes corporaciones y estamentos públicos ; la protección de diseñadores ambientales (urbanistas) en las figuras como Jane Pricotman del British Rail, Dick Petersen de BAA (autoridades de los aeropuertos), Tony Key en el British Telecom y Jeremy Rewse-Davies en el London Transport, ha dado lugar a numerosos encargos.

En Alemania el diseñador alemán Dieter Sieger de Sieger Desing, el fabricante Bulthaup y la firma Erco de lámparas son ejemplos de compañias alemanas con una excelente filosofía del diseño, como son apostar por la calidad, la intemporalidad y el respeto al medio ambiente.

EL PROCESO

La forma de encargar y la ejecución del trabajo de los interioristas varía de un país a otro y de todas formas está en constante evolución profesional. Empero hay un numero apreciado de innovaciones objeto de discusiones. Dr. Frank Duffy de DEGW diseñadores y arquitectos hace la distinción entre los interioristas de Norte América y los europeos. El modelo norteamericano divide la responsabilidad entre el diseñador de la estructura del edificio y del diseñador interiorista, esto, – nos explica –, permite un buen y robusto edificio que puede ser estrenado y reestrenado a lo largo de su existencia, y habilitado de diversas maneras por diferentes interioristas. pero esta práctica repugna a muchos arquitectos alemanes y escandinavos quiénes cuando reciben un encargo para diseñar un edificio quieren ocuparse de toda la obra exterior e interior hasta en los más mínimos detalles. Este sistema europeo incluye frecuentemente diseño – moda de mobiliario y accesorios – para el interior del edificio.

El conflicto entre la visión global del arquitecto y una más especializada mente artística del interiorista ha sido el aspecto más notable del diseño de los últimos 30 años.

Los altibajos entre diseñadores y arquitectos, dependen de las circunstancias económicas y tecnológicas. Por ejemplo, en Gran Bretaña, en 1980, los arquitectos tuvieron tanto trabajo con los nuevos proyectos de construcción de edificios, que los interioristas hicieron grandes incursiones en el comercio, el ocio y las oficinas. Actualmente, como la recesión golpea la industria británica de la construcción, los arquitectos luchan para ganar a los intrioristas el trabajo de la remodelación de interiores.

Al mismo tiempo, en España e Italia, hay un intento de cruzar las frontras del diseño – una mayor fluidez – un renacimiento del interiorismo, sustentado por diferentes influencias culturales.

El proceso en el lejano Oriente es distinto, especialmente en Japón donde Ken Walker explica que "las firmas de diseño y construcción van a lanzarse al diseño de interior si consiguen un contrato para edificar unos grandes almacenes." Esto puede convertirse en una dura competencia para los pequeños diseñadores independientes.

Una notable característica a nivel mundial es el crecimiento gradual de la especialización de los equipos de diseño de edificios multi-disciplinarios. Una fuerza creciente son los especialistas en hoteles de las misma forma que hay especialistas en acústica o en luminotecnia.

PERSPECTIVAS DE FUTURO

Los diseñadores de luminotecnia tienen garantizado un papel más importante en el futuro, debido a que el ahorro energético y las condiciones ambientales serán el punto de mira más importante de los 90. Actualmente los interioristas europeos están luchando por encontrar caminos que conserven la energía y los materiales pero las soluciones son todavía enormemente complejas.

En términos estilísticos, las predicciones de las balas de cristal, apuntan a quel el diseño de interior crecerá en diferentes direcciones que reflejarán las diferencias del mercado medio de los años 70 a los 90.

El crecimiento de los estilos locales equilibra el imperativo de la "apariencia" homogénea impuesta por las iniciativas de las multinacionales que comercian por todo el mundo.

Si hay un tema central que atañe a las creaciones futuras este es la "escala humana" : En Alemania, por ejemplo, Dieter Sieger habla de añadir un poco de alma y ambiente a la geometría básica del Modernismo y de crear diseño más centrado en la persona.

Pero los mayores cambios del interiorismo están unidos a los acontecimientos económicos y políticos. En 1997, Europa tendrá un mercado único de 320 millones de personas, 200 millones de las cuales estarán a una distancia la una de la otra de 3 horas de viaje. Su poder adquisivo será mayor que la economía global de América, y el comercio, el transporte y las infraestructuras de los servicios financieros son inmensos. Ello explica que tantos arquitectos y diseñadores americanos hayan abierto oficinas en Londres.

También hay que considerar el tema de la liberalización de las economías de la Europa del Este, esto conducirá inevitablemente a un mayor trabajo para los interioristas, una vez que las monedas fuertes se hayan estabilizado.

En el lejano Oriente existe ya habitualmente, un numero de centros comerciales internacionales en construcción, que darán lugar a una demostración del trabajo de diseño durante 4 años. Dondequiera que se mire, el negocío del diseño de interiores está en marcha. Hay buenos augurios para los 90.

LA PROGETTAZIONE D´INTERNI NEGLI ANNI NOVANTA

DI JEREMY MYERSON E WENDY SMITH

Diversi tipi di sviluppo economico, culturale e tecnologico hanno contribuito a portare alla ribalta internazionale la progettazione d'ambienti e l'architettura d'interni.

L'impeto tecnologico che ha introdotto nello studio di progettazione le tecniche di design coadiuvate dal computer, offrendo in tal modo una notevole produttività a grandi progetti e un approcio più scientifico e razionale alla disciplina, è un altro fattore chiave che ha contribuito a far emergere la consulenze di progettazione d'interni come una forza di primo piano all'interno non solo del mondo degli affari, ma anche di quello edilizio.

La tendenza culturale a riciclare vecchi edifici, tenendo in maggior conto il patrimonio storico e la conservazione, ha senza dubbio contribuito a fare commissionare ai progettisti d'interni importanti progetti di rinnovamento.

Ma tutta l'attività di progettazione d'interni registrata in Europa, nel Nord America e nei paesi intorno al pacifico è stata stimolata dall'orientamento del sottostante andamento economico. Gli aghi dei barometri economici erano tutti puntati nella direzione giusta per sostenere il livello di crescita.

ECONOMIA

Il mercato mondiale del design e dei servizi d'architettura è cresciuto con un ritmo impressionante. Secondo attendibili stime industriali il livello degli onorari risultante dai proventi del lavoro d'architettura - onorari che sono stati separati dai bilanci relativi alle spese di costruzione e di corporate image - è stato calcolato 6 miliardi di lire sterline su scala mondiale. Il Nord America rappresenta il mercato più grande, con onorari che complessivamente raggiugono all'incirca 3 miliardi di lire sterline ; l'Europa segue con 2 miliardi di lire sterline e si distingue per lo sviluppo più rapido dovuto alla prossima armonizzazione commerciale del 1992 ; mentre l'Estremo Oriente partecipa con 1 miliardo di lire sterline e si presenta come una regione dall'enorme potenziale, considerando le recenti iniziative politiche e commerciali.

Se si dividono i 6 miliardi di lire sterline fra le discipline, la parte del leone spetta all'architettura commerciale (4,1 miliardi di sterline) e alla progettazione d'interni con inclusa la vendita al dettaglio (1 miliardo di sterline). Il design grafico e quello di prodotti contribuiscono alle entrate degli onorari con quasi 1 miliardo di sterline. L'attività del progettista e dell'architetto d'interni si svolge ora in un mercato di emolumenti che otrepassa i 5 miliardi di lire sterline e che è per di più in costante crescita, trattando contratti di costruzione e di rinnovamento per un volume d'affari che si può stimare superiore ai 50 miliardi di lire sterline.

Come si è giunti a questo livello d'attività ? La spiegazione più immediata si trova nella crescente ricchezza delle nazioni - nella maggiore disponibilità di fondi da stanziare per il miglioramento delle abitazioni e delle strutture sia di lavoro che di ricreazione. La spiegazione più semplice di questo processo può essere ricavata rapportando la crescita, in larga parte statica, della popolazione allo sviluppo più pronunciato del prodotto nazionale lordo in quelle nazioni come la Germania Occidentale, la Spagna, la Gran Bretagna et il Giappone.

La richezza crescente ha incoraggiato società in tutto il mondo - sia che si tratti di grandi magazzini, catene d'alberghi o di imprese che si occupano della costruzione di uffici - a investire in arredamenti di tipo più sofisticato. Si è anche registrata una spinta da parte degli utenti. La gente, dopo tutto, è più istruita, viaggia di più e sta diventando più che mai esigente.

INDICATORI DI ORIENTAMENTO

Ma anche se i barometri economici sono tutti puntati nella giusta direzione, ci vuole pur sempre del coraggio e della convinzione da parte delle organizzazioni che dettano orientamenti e delle loro equipe di progettisti per creare progettazioni d'interni veramente innovative.

Una breve indagine sulle recenti innovazioni rivela che importanti sviluppi sono presenti in tutti e tre i principali mercati per l'achitettura d'interni. Quali sono i settori di punta nella architettura d'interni giopponese ? "Nella vendita al dettaglio e nel ramo alberghiero", risponde Ken Walker, il presidente del Walker Group/CNI progettisti americani, con una filiale anche a Tokyo.

"I giapponesi dimostrano un vivo interesse per le idee internazionali nuove e trattano le nuove idee come oggetti. Tutto è costruito in contrasto con tutto il resto. Tokyo dimostra di non avere assolumente il senso del design contestuale. I giapponesi tendono a predere qualcosa di Walker o di Nigel Coates oppure di Frank Gehry o di Philippe Starck, e poi semplicemente costruiscono una successione di innovazioni in competizione."

Queste innovazioni hanno però vita breve.

L'architetto inglese Nigel Coates, che ha svolto un notevole volume di lavoro in Giappone, occupandosi di progetti come il Caffè Bongo e l'Hotel Otaru Marritimo, parla con rammarico di come i clienti comincino ad apportare sostanziali cambiamenti prima ancora che il progettista abbia addirittura raggiunto l'aeroporto.

Ken Walker, tuttavia, mostra apprezzamento per società come la Sony e la Nissan che ritiene organizzazioni veramente in grado di dettare degli orientamenti e osserva che "in particolare le industrie automobilistiche giapponesi hanno trasformato i loro saloni d'esposizione in centri di idee."

Le società giapponesi hanno anche mostrato quello di cui sono capaci a Hong Kong, secondo Patrick Bruce, amministratore delegato della RSCG Conran Design Pacific. Tuttavia, secondo Bruce, l'opera più straordinaria dell'Estremo Oriente non è nè un grande magazzino, nè un albergo. E' l'aeroporto Chagi di Singapore che si distingue per "l'eccellenza del design e la relativa atmosfera." E' opera dei progettisti Chaix e Johnson, una ditta americana con una filiale a Singapore.

Ritornando in America, anche qui un lavoro che possa dettare nuovi orientamenti è il terminale delle United Airlines all'aeroporto O'Hare di Chicago, fa apprezzare l'opera di Murphy/Jahn a quei passeggeri che hanno la fortuna di transitarvici. Ma lo sforzo maggiore del design americano è concentrato al momento nel settore alberghiero e in quello della ricreazione.

Tuttavia, data la situazione precaria dell'economia statunitense, Ken Walker prevede che le possibilità per la progettazione d'interni americana negli anni Novanta consisteranno "più nel conquistare quote di mercato che nel mirare alla crescita di mercato." Non si deve certo fare molta fatica per trovare indicazioni della straordinaria fioritura della progettazione d'interni europea. La Francia e la Spagna hanno fornito gli esempi forse più spettacolari, ma anche la Gran Bretagna à stata al centro del fenomeno.

Il francesi sono stati favoriti in particolare da un tipo di patronato illuminato da parte dello Stato che i progettisti normalmente possono soltanto sognare di ricevere. Ma i progettisti d'interni e i creatori di mobili in Francia hanno per lo meno dimostrato di sapersi avvantaggiare delle occasioni presentate dai "grands projets" avviati da Mitterand e dal suo ministro per la cultura Jack Lang durante gli anni Ottanta.

Ingenti somme di denaro sono state elargite dal governo per sovvenzionare una serie di ambiziosi progetti di edifici pubblici, per dare avvio al processo che dovrebbe fare di Parigi uno dei principali punti di riferimento nel mondo per l'arte, l'architettura ed il design ed inoltre per fornire un modello al resto della Francia. I francesi hanno ora cominciato seriamente a presentarsi sul palcoscenico internazionale come leader nel mondo d'affari che ruota interno al design - uno sviluppo che è riflesso nell'acquisizione del Conran Desing Group, il marchio più famoso nel campo della progettazione d'interni, da parte della RCSG, il gigante delle comunicazioni francese.

Il progettisti spagnoli potranno anche non avere ancora l'impeto negli affari internazionali delle loro controparti francesi, ma senza dubbio si è assistito in Spagna a molte innovazioni artistiche nell'architettura d'interni, molte delle quali sono concentrate a Barcellona e derivano dalle tradizioni culturali e dalle fantasia catalana. Salvador Ballarin della McColl spagnola, sostiene che il principale lavoro innovativo si trova in "bar e ristoranti alla moda, compagnie finanziarie e di mass media." E' difficile che la Spagna finisca nell'anonimato internazionale, se si considerano le Olimpiadi del 1992 a Barcellona e l'Esposizione mondiale a Siviglia, anche se - con rammarico dei professionisti locali - un numero sempre crescente di architetti internazionali viene chiamato a lavorare ai progetti di design che sono associati con questi eventi. Inoltre anche le società italiane continuano a comissionare architettura d'interni ad alto livello - fra queste l'Olivetti e il gigante della moda GFT.

Il modo latino di accostarsi al desing è in netto contrasto con il modello anglosassone, più concreto ed empirico. Il boom della progettazione d'interni in Gran Bretagna, per esempio, non è tanto da attribuirsi all'innato gusto estetico della clientela : è dovuto piuttosto all'emergenza di una nuova generazione dirigenziale di design impiegata in importanti aziende ed enti pubblici : il patronato di progettisti d'ambienti da parte di figure come Jane Priestman alla British Rail, Dick Petersen alla BAA (l'ente aeroportuale), Tony Key alla British Telecom e Jeremy Rewse-Davies alla London Transport ha originato molte commissioni d'avanguardia.

Allo stesso tempo, il progettista tedesco Dieter Sieger della Sieger Design cita la ditta produttrice di cucine Bulthaup e la ditta di implanti d'illuminazione Erco come esempi di società tedesche con un'eccellente filosiofia di design. Sotto molti aspetti, la Germania ha le stesse caratteristiche di design della Scandinavia, in quanto entrambe puntano sulla qualità, sulla durabilità e sulle considerazione per l'ambiente.

PROCEDURA

Il modo in cui la progettazione d'interni opera, è commissionata ed eseguita varia di paese in paese, ed è in ogni caso in continuo mutamento professionale. Tuttavia, esiste un certo numero di orientamenti emergenti su cui è opportuno soffermarsi. Franck Duffy dello studio di architetti e progettisti britannici DECW fa una distinzione fra il modo di accostarsi alla progettazione d'interni nordamericano ed europeo.

Nel modello nordamericano la responsabilità viene divisa fra chi progetta la struttura di base e chi progetta gli interni ; questo, ci spiega il Dott. Durry, permette che un buon edificio solido sia utilizzato e riutilizzato diverse volte nel corso della sua esistenza, permette che sia adattato in modi differenti da progettisti diversi. Ma questa è un'idea aborrita da molti architetti tedeschi e scandinavi, che quando ricevono una commissione per il progetto di un edificio, intendono seguirlo occupandosene in tutti i minimi dettagli. Questo approccio europeo include spesso la progettazione di mobili ed accessori all'interno dell'edificio, costruiti appositamente per il cliente.

Il conflitto tra la grande visione d'insieme dell'architetto e l'arte più specialistica del progettista d'interni è stata una caratteristica costante della progettazione d'ambienti negli ultimi 30 anni. L'iniziativa è ora a appannaggio del progettista, ora dell'architetto a seconda delle circostanze economiche e tecnologiche. Negli anni Ottanta, gli architetti in Gran Bretagna, per esempio, sono stati occupati da così tanti progetti di costruzioni nuove, che i progettisti d'interni si sono orientati con successo verso il lavaro nel ramo della distribuzione, della ricreazione e degli uffici. Ora, nel momento in cui in Gran Bretagna l'industria edilizia è colpita dalla recessione, gli architetti si adoperano per riottenere il lavoro di ristrutturazione e d'interni. Nel frattempo, in Spagna e in Italia, si registra il tentativo di superare i confini del design - un accostamento alla progettazione d'interni più fluido, di tipo rinascimentale in cui vengono utilizzate molte influenze culturali. Il processo nell'Estremo Oriente è a sua volta differente, particolarmente in Giappone dove Ken Walker spiega che "imprese di progettazione e di costruzioni son pronte ad offrire gratuitamente il servizio di progettazione d'interni, se ottengono un contratto per la costrusione di un grande magazzino". Questo può rendere estremamente difficile il compito di vendere la consulenza indipendente di design per la distribuzione.

Una caratteristica che si rileva in tutto il mondo è l'evoluzione multidisciplinare del grado di specializzazione delle equipe di design. Gli specialisti d'alberghi rappresentano una forza crescente, così come i consulenti per l'illuminazione e gli esperti di acustica.

PROSPETTIVE FUTURE

Ai progettisti che si occupano dell'illuminazione è garantito un ruolo molto più importante nel futuro, perché l'attenzione negli anni Novanta sarà focalizzata su questioni come il risparmio energetico e i problemi ambientali. I progettisti d'interni in Europa stanno già sforzandosi di cercare modi di conservare l'energia e i materiali - ma le questioni che vi sono implicate sono tremendamente complesse. In termini stilistici, si prevede che la progettazione d'interni seguirà diverse direzioni di evoluzione riflettendo la frammentazione del mercato di massa degli anni Settanta e Ottanta in tanti segmenti. L'imperativo di una visione omogenea avviata da imprese multinazionali che operano su scala mondiale sarà controbilanciato dalla spinta crescente degli stili locali.

Se proprio ci dovrà essere un tema centrale per le prossime tendenze, questo sarà "la dimensione umana": in Germania, per esempio, Dieter Sieger parla di aggiungere dell'anima e dell'atmosfera alla geometria di base del Modernismo e di porre maggiormente la gente al centro del prerogative del design.

Ma i maggiori cambiamenti nella progettazione d'interni sono legati agli eventi economici e politici. L'Europa dopo il 1992 creerà un unico mercato di 320 milioni di persone, 200 milioni delle quali saranno distanziate fra di loro da non più di tre ore di viaggio. Il loro potere d'acquisto sarà più esteso di quello dell'intera economia americana - e le occasioni per la progettazione d'interni di creare una nuova infrastruttura per i servizi finanziari, di vendita al dettaglio e di trasporti sono immense. Non ci si meravigli affatto che così tanti studi di architettura e di progettazione statunitensi abbiano aperto delle filiali a Londra.

Inoltre, esiste anche la questione non trascurabile della liberalizzazione delle economie nei paesi dell'Europa dell'Est. Questo fatto produrrà inevitabilmente ulteriore lavoro non appena verrà risolto il problema delle valute convertibili.

Un certo numero di centri commerciali mondiali sono al momento in costruzione nell'Estremo Oriente, il che risulterà in parecchio lavoro per esposizioni entro quattro anni. Ovunque si guardi, l'attività di progettazione d'interni è in evoluzione. Lo si può considerare un buon auspicio per gli anni Novanta.

ALPHABETICAL INDEX

SUPPLEMENTARY LISTING
OF LEADING ARCHITECTS & DESIGNERS

EUROPE

BELGIUM - Telephone Code: 32

A + B CONCEPT
PL Delporte 2, 1060 Bruxelles
☎ 02-537 05 54 - Fax 02-537 06 02

A DESIGN
Rue G. Huberti 8, 1030 Bruxelles
☎ 02-242 00 38

ACTUEL
Rue du Menuet 10, 1080 Bruxelles
☎ 02-520 13 46

AERTS LEO
Stationsstraat 169, 2440 Geel
☎ 014-58 65 69

ARCHI CONCEPT
Rue du Moulin 8, 6000 Charleroi
☎ 071-772 31 91 - Fax 071-33 02 65

ARCHI TEXTE
Rue Adolphe Mathieu 64, 1050 Bruxelles
☎ 02-648 70 94

ARIA
Rue du Doyenne 83, 1180 Bruxelles
☎ 02-347 09 04

ASSOCIATION ARCHIT. INTER.
Sq de l'Atomium, B613 - ITM, 1020 Bruxelles
☎ 02-478 47 58 - Fax 02-478 37 66

ATELIERS DE GENVAL
Pl Communale 43, 1320 Genval
☎ 02-653 09 60 - Fax 02-654 17 46

AYER DECORATION
Bd de Waterloo 91, 1000 Bruxelles
☎ 02-537 04 95

BATAILLE CLAIRE
Venusstraat 14, 2000 Antwerpen
☎ 03-231 35 93

BOBBAERS JEAN-PIERRE
Dorpstraat 14, 3520 Zonhoven
☎ 02-537 41 14

BOGAERT BART
Winkelstraat 23, 9561 Steenhuize
☎ 054-50 09 79

BOSMAN ERIC + DOMINIQUE
Rue Monstreux 19, 1400 Nivelles
☎ 067-21 42 31

BOTTE EMMANUAL
Oude Zak 45, 8000 Brugge
☎ 050-33 79 76

GRUNELLE MARC
Av. Brugmann 14, 1060 Bruxelles
☎ 02-344 50 90

DE LAMINNE J.M. & ASSOC.
Belle Voie 23, 1300 Wavre
☎ 010-22 78 57

DECOBO
Hoveniersstr. 39, 2800 Mechelen
☎ 015-42 15 50 - Fax 015-42 29 06

DEPREZ KOEN
Rink 46, 1800 Sint Pieters Leeuw
☎ 02-377 52 99

DUBOIS XAVIER
Rue Moris 43, 1060 Bruxelles
☎ 02-538 98 79

GOFFIN MIREILLE
Rue Champ du Roi 78, 1040 Bruxelles
☎ 02-736 31 21

GROUP CREA
Rue T. Vanham 18, 1020 Bruxelles
☎ 02-427 39 72

IBENS PAUL
Beersgat 4, 2170 Wuustwezel
☎ 03-669 65 61

KEUP JEAN
Av. Macau 27, 1050 Bruxelles
☎ 02-647 41 51 - Fax 02-641 93 42

LEVY VICTOR
Rue Sans Souci 51, 1050 Bruxelles
☎ 02-513 65 39

LIZIN BERNARD
Rue Porcelein 20, 1070 Bruxelles
☎ 02-522 41 96

LONCKE PHILIPPE-ABITA
Rue A. Den Reep 28, 7700 Mouscron
☎ 056-33 47 49

POLAK ANDRE & JEAN
Av. Louise 140, 1050 Bruxelles
☎ 02-648 41 94

SIMONI VITTORIO
Hentjenslaan 9 A, 3511 Hasselt Kuringen
☎ 011-25 35 02 - Fax 011-87 21 00

SIPLET GEORGES
Chemin Tigelles 10, 1150 Bruxelles
☎ 02-770 51 71

STAPELS RENE
Av. F. Roosevelt 243, 1050 Bruxelles
☎ 02-673 27 35

TRACES
Rue de l'Eté 15, 1050 Bruxelles
☎ 02-640 61 20 - Fax 02-640 82 02

TRACTEBEL INGENIERIE
Av. Ariane 7, 1200 Bruxelles
☎ 02-773 91 11

VAN BEVEREN WIM
Nieuwstraat 6, 9290 Berlare
☎ 052-42 26 90

VAN DEN BERGHE BOS + DRIES
Meibloemstraat 14, 9000 Gent
☎ 091-26 29 22

VERANNEMAN EMIEL
Vandevoordeweg 2, 9770 Kruishoutem
☎ 091-83 53 41

WHITE DESIGN
Avenue L. Gribaumont, 1, 11500 Bruxelles
☎ 027-72 43 10 - Fax 027-72 43 08

DENMARK - Telephone Code: 45

BASTA KONTORINDRETNING
Hjortevangen 5, 2920 Charlottenlund
☎ 31 64 46 44 - Fax 31 64 09 98

BLATARN
St. Kongensgade 75B, 1264 Copenhagen K
☎ 33 13 60 22 - Fax 33 91 16 40

BUSK, BRUGGER & NIELSENA/S
Vestergade 4, 8000 Arhus C
☎ 86 18 55 11 - Fax 86 18 39 11

ERIK SOLBERG, INDRETNINGSARKITEKT
Faelledvej 19, 2200 Copenhagen N
☎ 35 37 75 05 - Fax 35 37 75 05

INTERIEUR
Gothersgade 91, 1123 Copenhagen K
☎ 33 13 15 56 - Fax 33 15 25 56

KAARE SOLVSTEN, ARKITEKT
Mejlgade 55, 8000 Arhus C
☎ 86 19 42 33

MANGOR & NAGEL
Mollestraede 4, 3400 Hillerod
☎ 42 25 55 50 - Fax 42 25 59 97

MG DESIGN
Gronningen 5, 5, 1270 Copenhagen K
☎ 33 15 22 72

MICHAEL PETERS GROUP, RETAIL
ARCHITECTURE AND INTERIORS/XMPR
Gl Lundtoftevej 1A, 2800 Lyngby/Copenhagen
☎ 42 88 85 55

MOGENS RULYKKES TEGNESTUE
Alekistevej 18, 2720 Vanlose
☎ 31 74 82 15 - Fax 31 74 96 10

W-INTERIOR & ARCHITECTURE
Fredericiagade 57, 1310 Copenhagen K
☎ 33 32 52 12 - Fax 33 32 74 57

EIRE - Telephone Code: 353

A & D WEJCHERT ARCHITECTS
23 Lower Baggot Street, Dublin 2
☎ (0)11610321 - Fax (0)11610203

BURKE-KENNEDY DOYLE & PARTNERS
6-7 Harcourt Terrace, Dublin 2
☎ (0)1 610399 - Fax (0)1 767385

DELANY MacVEIGH & PIKE
Owenstown House, Fosters Ave, Blackrock, Co. Dublin
☎ (0)1 832 571 - (0)1 832466

HUNT W KENNETH & ASSOCIATES
260 Merrion Road, Dublin 4
☎ (0)1 694 833 - Fax (0)1 692130

KEOGH PAUL ARCHITECTS
1 Johnson Place, Dublin 2
☎ (0)1 6791551

McHUGH O'COFAIGH
4 Mount Street Crescent, Dublin 2
☎ (0)1 767033 - Fax (0)1 619997

RYAN O'BRIEN HANDY ASSOCIATES
38 Percy Place, Dublin 4
☎ (0)1 680899 - Fax (0)1 680089

SCOTT TALLON WALKER
19 Merrion Square, Dublin 2
☎ (0)1 760621 - Fax (0)1 613300

TYNDALL HOGAN HURLEY
1 Mount Street, Crescent, Dublin 2
☎ (0)1 760915 - Fax (0)1 611015

FINLAND - Telephone Code: 358

ARKKITEHDIT OY
Nervanderinkatu 5 D, 00100 Helsinki
☎ 0-441 951 - Fax 0-441 955

ARKKITEHTIRYHMÄ ARRAK OY
Pohjoisesplanadi 21, 00100 Helsinki
☎ 0-625 511 - Fax 0-669 859

ARKKITEHTIRYHMÄ KRÅKSTRÖM OY
Tietäjäntie 4, 02130 Espoo
☎ 0-460 188 - Fax 0-460 108

ARKKITEHTITOIMISTO GRIPENBERG
& CO ARKITEKTKONTOR
Pohjantie 12, 02100 Espoo
☎ 0-461 744 - Fax 0-4553 939

ARKKITEHTITOIMISTO HELIÖVAARA JA UKSILA
Fabianinkatu 8, 00130 Helsinki
☎ 0-176722 - Fax 0-176632

ARKKITEHTITOIMISTO HELIN PEKKA & SIITONEN TUOMO
Bernhardinkatu 5 A, 00130 Helsinki
☎ 0-176966 - Fax 0-657110

ARKKITEHTUURITOIMISTO OLLI PARVIAINEN KY
Pohjantie 12, 02100 Espoo
☎ 0-460933 - Fax 0-461041

SISUSTUSSUUNNITTELU JE TEOLLINEN MUOTOILU
Oy SISTEM, Iso Roobertinkatu 20-22, 00120 Helsinki
☎ 0-170474 - Fax 0-636526

STUDIO NURMESNIEMI KY
Hopeasalmentie 27, 00570 Helsinki
☎ 0-6847055 - Fax 0-6848325

STUDIO TURKKA OY
Ruukinkuja 3, 02320 Espoo
☎ 0-8024144 - Fax 0-8024122

FRANCE Telephone Code: 33

A.B. DESIGN
8, rue de Prague, 75012 Paris
☎ 1 43 07 56 42

A.C.R. ARCHITECTURE INTERIEURE
36, bd de la Bastille, 75012 Paris
☎ **1 43 40 47 52/18 22**

A.D.5
14, rue Saint-Louis-en-L'Isle, 75004 Paris
☎ 1 43 25 72 39

A.X.L.
10, rue du Volga, 75020 Paris
☎ 1 40 09 14 50

AAA NET SUMMERTIME ARCHITECTURE
72, rue de Miromesnil, 75008 Paris
☎ 1 42 89 29 63

ABCOM IMAGE
374, rue de Vaugirard, 75015 Paris
☎ 1 48 42 30 30

ACTE ARCHITECTURE
2, rue de Lyon, 75012 Paris
☎ 1 43 44 33 25

ADAM CHRISTIAN
27, rue Saint-Fargeau, 75020 Paris
☎ 1 47 97 58 15

ADDISON DESIGN CONSULTANTS Ltd
16, rue Saint-Denis, 92100 Boulogne
☎ **1 30 21 95 31**

ADEST
202, rue Croix Nivert, 75015 Paris
☎ 1 46 51 70 30

A.D.S.A. & PARTNERS
74, rue du Faubourg Saint-Antoine, 75012 Paris
☎ **1 43 46 90 58 - Fax 1 43 47 28 47**

AGENCE BERNARD GRENOT
79 bis, rue Madame, 75006 Paris
☎ **1 45 48 70 45 - Fax 1 45 44 18 86**

AGENCE PASCAL DESPREZ
30, avenue Marceau, 75008 Paris
☎ 1 47 20 10 23

AGORA XXI
36, rue Fontaine, 75009 Paris
☎ 1 48 78 15 00

ANTIPODE
14, boulevard de Courcelles, 75017 Paris
☎ 1 43 80 96 97

ARCAM ALAIN CARRE DESIGN
11, rue Paul Lelong, 75002 Paris
☎ **1 42 60 36 60 - Fax 1 42 61 79 03**

ARCHIMEDE (GROUPE VITRAC DESIGN)
60, rue d'Avron, 75020 Paris
☎ **1 40 24 08 00 - Fax 1 40 24 08 12**

ARCHITECTURES
Château l'Escadrille, 33390 Cars-Bordeaux
☎ **57 42 15 18**

ARCHITECTURE INTERIEURE ALAIN MARCOT
5, rue Richepanse, 75008 Paris
☎ **1 47 03 46 00 - Fax 1 42 97 51 83**

ARCHITRAL
28, rue Broca, 75005 Paris
☎ **1 45 35 04 04 - Fax 1 43 36 38 98**
Tx BARRAU 205 616

ARTRIUM SARL
43, rue Monge, 75005 Paris
☎ **1 43 26 47 80 - Fax 1 46 34 07 69**
Tx 219 000 + Q86038 ARTRIUM

ARCHITECTURE COMMERCIALE
Tour les Parallèles 12, rue Jean-Baptiste Clément, 94200 Ivry
☎ 1 49 60 05 00

ARCHITECTURE DECORATION AMENAGEMENT
157, rue du Faubourg Saint-Antoine, 75008 Paris
☎ 1 45 63 22 90

ARCHITECTURAL GERARD BARRAU
16, rue de la Grande Chaumière, 75006 Paris
☎ 1 46 33 47 47

ARNAUL DANIEL
66, rue de Sèvres, 75005 Paris
☎ 1 45 66 40 84

ASYMETRIE
16, rue des Minimes, 75003 Paris
☎ **1 43 56 22 20 - Fax 1 43 56 75 67**

ATELIER JEAN-LUC CELEREAU
13-15, rue de la Verrerie, 75004 Paris
☎ **1 40 29 95 05 - Fax 1 40 29 00 96**

ATTIDU DECO
62, rue François Ier, 75008 Paris
☎ 1 42 56 65 18

AXE CONCEPT
41, rue de Bourgogne, 75007 Paris
☎ 1 47 05 71 74

B.E.D.
50-54, rue de Silly, 92513 Boulogne-Billancourt Cedex
☎ **1 49 09 75 75 - Fax 1 49 09 73 79**

BEINEIX MARIE-HELENE
184, avenue Charles de Gaulle, 92200 Neuilly-sur-Seine
☎ 1 47 38 28 22

B.E.L.F.
43, rue de Maubeuge, 75009 Paris
☎ 1 42 46 25 56

BERBESSON RACINE ET ASSOCIES
1, villa Juge, 75015 Paris
☎ **1 45 77 87 48 - Fax 1 45 77 78 34**

B.E.T. LOGER
13, rue Gandon, 75013 Paris
☎ 1 45 84 37 00

BALAND JEAN-CLAUDE
7, rue Saint-Anne, 34000 Montpellier
☎ 67 66 06 43

BAYLET
22, rue de la Pomme, 31000 Toulouse
☎ 61 22 05 79

BIGAND MARAIS
147, rue Saint-Martin, 75003 Paris
☎ 1 42 71 04 76

BIGE PATRICK
4, place Paul Langevin, 93200 Saint-Denis
☎ 1 48 21 17 98

BOIFFILS JACQUELINE
137, boulevard Saint-Germain, 75006 Paris
☎ 1 43 65 60 18

BOYER MICHEL
7, rue de la Banque, 75002 Paris
☎ 1 42 96 12 30

BRIGITTE DUMONT DE CHASSARD S.A.
108, rue Vieille-du-Temple, 75003 Paris
☎ **1 42 77 06 50 - Fax 1 42 77 65 70**

BUREAU D'ETUDES ARCHITECTURALES BACHOUD HECHT
6 bis, rue Leconte-de-Lisle, 75016 Paris
☎ **1 45 20 78 04 - Fax 1 45 20 60 62**

BUREAUX D'ETUDES PARALLELE
18, rue Mousset Robert, 75012 Paris
☎ 1 43 42 23 82

BURROWES GERVAIS
78, rue Albert, 75013 Paris
☎ 1 45 82 19 67

C.A.P. CONCEPT
44, rue Lamark - 75018 Paris
☎ 1 42 62 87 87

C.R.A.T.E.R.E.
36, rue de la Roquette, 75011 Paris
☎ 1 43 38 90 49

CABINET AARKA
1, rue Théodule-Ribot, 75017 Paris
☎ **1 47 66 33 64 - Fax 1 48 88 93 05**

CABINET AUBOIRON
126, boulevard Haussmann, 75008 Paris
☎ 1 42 93 69 39

CABINET BERTHET-POCHY
127, boulevard Malesherbes, 75017 Paris
☎ 1 47 66 29 98

CADESTIN MICHEL
122, av. Daumesnil, 75012 Paris
☎ 1 43 46 13 88

CANAL
7, rue Elzévir, 75003 Paris
☎ 1 42 78 22 50

CARRÉ NOIR
82, bd des Batignolles, 75017 Paris
☎ 1 42 94 02 27

CONCEPT JACQUES CARCHON & JEAN FOURNIER
47, rue de L'Arbre-Sec, 75001 Paris
☎ 1 42 60 08 94 / 42 60 77 41

CORAME
5, bd Poissonnière, 75002 Paris
☎ **1 42 36 19 91 - Fax 1 42 36 28 28**

COTTET BERNARD
10, rue Feuillantines, 75005 Paris
☎ 46 33 03 21

CRABTREE HALL PROJECTS LIMITED
Crabtree Hall/Plan Créatif
10, rue Mercœur, 75011 Paris
☎ **1 43 70 60 60 - Fax 1 43 70 96 29**

C.S.I.A. CHRISTOPHE SEGUIN INTERNATIONAL ART
27, rue Buffault, 75009 Paris
☎ **1 42 81 38 05**

DE PAZZIS GAUTIER
101, rue de Vaugirard, 75006 Paris
☎ 45 48 63 26

DELPIRE JEAN-JACQUES
7, rue Paul-Franchi, 91450 Soisy-sur-Seine
☎ 1 60 75 11 43

DESIGN ARCHITECTURAL
15 bis, rue du Général-de-Gaulle,
94480 Ablon-sur-Seine
☎ **1 45 97 43 41 - Fax 1 45 97 27 52 - Tx 264 918**

DESIGN SOLUTION
65, rue Rambuteau, 75004 Paris
☎ **1 42 77 03 63 - Fax 1 42 72 93 11**

DRAGON ROUGE
32, rue Pages, 92150 Suresnes
☎ 1 42 04 11 00

DUMONT JEAN-PIERRE
21, allée Paul-Sabatier, 31000 Toulouse
☎ 61 63 83 83

ECART
111, rue St-Antoine, 75004 Paris
☎ 1 42 78 88 35

ELIXIR
1, rue Gustave-Geoffroy, 75013 Paris
☎ 1 43 37 86 84

E.M.C.
15, allée des Eiders, 75019 Paris
☎ 1 40 05 02 02

ENFI DESIGN GROUPE
32/34, rue Kléber, 4e étage, 75116 Paris
☎ 1 45 00 80 32

ENVIRONNEMENT DESIGN
6, rue Jules-Simon, 92100 Boulogne
☎ 1 46 03 18 48

ÉRIC LIEURÉ
89, fg St-Antoine, 75011 Paris
☎ 1 43 42 39 49 - Fax 1 43 45 08 62

ESNAULT JEAN-FRANÇOIS
16, rue G.-de-Caillavet, 75015 Paris
☎ 1 45 79 33 99

ESPACE ET STRUCTURE
11, rue de Rochechouart, 75009 Paris
☎ 1 42 85 21 11

EXPO CREATION
17, rue Médéric, 75017 Paris
☎ 1 42 67 46 50

FALOCI PIERRE-LOUIS
9, bd Port-Royal, 75013 Paris
☎ 1 43 37 72 44

FATUS ROGER
51, rue Dareau, 75014 Paris
☎ 1 43 27 78 11

FOURNET COLETTE
141, bd J.F. Kennedy, 06600 Cap d'Antibes
☎ 93 61 94 44

FRANÇOIS ELIE DESIGN
49, rue Saint-Roch, 75001 Paris
☎ 42 96 23 10

GANE & TROUPEL
17, rue de Tournon, 75006 Paris
☎ 1 46 34 54 40

GANG
7, rue des Gabres, 06400 Cannes
☎ 93 68 10 60

GARCIN MARTY PERRIN
9, rue Béranger, 75003 Paris
☎ 40 27 87 47

GOVERNOR
4, quai des Célestins, 75004 Paris
☎ 1 42 77 16 61

GRAPHITE
114, rue de la Croix-Nivert, 75015 Paris
☎ 1 42 77 16 61

GRIOIS PHILIPPE
12, rue Lagarde, 75005 Paris
☎ 1 45 35 59 00

GROCHOWICKI MICHEL
17, avenue d'Arras-Marconne, 62140 Hesdin
☎ 21 86 82 58

HART-LABORDE
174, avenue Charles-de-Gaulle,
92200 Neuilly-sur-Seine
☎ 1 46 24 76 89 - Fax 1 47 45 50 42 -
Tx HARTLAB 620 049 F

HEBEY ISABELLE
13, rue Villherhardouin, 75003 Paris
☎ 1 42 72 80 79

HERTRICH MARC
13, rue Marie et Louise, 75010 Paris
☎ 1 42 45 69 27

IMHOTEP ARCHITECTURE INTÉRIEURE
5, rue Civry, 75016 Paris
☎ 1 46 51 13 42

IN'16
Rue Louis-Dardenne, 92170 Vanves
☎ 1 46 44 85 06

INTER ART
70, rue Michel-Ange, 75016 Paris
☎ 1 46 51 42 71

INTÉRIEUR DESIGN
30, rue Gaston-Charle, 94120 Fontenay-sous-Bois
☎ 1 48 73 87 05

JOUANNET MICHEL
12, rue Aubriot, 75004 Paris
☎ 1 42 78 30 20

KAGEYAMA HIROKO
13, rue Mazarine, 75006 Paris
☎ 1 43 25 91 27

L'UTEAU
31, bd Exelmans, 75016 Paris
☎ 1 45 27 16 21

LANDORS
19, rue Valette, 75005 Paris
☎ 1 40 46 97 97

LECONTE MICHEL
34, rue d'Antar, 78680 Epone

LOBBE GENEVIÈVE
73, rue Claude-Bernard, 75005 Paris
☎ 1 45 44 61 59

LONSDALE DANIEL BONNEMAISON
78, bd de la République, 92100 Boulogne
☎ 1 46 21 66 11

LYNN WILSON ASSOCIATES INC
Lynn Wilson Assoc., Paris
☎ 1 40 49 02 34 - Fax 1 40 49 02 73

MEDIANE INTERNATIONAL
37, bd Latour-Maubourg, 75007 Paris
☎ 1 47 05 45 38

NOIR PHILIPPE & DE VICHET CHRISTINE
23, rue des Jeuneurs, 75002 Paris
☎ 1 45 08 53 12/ 40 26 48 55

PALISSAD
14, rue Rémy Dumoncel, 75014 Paris
☎ 1 43 22 60 21

P.H.I. SA
8, avenue du Maine, 75015 Paris
☎ 1 42 22 47 24

PIERREJEAN JACQUES
10, rue Jules-Valles, 75011 Paris
☎ 1 43 67 48 64

PLAN CREATIF
10, rue Mercœur, 75011 Paris
☎ 1 43 70 60 60

POULPIQUET DE BRESCANVEL JEAN-MICHEL
1, rue Desnouettes, 75015 Paris
☎ 1 45 32 49 57

PPH VOLUME
10, rue Duvergier, 75019 Paris
☎ 1 40 35 43 45 - Fax 1 40 35 43 47

RICHARD ALAIN
15/17, rue Cels, 75014 Paris
☎ 1 43 22 34 35

RSCG SOPHA DESIGN
8, rue Rouget-de-Lisle, 92130 Issy-les-
Moulineaux
☎ 1 40 93 93 94 - Fax 1 46 62 60 72 - Tx 631 262

S.N.A.I.
56, rue de Bourgogne, 75007 Paris
☎ 1 45 51 37 43

SANTINI PAOLO
88, rue Saint-Martin, 75004 Paris

SHINING STRATÉGIE DESIGN SEN SUPTA
26, rue Benard, 75014 Paris
☎ 1 40 44 93 27

SOCIÉTÉ GETRAD
6, rue Brey, 75017 Paris
☎ 1 47 63 41 94/ 47 63 41 94

SOCIÉTÉ INTER-ART
70, rue Michel-Ange, 75016 Paris
☎ 1 46 51 42 71

SOCIÉTÉ KERBOZ
27, rue Hippolyte-Maindron, 75014 Paris

SOCIÉTÉ PHILTRE
137, rue du fg Saint-Antoine, 75011 Paris
☎ 1 43 43 80 63

SOCIÉTÉ SPHÈRE
16, rue Wallons, 75013 Paris
☎ 1 45 35 16 20

SOCIÉTÉ STARCK
3, rue de la Roquette, 75011 Paris
☎ 1 40 21 72 54

SOCIÉTÉ TECTES
7, rue Bayard, 75008 Paris
☎ 1 42 25 26 07

SPORTES RONALD
17, quai Voltaire, 75007 Paris
☎ 1 42 60 99 31

TECUOVA
12, rue Pestalozzi, 75005 Paris
☎ 1 43 37 99 58

THUAL JACQUES
51, avenue Montaigne, 75008 Paris

WOLFF OLINS/HAMILTON
Wolff Olins
72, rue du Fg Saint-Honoré, 75008 Paris
☎ 1 40 07 86 06 - Fax 1 40 07 80 40

GERMANY - Telephone Code: 49

BORN & STRUKAMP MESSEBAU GmbH
Grossenbaumer Weg 9, 4000 Düsseldorf 30
☎ (0) 211 411025 - Fax (0) 211 424053

FITCH-RS
Bahnofstrasse 20, 6200 Wiesbaden
☎ 61 21 30 90 61 - Fax 61 21 30 20 07

MICHAEL PETERS GROUP, RETAIL
ARCHITECTURE AND INTERIORS/XMPR
Bilker Strasse 32, 4000 Düsseldorf
☎ (0) 211 13 35 91

PETER SCHMIDT VEIT MAHLMANN DESIGN
GmbH
Badestrasse 19, 2000 Hamburg 13
☎ (0) 40 44 38 67/ 41 76 - Fax (0) 40 44 68 30

SIEGER DESIGN
Schloss Harkotten, 4414 Sassenberg 2
☎ (0) 5426 2796/ 2816 - Fax (0) 5426 3875

STUDIO 2A S.A.S. c/o blu consult
Holzstrasse 11, 800 Munich
☎ (0) 89 2607799 - Fax (0) 89 260 7586

ttsp
Wilhelm - Leuschner Strasse 7,
6000 Frankfurt-am-Main 1
☎ (0) 69 25 33 08 - Fax (0) 69 25 33 84

Associations in Germany

BUND DEUTSCHER ARCHITEKTEN (BDA)
Ippendorfer Allee 14b, 5300 Bonn 1
☎ (0) 228 28 50 11

PRASIDIUM BUND DEUTSCHER INNENARCHITEKTEN (BDIA)
Hannoversche Str. 79, 3004 Isernhagen 1
☎ (0) 511 61 87 3

DEUTSCHER DESIGNER CLUB (DDC)
Fullerstrasse 4, 6370 Oberursel/f fm
☎ (0) 6171 40 30

VERBAND DEUTSCHER
INDUSTRIE-DESIGNER e.V
Altestadt 9, 4000 Düsseldorf 1
☎ (0) 211 804 48

AARDEWERK & PARTNERS
Princess Mariestr. 13 A, 2514 KC DEN HAAG
☎ 070-64 62 26

ALBERTS & VAN HUUT
Keizersgracht 169, 1016 DP Amsterdam
☎ 020-22 00 82 - Fax 020-24 04 06

ASNOVA
Korte Lauwerstraat 9, 3512 VE Utrecht
☎ 030-32 20 29 - Fax 030-32 20 29

AVI
Stationstraat 58, 5664 AT GELDEROP
☎ 073-13 27 11

BNI
Waterlooplein 219, 1011 PG Amsterdam
☎ 020-27 68 20

BOESTEN VAN VLIET HENNY
Veursestraatweg 90, 2265 CE Leidschendam
☎ 070-20 41 04

BOLHUIS LAMBECK
Spui 24, 1012 XA Amsterdam
☎ 020-26 10 18

BOZELL DESIGN
Bovenkerkerweg 2, 1185 XE Amstelveen
☎ 020-47 66 76 - Fax 020-47 71 91

BRS PREMSELA VONK
Nieuwe Prinsengracht 89, 1018 VR Amsterdam
☎ 020-26 20 30 - Fax 020-26 50 79

BUDDING FELS JOKE
Herengracht 162, 1016 BP Amsterdam
☎ 020-20 41 39

DAM CEES
Singel 148, 1015 AG Amsterdam
☎ 020-23 47 55

DE JONG HASKO
Leliegracht 56, 1015 DJ Amsterdam
☎ 020-20 63 55

DE VLAMING FENNIS DINGEMANS
Huizingalaan 189, 3572 LL Utrecht
☎ 030-73 05 55 - Fax 030-73 16 24

DKS
Piazzacenter 404, 5600 HE Eindhoven
☎ 040-44 84 79

DUINTJER
Ulenpas 18, 1082 LC Amsterdam
☎ 020-44 28 91

EGM ARCHITECTEN
**Laan der Verenigde Naties 9, Postbus 298,
3300 AG Dordrecht
☎ 078-33 06 60 - Fax 078-14 00 71**

FUKKEN SYBRANT
Kolenbranderstr. 24, 2984 AT Ridderkerk
☎ 01804-1 07 22 - Fax 01804-1 57 78

GOOSEN AD
Stationstraat 4, 5038 ED Tilburg
☎ 013-43 33 34

GROENHOUT ARCHI. GROEP 69
Keizersgracht 450, 1016 GD Amsterdam
☎ 020-23 26 11

HART FRED
Radboudkwartier 193, 2340 GH Utrecht
☎ 030-32 13 37

HARTSUYKER E. IR.
Van Diemenstraat 158, 1013 CN Amsterdam
☎ 020-25 43 20

HIDDE CONSULTANTS
**Herengracht 162, 1016 BP Amsterdam
☎ 020-38 21 37 - Fax 020-38 21 38**

HOOGSTAD VAN TILBURG
Wijnhaven 8, 3011 WP Rotterdam
☎ 010-414 16 77 - Fax 010-412 04 40

HOOPER ARCHITEKTENBURO
DR. Hub V. Doorneweg 97, 5026 RB Tilburg
☎ 013-68 27 17 - Fax 013-63 24 34

INTEREXPO
Thomas Jeffersonlaan 647, 2285 AZ Rijswijk
☎ 070-94 35 36 - 070-94 54 64

JOWA IMRE
Prinsengracht 526, 1017 KJ Amsterdam
☎ 020-24 43 80

KHO LIANG IE ASSOCIATES
Valeriusstraat 55, 1071 MD Amsterdam
☎ 020-662 64 08 - Fax 020-662 29 19

KROEZE RUYS
Parkstraat 69 A, 2514 JE Den Haag
☎ 070-45 24 02

KUBUS
Kralingseplaslaan 118, 3061 DH Rotterdam
☎ 010-52 42 27

KUIJT JAN
Spui 23 - 27, 1012 WX Amsterdam
☎ 020-22 09 93

LELIEVELDT H.
Hoflaan 121, Rotterdam
☎ 010-413 01 46

MICHAEL PETERS GROUP/XMPR
**Koningslaan 54, 1075 AE Amsterdam
☎ 020-758 551**

MIN 2 PRODUKTIES
Oude Bergerweg 1, 1862 KH Bergen NH
☎ 02208-9 45 37

OPERA
Baronielaan 85, 4818 PC Breda
☎ 076-147 5 96 - Fax 076-14 82 78

PARRY ROB
Laan.V.Nieuw Oost Einde 35-37, 2274 EA Voorburg
☎ 070-86 72 46

PEEK DICK
Oranje Nassaulaan 14, 1075 AN Amsterdam
☎ 020-664 98 81

SCHOENMAKERS LEO
Roerstraat 65, 5626 DS Eindhoven Acht
☎ 040-62 33 47

SPAANDERMAN J.
Noordzijde Zoom 1, 4313 AA Bergen op Zoom
☎ 01640-5 30 00

V SANTEN VOLLEBREGT V TONGEREN
Entrepotdok 28, 1018 AD Amsterdam
☎ 020-22 57 70 - Fax 020-20 62 57

VAN ANDEL LEIJSEN
ZIJLWEG 77, HAARLEM
☎ 023-28 83 63 - Fax 023-31 22 04

VAN DER MASCH SPAKLER W.
DE Ruyterlaan 24, 6881 GV Velp
☎ 085-61 89 37

VAN DER VELDEN BEN
Kralingseplaslaan 20, 3062 DB Rotterdam
☎ 010-452 15 11

VAN DER WIJST MARIJKE
NWE Herengracht 101, 1011 RZ Amsterdam
☎ 020-25 04 09

VAN HENGSTUM & KOOYMANS
Leonardus V. Veghelstr. 6, 5212 AE Den Bosch

VAN LONKHUIJSEN JOHAN
Willemsparkweg 180, 1071 HV Amsterdam
☎ 020-79 60 57

VAN OORT V.D. BERG MIEKE
Krakeling 4, 2121 BM Bennebroek
☎ 02502-68 18

VAN RIJN PETER
Schiedamseweg Ben. 535, 3028 BW Rotterdam
☎ 010-462 05 88

VEENENDAAL & BOS
Concertgebouwplein 9, 1071 LL Amsterdam
☎ 020-71 68 86 - Fax 020-76 80 48

VOSSEN STUDIO
Keizergracht 109, 1015 CJ Amsterdam
☎ 020-23-10-19

ITALY - Telephone Code : 39

GAE AULENTI
4 Piazza S.Marco, 20121 Milan
☎ (0)2 869 2762

MARIO BELLINI
11 Corso Venezia, 20121 Milan
☎ (0)2 760 07390

RODOLFO BONETTO
55 Ripa di Porta Ticinese, 20143 Milan
☎ (0)2 894 011156

ANDREA BRANZI
22A Via Solferino, 20121 Milan
☎ (0)2 659 2227/ 655 7351

STEFANO CASCIANI
78 Viale Umbria, 20135 Milan
☎ (0)2 545 9325

ACHILLE CASTIGLIONI
27 Piazza Castello, 20121 Milan
☎ (0)2 805 3606

ALDO CIBIC
28 Via Legnano, 20121 Milan
☎ (0)2 657 1948/ 659 7293/ 659 7328/ 290 01110

ANTONIO CITTERIO
14 Via Maroncelli, 20154 Milan
☎ (0)2 655 9888

ADALBERTO DAL LAGO
34 Via Aurelio Saffi, 20123 Milan
☎ (0)2 4819 5610

MICHELE DE LUCCHI
7 Via Goito, 20121 Milan
☎ (0)2 655 7013

MARTINO FERARRI
46 Via San Marco, 20123 Milan
☎ (0)2 655 5311/ 657 0286

GREGOTTI ASSOCIATI
20 Via Bandello, 20123 Milan
☎ (0)2 481 4141

MASSIMO IOSA GHINI
6 Via Poma, 20129 Milan
☎ (0)2 76 110596

VERONICA LEVIS
9 Via Lazzaro Palazzi, 20156 Milan
☎ (0)2 220 278

ITALO LUPI
39 Via Vigevano, 20144 Milan
☎ (0)2 894 03950

ROBERTO MAGRIS
24 Via XXIV Maggio, 50129 Florence
☎ (0)55 474 925

MASSIMO MOROZZI
85 C.so Garibaldi, 20121 Milan
☎ (0)2 654 148

LORENZO PAPI
26 Via G. Capponi, 50121 Florence
☎ (0)55 588 208

**MICHAEL PETERS GROUP, RETAIL
ARCHITECTURE AND INTERIORS/XMPR**
Via Dante 4, 20121 Milan
☎ (0)2 7202 0181

FRANCO RAGGI
5 Via Cornaggia, 20123 Milan
☎ (0)2 866 263

HELEN RAINEY
8 Via Tadino, 20124 Milan
☎ (0)2 2940 0814

LEONARDO RICCI
21 Via di Monte Rinaldi, 50139 Florence
☎ (0)55 400 062

ALDO ROSSI
1 Via Maddalena, 20121 Milan
☎ (0)2 865 440

CLAUDIO SALOCCHI
3 Via Filippetti, 20122 Milan
☎ (0)2 551 3576/ 5519 1963

SOTTSASS ASSOCIATI
9 Borgo Nuovo, 20122 Milan
☎ (0)2 655 2676

GEORGE SOWDEN
46/B Corso di Porta Nuova, 20121 Milan
☎ (0)2 53089/ 653 758

STUDIO 2A S.A.S.
Via Novara 13, 20013 Magenta, Milan
☎ **(0)2 979 31 77 - Fax (0)2 979 42 76**

CRISTIANO TORALDO DI FRANCIA
2/B Via Mulina S. Andrea, 50136 Florence
☎ (0)55 691 228

CARLA VENOSTA
6 Via Lovanio, 20121 Milan
☎ (0)2 659 7170

MARCO ZANUSO JR
111 Corso di Porta Romana, 20122 Milan
☎ (0)2 551 0593

SPAIN - Telephone Code: 34

ARCHIMEDE (GROUP VITRAC DESIGN)
Madrid: B.F.L. S.A.
☎ **1 593 83 17 - Fax 1 446 22 19**

ALFREDO ARRIBAS
Balmes, 345 1°2ª, 08008 Barcelona
☎ (9) 3 417 33 37 - Fax (9) 3 417 35 91

SANDRA BABSKY
Trim 6 BO, Gral Varela, 35 2° PTA 4, 28020 Madrid
☎ (9) 1 279 66 91 - Fax (9) 1 571 06 37

JAUME BACH
Hercegovina, 24 Pral, 1ª, 08006 Barcelona
☎ (9) 3 200 70 66 - Fax (9) 3 200 73 96

BERNADI
Reina Victoria, 6-10, 08021 Barcelona
☎ (9) 3 201 64 17

BIAIX SA
Rambla de Cataluña, 90 2°4ª, 08008 Barcelona
☎ **(9) 3 215 89 67 - Fax (9) 3 487 28 10**

RICARDO BOFILL
Av. Industria, 14, 08960 St Just Desvern, Barcelona
☎ (9) 3 371 59 50 - Fax (9) 3 371 18 16

BONAMUSA HOMS, ANTONIO
Ganduxer, 5-15 PTA 7 pasillo a puerta 10, 08021 Barcelona
☎ (9) 3 201 14 22

CASADESUS, SA
Via Augusta, 236, 08021 Barcelona
☎ (9) 3 202 01 99 - Fax (9) 3 202 01 66

CASA Y JARDIN
Padilla, 21-19, 28006 Madrid
☎ (9) 1 276 76 04

MARITA COLL
Manila, 61 bajos 2°
08034 Barcelona
☎ (9) 3 205 79 57 - Fax (9) 3 205 78 57

LUIS CORBELLA
Spaintex, Claudio Coello, 79 1°, 28001 Madrid
☎ (9) 1 575 11 47

TITO DALMAU
P° Picasso, 12 2°2ª, 08003 Barcelona
☎ (9) 3 319 68 90

DECO STIL S.A.
c/o Santa Ana 2, 08002 Barcelona
☎ **(9) 3 301 02 48/02 90/00 05**
Fax (9) 3 412 33 38

HORACIO DOMINGUEZ LOPEZ
Sextante, 33, 28023 Madrid
☎ (9) 1 207 04 43/ 4

ESTUDI OBERT DE DISSENY
Buenos Aires, 4 12 entlo 3°, 08029 Barcelona
☎ (9) 3 322 36 18

DOUS, SA DE DISSENY I CONSTRUCCIO
Rambla de Cataluña, 42 4° 1ª, 08007 Barcelona
☎ (9) 3 301 99 22

EQUIP 63
San Juan Bosco, 53 Bajos, 08017 Barcelona
☎ (9) 3 204 64 15

FITCH RS DESIGN CONSULTANTS
Serrano 240 5°, Madrid 28016
☎ **(9)1 457 07 81 - Fax (9)1 457 20 79**

ENRIQUE FRANCH
Commercio, 27 pral. 1ª, 08008 Barcelona
☎ (9) 3 319 11 66

DANIEL FREIXES
Carme, 44 3° 2ª, 08001 Barcelona
☎ (9) 3 301 42 97 - Fax (9) 3 301 48 58

RAMON GODO & MIGUEL CARLOS JORDA
Paseo de Entenza, 1 Pral, 08021 Barcelona
☎ (9) 3 318 60 70

CARLOS GOMEZ VACAS
Nuñez de Balboa, 114 AP. 811, 28006 Madrid
☎ (9) 1 261 61 99

FEDERICO GONZALEZ
Europa, 12 Entlo 1°, 08028 Barcelona
☎ (9) 3 330 40 50

JORDI GONZALEZ
Teodora Lamadrid, 52-60 Esc. E Entlo 1°, 08022 Barcelona
☎ (9) 3 211 34 92

GREI
Balmes 23, 08006 Barcelona
☎ (9) 3 318 61 66

LIEVORE ALBERTO
Pza. Ramon Berenguer El Grande, 1 AT, 08002 Barcelona
☎ (9) 3 310 32 92 / 30 36 - Fax (9) 3 315 38 25

MANBAR
Via Augusta 61, 08006 Barcelona
☎ (9) 3 218 64 50 - Fax (9) 3 217 34 37

MANUEL DE CENDRA Y APARICIO
DE CENDRA DISEÑO, SA
P° de la Castellana, 114, 28047 Madrid
☎ (9) 1 261 90 83 / 82

CARLOS MANZANO
Jorge Juan, 11 2° Izda, 28001 Madrid
☎ (9) 1 431 22 43 / 23 70

McCOLL GROUP INTERNATIONAL
Associate Office
Marques de Riscal n° 6, 28010 Madrid
☎ (9) 1 308 27 64

MICHAEL PETERS GROUP, RETAIL
ARCHITECTURE AND INTERIORS/XMPR
Velasquez 24, 5 D, 28001 Madrid
☎ (9) 1 575 39 64

ODESA
Laforja, 67 1° 2ª, Llorens Querol, 08021 Barcelona
☎ (9) 3 414 40 02

OJINAGA, SCP
Raset, 29 Bajos, 08021 Barcelona
☎ (9) 3 201 82 22 - Fax (9) 3 201 73 41

PASCUA ORTEGA
Lope de Vega, 24 Bajo, 28014 Madrid
☎ (9) 1 429 15 51

PENNINGTON ROBSON LTD
Plaza Santa Eulalia, 7-6, 07001 Palma de
Mallorca
☎ (0) 71 72 04 41 - Fax (0) 71 72 04 41

PEPE CORTES I LEON
Santa Teresa, 6, 08004 Barcelona
☎ (9) 3 218 79 32 / (9) 3 204 94 20 - Fax (9) 3 237 92 17

JOQUIM PRATS
Valencia, 560-562 PTA. 2°, 08026 Barcelona
☎ (9) 3 447 09 36 / 32 20 - Fax (9) 3 447 16 03

SANTIAGO ROQUETA
Paris, 207 3° 2ª, 08008 Barcelona
☎ (9) 3 237 76 36

EDUARDO SAMSO
Gran Via Carlos III, 87-89, 08028 Barcelona
☎ (9) 3 339 98 93

SERRANO & LEBEÑA
San Pedro Martir, 2 1° 8ª, 08012 Barcelona
☎ (9) 3 415 35 94

SICO, SA
Rafaël Salanova
☎ (9) 3 209 93 55

PACO TERÁN
Velazquez, 51, 28001 Madrid
☎ (9) 1 435 95 55

SWEDEN - Telephone Code : 46

ABAKO ARKITEKTKONTOR AB
Byggnad 57, Nya Varvet, 42171 Vastra Frolunda
☎ (0) 31 69 10 10

ABERLARDO GONZALEZ ARKITEKTKONTOR
Hyregatan 7, 30293 Malmo
☎ (0) 40 23 25 08

AGORA ARKITEKTER AB
Kaptensgatan 6, 11457 Stockholm
☎ (0) 8 665 30 15

AHLIN/JOHNSON ARK
Drottensg. 2, 22223 Lund
☎ (0) 46 13 72 88

ALENIUS SILFVERHIELM AHLUND ARKITEKTKONTOR AB
Gotgatan 32 og, 11621 Stockholm
☎ (0) 8 42 99 43

AOS ARKITEKTKONTOR
Norrlandsgatan 18, 11143 Stockholm
☎ (0) 8 24 11 80

ARKIMEDES AB
Nybrogatan 25 A, 11439 Stockholm
☎ (0) 8 666 02 20

BERG-ARKKONTOR AB
Kommendorsgatan 30, 11448 Stockholm
☎ (0) 8 67 05 00

BI AND LARS NORINDER AB
Sjofararvagen 16, 13200 Saltsjo-Boo
☎ (0) 8 715 33 32

COORDINATOR ARKITEKTER AB
Box 1218 (Brunnsgrand 3), 11182 Stockholm
☎ (0) 8 22 08 20

ETV ARKITEKTKONTOR AB
Kornhamnstorg 6, 11127 Stockholm
☎ (0) 8 24 24 70

FFNS ARKITEKTER I GOTEBORG
Box 2213, 40314 Goteborg
☎ (0) 31 17 50 80

FFNS INREDNINGSARK AB
Box 5503, 11485 Stockholm
☎ (0) 8 700 30 00

JONAS BOHLIN ARKITEKTKONTOR
Nybrogatan 25, 11439 Stockholm
☎ (0) 8 662 32 37

LENNART JANSSON ARKITEKTKONTOR AB
Vasterlanggatan 27, 11129 Stockholm
☎ (0) 8 14 04 90

LISS & MOSSBERG INREDNINGSARKITEKTER AB
Kindstugatan 16, 11131 Stockholm
☎ (0) 8 23 01 20

MADE ARKITEKTKONTOR AB
Nybrogatan 25, 11439 Stockholm
☎ (0) 8 67 96 55

MCM ARKITEKTER AB
Regeringsgatan 97, 11139 Stockholm
☎ (0) 8 21 56 60

NYRENS ARKITEKTKONTOR AB
Ferkens grand 3, 4tr, 11130 Stockholm
☎ (0) 8 14 24 50

PENNINGTON ROBSON Ltd
Pennington Robson/Rupert Gardner AB,
Sibylegatan 53, 11443 Stockholm
☎ (0) 8 66 51 910 - Fax (0) 8 86 27 0 26

SKALA ARKITEKTER AB
Malmgardsvagen 28, 11638 Stockholm
☎ (0) 8 743 03 75

SVENSKA RUM INREDNINGSARKITEKTER
Barnhusgatan 4, 11123 Stockholm
☎ (0) 8 23 42 20

WHITE ARKITEKTER AB
Drottningg. 5, Box 2502, 40317 Goteborg
☎ (0) 31 17 34 60

ZEBRA INREDNINGS ARK AB
St Paulsg 29, 11648 Stockholm
☎ (0) 8 702 05 30

SWITZERLAND - Telephone Code: 41

ARCHITECTURES/HOLENSTEIN JOHANNES
Minervastrasse 117, 8032 Zurich
☎ 01 38 39 117 - Fax 01 38 39 117

BACHMANN URS
c/o Keller + Bachmann, Munstergasse 12/14, 8001 Zurich
☎ 01 251 07 30

BERGMAIER CHRISTIAN
Les Dolles, 1812 RIVAZ/VD
☎ 021 946 16 46

BERTOSSA GABRIELE
Viale Portone, 6500 Bellinzona
☎ 092 26 13 77

BIERI HANSPETER
Designo AG, Pfeffingerstrasse 50, 4053 Basel
☎ 061 701 59 13

BURI MICHEL
32, av. de Frontenex, 1207 Genève
☎ 022 35 46 86

BURKI ANDREAS
Werkgruppe, Gerberngasse 21b, 3011 Bern
☎ 031 22 05 07

CAHEN ANTOINE
2, place du Nord, 1005 Lausanne
☎ 021 20 58 07

CAVADINI CLAUDIO
Via Borromini 18, 6900 Lugano
☎ 091 56 85 75

DENZ ANDRE
Seestrasse 127, 8704 Herrliberg
☎ 01 915 13 61

DE SEPIBUS HANSPETER
Bahnhofquai 11, 8001 Zurich
☎ 01 221 22 10

FELLMANN HANSRUEDI
Widenholzstrasse 1, 8304 Wallisellen
☎ 01 830 40 30

FROSSARD CLAUDE
6, rue de la Barre, 1005 Lausanne
☎ 021 20 58 07

HAUSSMANN ROBERT
Mittelstrasse 47, 8008 Zurich
☎ 01 251 03 50

HEUFF ANDREE
9, ch des Clochetons, 1004 Lausanne
☎ 021 24 71 17

HUBER VERENA
Bergstrasse 125, 8032 Zurich
☎ 01 252 07 40

KELLER FRITZ
c/o Keller + Bachmann, Munstergasse 12/14, 8001 Zurich
☎ 01 251 07 30

MILANI FRANCESCO
Via Monte Tabor 4, 6512 Giubiasco
☎ 092 27 46 55

NEUENSCHWANDER MANFRED
Sonnenrain 6, 8700 Kusnacht
☎ 01 910 15 11

WYSS BENEDIKT
Designo AG, Pfeffingerstrasse 50, 4053 Basel
☎ 061 701 59 13

UNITED KINGDOM - Telephone Code: 44

20/20
The Forum, 74-80 Camden Street, London NW1 0EG
☎ 071 383 7071 - Fax 071 383 7140

ABBEY HANSON ROWE INTERNATIONAL
4 Bloomsbury Place, London WC1A 2QA
☎ 071 636 4819

ADDISON DESIGN CONSULTANCY LTD
60 Britton Street, London EC1M 5NA
☎ 071 250 1887 - Fax 071 251 3712

ADDISON MARC
23 Emerald Street, London WC1N 3QL
☎ 071 831 2800 - Fax 071 831 0274

AMOS BROOME ASSOCIATES PLC
Old Bridge Street, Hampton Wick, Surrey, KT1 4BN
☎ 081 977 7333 - Fax 081 977 8346

THE ANDERLYN CONSULTANCY
209 Harrow Road, London W2 5EG
☎ 071 266 3779 - Fax 071 266 3706

ANSELL & BAILEY
2 Fitzroy Square, London W1P 5AH
☎ 071 387 0141 - Fax 071 387 7460

ARDIN & BROOKS & PARTNERS
73 Upper Richmond Road, Putney, London SW15 2SZ
☎ 081 874 9011 - Fax 081 871 2807

AUKETT ASSOCIATES
127 Albert Bridge Road, London SW11 4PL
☎ 071 352 0142 - Fax 071 924 1125

AUSTIN-SMITH : LORD
10-12 Carlisle Street, London W1V 5RF
☎ 071 734 6161 - Fax 071 439 2043

AVERY ASSOCIATES ARCHITECTS
8-9 Stephen Mews, London W1P 1PP
☎ 071 637 4243 - Fax 071 580 7333

AXIS DESIGNER
2 Cosser Street, London SE1 7BU
☎ 071 928 7801 - Fax 071 620 0238

BDFS GROUP
41-43 Mitchell Street, London EC1V 3QD
☎ 071 253 6172 - Fax 071 608 2155

BDP DESIGN
P.O. Box 4WD, 16 Gresse Street, London W1A 4WD
☎ 071 631 4733 - Fax 071 631 0393

B.M. TREVILLION INTERIORS
12 Ladysmith Road, Enfield, EN1 3AA
☎ 081 367 9494 - Fax 081 367 7785

B.S.B. DESIGN LTD
Emberford Studios, 8 Summer Road, East Molesey,
Surrey, KT8 9LS
☎ 081 398 2847 - Fax 081 941 6909

BAKER SAYER
5 Banbury Court, Floral Street, London WC2E 9BZ
☎ 071 836 4840 - Fax 071 497 2568

BARSBY PRINCE & PARTNERS LTD
Ashville Way, Whetstone, Leicester LE8 3NN
☎ 0533 848448 - Fax 0533 867491

BERESFORD SHERMAN DESIGN
47-49 Durham Street, London SE11 5JW
☎ 071 735 2020 - Fax 071 735 5363

BEACHMOUNT LTD
Waterside Drive, Langley Business Park, Langley,
Berkshire SL3 6EZ
☎ 0753 40660 - Fax 0753 47138

THE BELL SLATER PARTNERSHIP
287 Upper Richmond Road, London SW15 6SP
☎ 081 785 3030 - Fax 081 788 2934

BOWES DARBY DESIGN ASSOCIATES
4th Floor, 136 Tooley Street, London SE1 2TU
☎ 071 378 0637 - Fax 071 378 0692

BRADSHAW ROWSE & HARKER
25 Shelton Street, London WC2H 9HT
☎ 071 631 3001 - Fax 071 636 1419

STANLEY BRAGG PARTNERSHIP
Abbeygate One, 8 Whitewell Road, Colchester, CO2 7DF
☎ 0206 571371 - Fax 0206 765242

BRENNAN & WHALLEY LTD
131 Kingston Road, London SW19 1LT
☎ 081 542 0750 - Fax 081 543 7970

EDWARD BRISCOE & PARTNERS
182-194 Union Street, London SE1 0LH
☎ 071 928 2344 - Fax 071 620 0304

BROADWAY MALYAN
Weybridge Business Park, Addlestone Road, Weybridge,
Surrey, KT15 2UN
☎ 0932 845599 - Fax 0932 856206

BROCK CARMICHAEL ASSOCIATES
Federation House, Hope Street, Liverpool, L1 9BS
☎ 051 709 1087 - Fax 051 709 6418

DAVID BROWN & PARTNERS
51 High Street, Hampton, Middlesex, TW12 2SX
☎ 081 941 2112 - Fax 081 941 1742

BUSINESS DESIGN GROUP
The Meeting House, Lewins Mead, Bristol, BS1 2NN
☎ 0272 279137 - Fax 0272 298878

ROBERT BYRON ARCHITECTS
78 Fentiman Road, London SW8
☎ 071 735 1911 - Fax 071 735 1843

CAMPBELL, HELLOWELL, DUNCAN
Studio 19, The Waterside, Wharf Road, London N1 7XB
☎ 071 251 2900 - Fax 071 250 0271

BAXTER CLARK AND PAUL
2 Bow Lane, London EC4M 9EE
☎ 071 248 0751 - Fax 071 329 0091

CARTER DESIGN GROUP LTD
North Lane, Foxton, Market Harborough,
Leicestershire, LE16 7RF
☎ 0858 33322 - Fax 0858 84239

CECIL DENNY HIGHTON
Axtell House, 23-24 Warwick Street, London W1R 5RB
☎ 071 734 6831 - Fax 071 734 0508

CHAPMAN TAYLOR PARTNERS
96 Kensington High Street, London W8 4SG
☎ 071 938 3333 - Fax 071 937 1391

CHECKLAND KINDLEYSIDES
Fowke Street, Rothley, Leicester, LE7 7PJ
☎ 0533 374282 - Fax 0533 374649

CHIPPERFIELD ASSOCIATES
1A Cobham Mews, Agar Grove, London NW1
☎ 071 267 9422 - Fax 071 267 9347

JOHN CLARK ASSOCIATES
Kings Court, 2-16 Goodge Street, London W1P 1FF
☎ 071 637 5100 - Fax 071 580 0747

COCHRANE McGREGOR LTD
3 St Andrews Square, Edinburgh, EH2 2BD
☎ 031 557 4022 - Fax 031 556 7559

COLEY PORTER BELL
4 Flitcroft Street, London WC2H 8DJ
☎ 071 379 4355 - Fax 071 379 5164

THE COMPANY OF DESIGNERS FFNS
39 Charlton Street, London NW1 1JE
☎ 071 388 3722 - Fax 071 387 6139

RSCG CONRAN DESIGN
22-24 Torrington Place, London WC1E 7HJ
☎ **071 631 0102 - Fax 071 255 2049**

CORSTORPHINE & WRIGHT LTD
10 Church Street, Warwick, CV34 4AB
☎ 0926 402323 - Fax 0926 495318

COVELL MATTHEWS WHEATLEY
19 Bourdon Place, London W1X 9HZ
☎ **071 409 2444 - Fax 071 493 8998**

CRABTREE HALL
70 Crabtree Lane, London SW6 6LT
☎ **071 381 8755 - Fax 071 385 9575**

DAVID DAVIES ASSOCIATES
12 Goslett Yard, London WC2H OEE
☎ 071 437 9070 - Fax 071 734 0291

DEACON EDGE
131 High Holborn, London WC1V 6PS
☎ 071 405 8873 - Fax 071 405 8874

DEGW
Porters North, 8 Crinan Street, London N1 9SQ
☎ 071 239 7777 - Fax 071 278 3713

THE DESIGN ASSOCIATES
67 Neal Street, London WC2H 9PJ
☎ 081 836 9719 - Fax 081 836 1123

DESIGN AXIS
14-15 Perserverance Works, 38 Kingsland Road, London
E2 8DD
☎ 071 739 4399 - Fax 071 739 7830

THE DESIGN CONSULTANCY LTD
62 Lordship Road, London N16 0QT
☎ 081 802 3059

DESIGN HOUSE
120 Parkway, London NW1 7AN
☎ **071 482 2815 - Fax 071 267 7587**

THE DESIGN SOLUTION
20 Kingly Court, London W1R 5LE
☎ **071 434 0887 - Fax 071 434 0269**

DESIGNWORK
10/13 King Street, Covent Garden, London WC2E 8HZ
☎ 071 240 0030 - Fax 071 836 5647

DI DESIGN AND DEVELOPMENT LTD
12 Dryden Street, London WC2E 9NA
☎ **071 836 1853 - Fax 071 379 4727**

DIN ASSOCIATES
6 South Lambert Place, London SW8 1SP
☎ 071 582 0777 - Fax 071 582 3080

MICHAEL DOWD
10 Barley Mow Passage, Chiswick, London W4
☎ 081 994 6477 - Fax 081 994 1533

DY DAVIS DESIGN LTD
36 Paradise Road, Richmond, Surrey TW9 1SE
☎ 081 948 5544 - Fax 081 948 8480

EPR DESIGN LTD
56-62 Wilton Road, London SW1V 1DE
☎ **071 834 2299 - Fax 071 834 7524**

EVA JIRICNA ARCHITECTS
7 Dering Street, London W1R 9AB
☎ 071 629 7077 - Fax 071 491 3370

EZRA ATTIA AND ASSOCIATES
3 Belsize Place, London NW3 5AL
☎ 071 431 2627 - Fax 071 794 0198

F.M. DESIGN
1A Lonsdale Square, Islington N1 1EN
☎ 071 242 2712 - Fax 071 831 6733

FAIRHURSTS
P.O. Box 24, Bank Chambers, Faulkner Street,
Manchester, M60 1EH
☎ 061 236 7722 - Fax 061 236 2226

FARMER DESIGN GROUP
33 Gresse Street, London W1P 1PN
☎ 071 436 3443 - Fax 071 436 3861

FIRST ARCHITECTURE GROUP PLC
12/18 Grosvenor Gardens, London SW1 0DH
☎ 071 824 8215 - Fax 071 730 4816

FITCH RS DESIGN CONSULTANTS
Porters South, 4 Crinan Street, London N1 9UE
☎ **071 278 7200 - Fax 071 833 1014**

FITZROY ROBINSON PARTNERSHIP
77 Portland Place, London W1N 4EP
☎ 071 636 8033 - Fax 071 580 3996

FOSTER ASSOCIATES
Riverside Three, 22 Hester Road, London SW11 4AN
☎ 071 738 0455 - Fax 071 637 2640

IAN FRASER, JOHN ROBERTS & PARTNERS LTD
1 Devonshire Street, London W1N 1FX
☎ 071 637 4141 - Fax 071 637 2629

FREDERICK GIBBERD COOMBES & PARTNERS
117-121 Curtain Road, London EC2A 3AD
☎ 071 739 3400 - Fax 071 739 8948

FURNEAUX STEWART
24 Beaumont Mews, London W1N 3LN
☎ **071 935 5724 - Fax 071 486 0304**

THE GMW PARTNERSHIP
239 Kensington High Street, London W8 6SL
☎ **071 937 8020 - Fax 071 937 5815**

GODFREY GILES & CO (LONDON) LTD
Southbank House, Black Prince Road, London SE1 7SY
☎ 071 735 6025 - Fax 071 735 1555

GODSMARK & GORDON
35 Rheidol Mews, London N1 8NU
☎ 071 226 9147 - Fax 071 354 5465

HLM ARCHITECTS LTD
1 Old Lodge Place, St Margarets, Twickenham,
Middlesex TW1 1RQ
☎ 081 744 1666 - Fax 081 744 2964

THE HALPERN PARTNERSHIP
Leonard House, 9-15 Leonard Street, London EC2A 4HP
☎ 071 251 0781 - Fax 071 251 9204

HANSON NOBLE & ASSOCIATES
55 Charlotte Road, London EC2A 3QT
☎ 071 739 0444 - Fax 071 739 2955

HARPER AND SPERRING
4 Firs Street, Dudley, West Midlands, DY2 7DN
☎ 0384 252622 - Fax 0384 456224

HEERY ARCHITECTS AND ENGINEERS LTD
49 Russell Square, London WC1B 4JP
☎ 071 631 4710 - Fax 071 323 2819

HENRION, LUDLOW & SCHMIDT LTD
12 Hobart Place, London SW1W OHH
☎ 071 235 5466 - Fax 071 235 8637

THE JOHN HERBERT PARTNERSHIP
8 Berkeley Road, London NW1 8YR
☎ 071 722 3932 - Fax 071 586 7048

HODGE ASSOCIATES LTD
3 Lambton Place, London W11 2SH
☎ 071 727 8600 - Fax 071 727 6195

HOLMES WRIGHT PARTNERSHIP
43 Coronet Street, London N1 6HD
☎ 071 739 9428 - Fax 071 739 9558

HOP STUDIOS
2 Jamaica Road, London SE1 2BX
☎ 071 252 0808 - Fax 071 237 7199

THE PETER INSTON DESIGN CO
48-52 Birmingham Road, Bromsgrove, Worcester B61 00D
☎ 0527 579321 - Fax 0527 579325

INTERIOR CONSULTANCY SERVICES LTD
Tyttenhanger House, St Albans, Herts AL4 OPG
☎ 0727 23633 - Fax 0727 26488

INTRADESIGN INC.
c/o Robinson Conn Partnership, 68 Alma Road,
Windsorn Berkshire
☎ 075 383 0055 - Fax 075 385 0913

ISHERWOOD & CO
12 Brewhouse Street, London SW15 2NR
☎ 081 785 2255 - Fax 081 788 4542

THE JENKINS GROUP
9 Tufton Street, London SW1P 3QB
☎ 071 799 1090 - Fax 071 222 6751

LESLIE JONES ARCHITECTS
Leslie House, 3-4 Bentinck Street, London W1M 5RN
☎ 071 935 5481 - Fax 071 487 3820

KATZ, VAUGHAN, MEYER & FELTHAM
162 Ewell Road, Surbiton, Surrey KT6 6HG
☎ 081 390 4658 - Fax 081 399 8980

LANDOR ASSOCIATES
3 Hill Street, Berkeley Square, London W1X 7FA
☎ 071 409 0722 - Fax 071 491 1258

LEVER DESIGN
Arch 74, Ranelagh Gardens, London SW6 3UR
☎ 071 736 0452 - Fax 071 371 0331

LEES ASSOCIATES
5 Dryden Street, Covent Garden, London WC2E 9NW
☎ 071 240 2430 - Fax 071 379 4280

LEWIS & HICKEY ARCHITECTS
Pitt House, 120 Baker Street, London W1M 2HL
☎ 071 935 2948 - Fax 071 935 1528

LEY COLBECK & PARTNERS
Charter House, Park Street, Ashford, Kent TN24 8EH
☎ 0233 622226 - Fax 0233 621870

LYNN WILSON ASSOCIATES INC
McColl/Wilson, London
☎ 071 935 4788 - Fax 071 224 3424

McCOLL GROUP INTERNATIONAL
64 Wigmore Street, London W1H 9OJ
☎ 071 935 4788 - Fax 071 935 0865

McILROY COATES LTD
10 Bernard Street, Leith, Edinburgh E86 6PP
☎ 031 226 2891 - Fax 031 220 1890

MARKETPLACE DESIGN PARTNERSHIP Ltd
Pulpit House, 1 The Square, Abingdon,
Oxfordshire OX14 5SX
☎ 0734 599924 - Fax 0734 500511

MAURICE BROUGHTON ARCHITECTS
38/39 South Molton Street, London W1Y 1HD
☎ 071 493 0456 - Fax 071 629 3856

MAURICE PHILLIPS ASSOCIATES
1 Auckland Street, London SE11 5HU
☎ 071 793 0696 - Fax 071 793 0603

JOHN MICHAEL DESIGN
20 Queen Elizabeth Street, London SE1
☎ 071 357 6002 - Fax 071 403 9938

MINALE TATTERSFIELD & PARTNERS
The Courtyard, 37 Sheen Road, Richmond, Surrey TW9 1AJ
☎ 081 948 7999 - Fax 081 948 2435

MORRISON DESIGN LTD
St Alkmunds House, 103 Belper Road, Derby DE1 3ES
☎ 0332 363355 - Fax 0332 291441

PAUL MULLINS ASSOCIATES LTD
The Forum, 74-80 Camden Street, London NW1 OEG
☎ 071 387 5633 - Fax 071 387 3454

MURDOCH ASSOCIATES
2-10 Magdelen Street, London SE1 2EN
☎ 071 962 1122 - Fax 071 962 1125

NORMAN JONES SONS & RIGBY
57-59 Hoghton Street, Southport, Merseyside PR9 OPG
☎ 0704 31252 - Fax 0704 32833

OYA INTERIOR
Fox House, 46 Oxford Street, Leicester LE1
☎ 0533 558084 - Fax 0533 541184

THE PD DESIGN COMPANY LTD
The Grange, Wigston, Leicester LE8 1NN
☎ 0533 810018 - Fax 0533 813010

PENNINGTON ROBSON LTD
Tea Warehouse, 10a Lant Street, London SE1 1QR
☎ 071 378 0671 - Fax 071 378 0531

PENTAGRAM DESIGN LTD
11 Needham Road, London W11 2RP
☎ 071 229 3477 - Fax 071 727 9932

PENTANGLE INTERIORS
23 Bucklersbury, Hitchin, Herts SG5 1BG
☎ 0462 422338 - Fax 0462 420918

PETER LEONARD ASSOCIATES
535 Kings Road, London SW10 0SZ
☎ 071 352 1717 - Fax 071 351 4307

MICHAEL PETERS (RETAIL) LTD/XMPR
151 Freston Road, London W10 6TH
☎ **071 229 1010 - Fax 071 792 9462**

PIERRE D'AVOINE ARCHITECTS
Tapestry Court, Mortlake High Street, London SW14 8KJ
☎ 081 878 9455 - Fax 081 876 6506

PORTLAND DESIGN ASSOCIATES
90-92 Great Portland Street, London W1N 5PB
☎ 071 436 5301 - Fax 071 631 1242

RANSLEY & ASSOCIATES
3 The Billings, Walnut Tree Close,
Guildford, Surrey GU1 4UL
☎ 0483 301491 - Fax 0483 301121

RAYLIAN LONDON LTD
Becketts Wharf, Off Lower Teddington Road,
Hampton Wick KT1 4ER
☎ 081 747 1606 - Fax 081 994 5232

RENTON HOWARD WOOD LEVIN PARTNERSHIP
77 Endell Street, London WC2H 9AJ
☎ 071 379 7900 - Fax 071 836 4881

STEWART K RIDDICK & PARTNERS
Stewart House, 930 High Road, London N12 9RT
☎ 081 446 4131 - Fax 081 446 3689

RETAIL DESIGN & BUILD LTD
Hope Street, Netherton, Dudley, West Midlands DY2 8RS
☎ 0384 458885 - Fax 0384 458819

RICHMOND INSTON
52-70 Shorts Gardens, London WC2H 9AB
☎ **071 379 6556 - Fax 071 240 1915**

ROBERTS WEAVER DESIGN LTD
7 Westbourne Grove Mews, London W11 2SA
☎ 071 221 4420 - Fax 071 727 1880

ROCK TOWNSEND
35 Alfred Place, London WC1E 7DP
☎ 071 637 5300 - Fax 071 580 6080

RICHARD ROGERS PARTNERSHIP LTD
Thames Wharf, Rainville Road, London W6 9HA
☎ 071 385 1235 - Fax 071 385 8409

ROLFE JUDD
Old Church Court, Claylands Road, London SW8 1NZ
☎ 071 582 7070 - Fax 071 735 5141

THE RPW PARTNERSHIP
77 Weston Street, London SE1 3RS
☎ **071 378 8001 - Fax 071 403 6386**

RUDDLE WILKINSON PARTNERSHIP
84 Lincoln Road, Peterborough, Cambridgeshire PE1 2SW
☎ 0733 314314 - Fax 0733 52242

SBT DESIGNWORK
43 King Street, London WC2E 8RJ
☎ 071 240 0030 - Fax 071 831 1231

SALMON SPEED
Tuscan Studios, 14 Muswell Hill Road, London N6 5UG
☎ 081 444 1041 - Fax 081 883 2226

SAMPSON/TYRRELL LTD
6 Mercer Street, London WC2H 9QG
☎ 071 379 7124 - Fax 071 836 1930

SEWARD GLYNN MARSH LTD
Ransomes Wharf, 33 Parkgate Road, London SW11
☎ 071 585 0050 - Fax 071 924 1475

SEYMOUR HARRIS PARTNERSHIP
4 Greenfield Crescent, Edgbaston, Birmingham B15 3BQ
☎ 021 454 4571 - Fax 021 454 5403

RSCG SOPHA DESIGN
RSCG Design Group - RSCG Conran Design,
London
☎ **071 631 0102 - Fax 071 255 2049**

SHEPPARD ROBSON
77 Parkway, Camden Town, London NW1 7PU
☎ **071 485 4161 - Fax 071 267 3861**

MICHAEL SHERIDAN & Co Ltd
40 Nelson Street, Leicester LE1 7BA
☎ 0533 544224 - Fax 0533 556322

SKS ARCHITECTS
Thavies Inn House, 5 Holborn Circus, London EC1N 2HN
☎ 071 583 8811 - Fax 071 583 0495

THE SIMONS DESIGN GROUP LTD
245 Old Marylebone Road, London NW1 5QT
☎ 071 229 9556 - Fax 071 221 3671

SPICER, KAPICA & KENNETH WOOD ASSOCS
82 Portsmouth Road, Surbiton, Surrey KT6 5PT
☎ 081 399 3030 - Fax 081 399 9809

SPRINGBOARD DESIGN
5 Ninetree Hill, Bristol, BS1 3SB
☎ 0272 244408 - Fax 0272 428943

TSBW
34 Gresse Street, London W1P 2AH
☎ 071 631 0408 - Fax 071 631 3208

TAYBURN DESIGN GROUP
25 Chester Street, Edinburgh, EH3 7EN
☎ 031 225 4707 - Fax 031 225 5193

THOMPSON & SICOMORI ARCHITECTS
63 Bayham Place, London NW1 0ET
☎ 071 388 2612 - Fax 071 388 5276

TIBBATS & Co
1 St Pauls Square, Birmingham B3 1QU
☎ **021 233 2871 - Fax 021 236 8705**

TILNEY LUMSDEN SHANE LTD
5 Heathmans Road, London SW6 4TJ
☎ **071 731 6946 - Fax 071 736 3356**

TRICKETT ASSOCIATES
The Factory, 84 Marchmont Street, London
WC1N 1HE
☎ **071 388 6586 - Fax 071 387 4287**

THROUGHTON McASLAN Ltd
186 Campden Hill Road, London W8 7TH
☎ 071 727 2663 - Fax 071 221 8835

ttsp
90-98 Goswell Road, London, EC1V 7DB
☎ 071 490 8899 - Fax 071 490 5845

WPP GROUP PLC
27 Farm Street, London W1X 6RD
☎ 071 408 2204 - Fax 071 493 6819

WALKER GROUP/CNI
24 St Johns Street, London EC1M 4AY
☎ 071 253 2844 - Fax 071 253 3887

WHITMORE THOMAS LTD
22 Jay Mews, London SW7 2EP
☎ 071 581 8866 - Fax 071 225 1079

WILLIAMSON DAWE DESIGN
61-63 Borough Street, Castle Donnington, Nr Derby DE7 2LB
☎ 0332 811674 - Fax 0332 850225

WILSON MASON AND PARTNERS/CHANDOS DESIGN LTD
3 Chandos Street, Cavendish Square, London W1M 0JU
☎ 071 637 1501 - Fax 071 631 0325

WIMBERLY ALLISON TONG & GOO
Waldron House, 57 Old Church St,
London SW3 5BS

WOLFF OLINS/HAMILTON
22 Dukes Road, London WC1R 9AB
☎ 071 387 0891 - Fax 071 388 6639

YRM INTERIORS
24 Britton Street, London EC1M 5NQ
☎ 071 253 4311 - Fax 071 250 1688

NORTH AMERICA

CANADA & USA - Telephone Code : 1

9 TEK Ltd DEVELOPMENT CONSULTANTS
8501 N 84th Place, Scottsdale, AZ 85258
☎ (602) 948 25 06

JAMES ADAMS & ASSOCIATES
206B Riverside Avenue, Newport Beach, CA 92663
☎ (714) 645 17 91

A.D.S.A. & PARTNERS
B.M.E.S. 215 East 80th St Suite 2M,
New York, NY 10021
☎ (212) 737 35 25 - Fax (212) 737 36 47

ADDISON DESIGN CONSULTANTS Ltd
112 East 31st Street, New York, NY 10016
☎ (212) 532 61 66 - Fax (212) 532 32 88

AIELLO ASSOCIATES
1441 Wazee, Denver, CO 80202
☎ (303) 892 70 24

DENNIS ALLEMAND & ASSOCIATES DESIGN
8090 West Selma Avenue, Los Angeles, CA 90046
☎ (213) 656 89 44

ALMASIAN ASSOCIATES Inc.
167 Washington St, Sherborn, MA 01770
☎ (508) 655 28 40

ARCHITECTS COLLABORATIVE
46 Bratle St, Cambridge, MA 02138
☎ (617) 868 42 00

ARCHITECTURAL INTERIORS
600 W Fulton, Chicago, IL 60606
☎ (312) 454 91 00

AUMILLER YOUNGQUIST, PC
800 E NW Highway, Mt Prospect, IL 60056
☎ (708) 253 37 61 - Fax (708) 394 83 20

THE AUSTIN COMPANY
3650 Mayfield Road, Cleveland, OH 44121
☎ (216) 382 66 00

WALTER M. BALLARD & ASSOCIATES
65 Bleecker St, New York, NY 10012-2470
☎ (212) 505 63 00

BALLINGER
The Curtis Center, Independence Sq W, Philadelphia,
PA 19106
☎ (215) 592 09 00

BARRY DESIGN ASSOCIATES
1333 Westwood Blvd, Los Angeles, CA 90024
☎ (213) 478 60 81 - Fax (213) 312 99 26

MELVIN BEACHER & PARTNERS
347 Fifth Ave, New York, NY 10016
☎ (212) 889 65 95

BOOKHAM/EISENMAN
16811 Milliken Ave, Irvine, CA 92714
☎ (714) 660 12 60

BENGTSSON INTERNATIONAL
10704 Hunters Valley Road, Vienna, VA 22180
☎ (703) 938 40 20

BENT SEVERIN & ASSOCIATES
815 Eddy, San Francisco, CA 94109
☎ (415) 929 05 10

BEYER BLINDER BELLE
41 East 11th Street, New York, NY 10003
☎ (212) 777 78 00 - Fax (212) 475 74 24

ANDREW BLACKMAN
121 East 36th Street, New York, NY 10016
☎ (212) 683 48 84

BONSIGNORE BRIGNATI & MAZZOTTA
275 Seventh Ave, New York, NY 10001
☎ (212) 633 14 00

BORDELON DESIGN
Two Shell Plaza, Houston, TX 77002
☎ (713) 236 84 26 - Fax (713) 236 05 12

BRAND & ALLEN ASSOCIATES
4455 North Braeswood, Houston, TX 77096
☎ (713) 667 59 28

BUSINESS SPACE DESIGN
111 So Jackson St, Seattle, WA 98104
☎ (206) 223 51 63 - Fax (206) 621 23 01

BUTLER ROGERS BASKETT
381 Park Ave So, New York, NY 10016
☎ (212) 686 06 77

BUTTRICK WHITE & BURTIS
475 Tenth Ave 7Fl, New York, NY 10018
☎ (212) 967 33 33

CALLISON PARTNERSHIP
1420 5th Ave #2400, Seattle, WA 98101
☎ (206) 623 46 46

CANNON
2170 Whitehaven Rd, Grand Island, NY 14072
☎ (716) 773 68 00

CBT/CHILDS BERTMAN TSECKARES
306 Dartmouth, Boston, MA 02116
☎ (617) 262 43 54

CHAIX & JOHNSON Inc.
1850 Sawtelle Blvd, West Los Angeles, CA 90025
☎ (213) 445 87 10

CHAPMAN & BIBER
422 Morris Ave, Summit, NJ 07901
☎ (201) 273 88 77

ALEX CHAPMAN DESIGN Ltd
49 Spadina Ave Suite 507, Toronto, Ontario, Canada,
M5V 2J1
☎ (416) 597 15 76

CONCEPT DESIGN GROUP
615 Piikoi St, Suite 1406, Honolulu, HI 96814
☎ (808) 523 76 30 - Fax (808) 531 17 06

CONCEPT INTERIOR CONSULTANTS
5706 Corsa Ave #107, West Lake Village, CA 91362
☎ (818) 597 00 34

CONCEPTS 4 Inc.
300 Continental Blvd, Suite 320, El Segundo, CA 90245
☎ (213) 640 02 90

RICHARD CROWELL ASSOCIATES
1860 Ala Moana Blvd, Suite 410, Honolulu, HI 96815
☎ (808) 946 48 68

CRS SIRRINE Inc.
PO Box 22427, Houston, TX 77227-2427
☎ (713) 552 20 00

MARSHALL CUMMINGS & ASSOCIATES
43 Davies Ave, Toronto, Ontario, M4M 2A9
☎ (416) 461 35 63 - Fax (416) 461 58 54

COVELL MATTHEWS WHEATLEY
ARCHITECTS Ltd
Tribble Harris Li Inc., 730 Fifth Avenue, Suite
604, New York, NY 10019
☎ (212) 262 71 80

JAMES D'AURIA ASSOCIATES ARCHITECTS
12 W 27, New York, NY 10001
☎ (212) 725 56 60

LEO A. DALY
8600 Indian Hills Drive, Omaha, NE 68114
☎ (402) 391 81 11

DAROFF DESIGN INC. & DDI ARCHITECTS
2300 Ionic St, Philadelphia, PA 19103
☎ (215) 636 99 00

DAVIS, BRODY & ASSOCIATES
315 Hudson, New York, NY 10013
☎ (212) 633 47 00

DESIGN 1 INTERIORS
2049 Century Park East, Los Angeles, CA 90067
☎ (213) 553 50 32 - Fax (213) 785 04 45

DESIGN CONTINUUM INCORPORATED
1801 Peachtree Road NE, Atlanta, GA 30309
☎ (404) 350 24 00

DESIGN INTERNATIONAL
D.I. Design & Development Consultants Ltd,
20 South Charles Street, Baltimore,
Maryland 21201
☎ (301) 962 05 05 - Fax (301) 783 08 16

DESIGN TREND INTERNATIONAL INTERIORS
3030 LBJ Freeway #230 L.B.4, Dallas, TX 75234
☎ (214) 243 35 55

DEUPI & ASSOCIATES Inc.
1101 17th St NW #200, Washington, DC 20036
☎ (202) 872 80 20

DILEONARDO INTERNATIONAL Inc.
2346 Post Road, Warwick, RI 02886-2242
☎ (401) 732 29 00

DORF ASSOCIATES
106 East 19th St, New York, NY 10003
☎ (212) 473 96 67 - Fax (212) 529 32 50

DOROTHY DRAPER AND ASSOCIATES
60 E 56, New York, NY 10022
☎ (212) 758 28 10

DYER/BROWN & ASSOCIATES Inc.
75 Broad St, Boston, MA 02109
☎ (617) 426 16 80

ELLERBE BECKET Inc.
1 Apple Tree Square, Minneapolis, MN 55425
☎ (612) 853 2061 - Fax (612) 853 23 90

BARBARA ELLIOTT INTERIORS Inc.
1038-1 Shary Circle, Concord, CA 95418
☎ (415) 798 85 50

ERIC LIEURÉ
Eric Lieuré/Butler Rogers Baskett,
381 Park Avenue South, New York, NY 10016
☎ (212) 686 96 77 - Fax (212) 213 21 70

FALICK/KLEIN PARTNERSHIP Inc.
5847 San Felipe #1900, Houston, TX 77057
☎ (713) 782 90 00

CW FENTRESS AND ASSOCIATES
1800 Grant St, Denver, CO 80203
☎ (303) 830 21 00

FITCH RS DESIGN CONSULTANTS
Fitch Richardsonsmith, 10350 Olentangy River
Road, PO Box 360, Worthington, OH 43085
☎ (614) 885 34 53 - Fax (614) 885 42 89

FITZPATRICK DESIGN GROUP
2109 Broadway, Suite 203, New York, NY 10023
☎ (212) 580 58 42

EARL R. FLANSBURGH + ASSOC.
77 No Washington St, Boston, MA 02114
☎ (617) 367 39 70

FORBES-ERGAS DESIGN ASSOC.
138 9th Ave, New York, NY 10011
☎ (212) 727 11 10

FORD & EARL ASSOCIATES Inc.
28820 Mound Road, PO Box 628, Warren, MI 48090
☎ (313) 536 19 99

GENSLER & ASSOCIATES
550 Kearney St, San Francisco, CA 94108
☎ (212) 581 96 00

GIFFELS ASSOCIATES Inc.
25200 Telegraph, Southfield, MI 48086-5025
☎ (313) 355 46 00

GN ASSOCIATES
595 Madison Avenue, New York, NY 10022
☎ (212) 935 29 00

THE GRAD PARTNERSHIP
One Gateway Center, Newark, NJ 07102
☎ (201) 621 17 00

GRAHAM-SOLANO Ltd
282 Mont Vale Ave, Woburn, MA 01801
☎ (617) 935 34 44

JON GREENBERG & ASSOCIATES
2338 Coolidge Highway, Berkley, MI 48072
☎ (313) 548 80 80 - Fax (313) 548 46 40

GWATHMEY SIEGEL & ASSOCIATES ARCHITECTS
475 10th Ave, New York, NY 10018
☎ (212) 947 12 40

HAMBRECHT & TERRELL INTERNATIONAL
860 Broadway, New York, NY 10003
☎ (212) 254 12 29

THOMAS HAMILTON & ASSOCIATES
11000 Staples Mill Rd, Glen Allen, VA 23060
☎ (804) 798 43 39

HEERY INTERIORS/INTERNATIONAL
999 Peachtree, Atlanta, GA 30367
☎ (404) 881 98 80

MARGARET HELFAND ARCHITECTS
32 E 38 St, New York, NY 10016
☎ (212) 779 72 60

HELLMUTH, OBATA & KASSABAUM
1831 Chestnut, St. Louis, MO 63103
☎ (314) 421 20 00

HIRSH BEDNER
3216 Nebraska Avenue, Santa Monica, CA 90404
☎ (213) 829 90 87

HKS Inc.
1111 Plaza of America No, Dallas, TX 75201
☎ (214) 969 55 99 - Fax (214) 969 33 97

STEPHEN ROBERTS HOLT ASSOCIATES
13 Central St, Manchester, MA 01944
☎ (508) 526 12 81

VICTOR HUFF AND ASSOCIATES
2675 So Abilene, Denver, CO 80014
☎ (303) 751 73 33 - Fax (303) 751 11 02

ALBERT HUI DESIGN ASSOCIATES
636 King St West 2nd Fl, Toronto, Ontario, M5V 1M7
☎ (416) 869 08 94

INDEX THE DESIGN FIRM
5701 Woodway, Houston, TX 77057
☎ (713) 977 25 94

INTEGRATED SERVICES CORPORATION
30 West 56 St, New York, NY 10019
☎ (212) 246 30 51

INTERIOR ARCHITECTS
350 California St #1500, San Francisco, CA 94104
☎ (415) 434 33 05

INTERIOR ARCHITECTS
305 E 47 St, New York, NY 10017
☎ (212) 888 20 80

INTERIOR DESIGN DEVELOPMENT
3188 Airway Avenue, Costa Mesa, CA 92626
☎ (714) 556 80 80

INTERIOR DESIGN Inc.
1440 So Sepulveda Blvd Ste 216, Los Angeles, CA 909025
☎ (213) 473 53 58

INTERNATIONAL DESIGN GROUP
188 Avenue Road, Toronto, Ontario, M5R 2JI
☎ (416) 961 18 11

INTRA-SPEC
200 E Culver Blvd, Playa Del Rey, CA 90293
☎ (213) 821 03 69

INTRADESIGN
910 No La Cienega Blvd, Los Angeles, CA 90069
☎ (213) 652 6114 - Fax (213) 652 69 45

ISD INCORPORATED
305 E 46 St, New York, NY 10017
☎ (212) 751 08 00

JOYCE/SNOWEISS DESIGN GROUP
2675 So Bayshore Drive, Coconut Grove, FL 33133
☎ (305) 858 41 14

KASLER & ASSOCIATES Inc.
Bank One Center Tower, 111 Monument Circle, Suite 4500,
Indianapolis, IN 46204-5145
☎ (317) 636 80 48

KOHN PEDERSEN FOX CONWAY ASSOC.
251 W 57 14 FL, New York, NY 10019
☎ (212) 397 11 00

CAROLE KORN INTERIORS
825 So Bayshore Drive, Penthouse Tower 3,
1001 Front Street, San Francisco, CA 94111
☎ (305) 375 80 80 - Fax (305) 374 55 22

W. LEE INTERIOR DESIGN Inc.
523 The Queensway, Suite 102, Toronto, Canada, M8Y 1J7
☎ (416) 252 71 15

LEE-ROVTAR ASSOCIATES
2403 Main, Santa Monica, CA 90405-3515
☎ (213) 392 83 25

LOONEY, BENSON, HLAVATY
2200 Ross Ave, Suite 700, Dallas, TX 75201
☎ (214) 220 47 77

LYNN WILSON
111 Majorca Avenue, Coral Gables,
Florida 33134
☎ (305) 442 40 41 - Fax (305) 443 42 76

SAM LOPATA
27 West 20, New York, NY 10011
☎ (212) 691 79 24

M.D.I. DESIGN CONSULTANTS Inc.
64 Jefferson Avenue, Suite #2, Toronto, Ontario, M6K 1Y3
☎ (416) 533 46 42

MANCINI DUFFY
1 World Trad Center, New York, NY 10048
☎ (212) 938 12 60

P. MICHAEL MARINO ARCHITECT
434 6th Ave 6th Fl, New York, NY 10011
☎ (212) 353 21 00

PETER MARINO ARCHITECT
150 E 58 St, New York, NY 10022
☎ (212) 752 54 44

McCOLL GROUP INTERNATIONAL
(Associate Office)
111 Majorca Avenue, Coral Gables, Fla.
☎ (305) 442 40 41

MEDIA FIVE LIMITED
345 Queens Street, Honolulu, HI 96800
☎ (808) 524 20 40

THE MILLER ORGANIZATION Inc.
149 Madison Ave 11th Fl, New York, NY 10016
☎ (212) 685 77 00

J.T. NAKAOKA
1900 So Sepulveda Blvd, Los Angeles, CA 90025
☎ (213) 479 48 73

MORRIS NATHANSON DESIGN
163 Exchange St, Pawtucket, RI 02860
☎ (401) 723 38 00 - Fax (401) 723 38 13

NBBJ/ROSENFIELD
58 W 40 16th Fl, New York, NY 10018
☎ (212) 391 90 10

NISHIMI WOMACK AND CARROLL
8075 West Third St, Los Angeles, CA 90048
☎ (213) 935 80 75

NOBUTAKA ASHIHARA ASSOCIATES
37 Murray St 3rd Fl, New York, NY 10007
☎ (212) 233 17 83

JAMES NORTHCUTT ASSOCIATES
717 LaCienga Blvd, Los Angeles, CA 90069
☎ (213) 659 85 95 - Fax (213) 659 71 20

ONE DESIGN CENTER Inc.
PO Box 29426, Greensboro, NC 27429
☎ (919) 288 01 34

PAPADATOS MOUNDIS ASSOC. PC
305 E 46th St, New York, NY 10017
☎ (212) 308 25 00

CHARLES PATTEN ARCHITECTS
1123 Broadway, New York, NY 10010
☎ (212) 929 03 38

RJ PAVLIK Inc.
1301 E Broward Blvd, Ft Lauderdale, FL 33301
☎ (305) 523 33 00

PERKINS & WILL
123 Wacker, Chicago, IL 60606
☎ (312) 977 11 00

PERRY, DEAN, ROGERS & PARTNERS
177 Milk St, Boston, MA 02109
☎ (617) 423 01 00

PFF/CONTRACT, Inc.
290 Easy St, Simi Valley, CA 93065
☎ (805) 583 07 22 - Fax (805) 583 02 79

PHH ENVIRONMENTS
716 So Olive St, 1st Fl, Los Angeles, CA 90014
☎ (213) 489 42 28

WARREN PLATNER ASSOCIATES
18 Mitchell Drive, New Haven, CT 06511
☎ (203) 777 64 71 - (203) 562 45 30

JOHN PORTMAN & ASSOCIATES
231 Peachtree St, NE, Suite 200, Atlanta, GA 30303
☎ (404) 522 88 11 - (404) 223 08 53

Q5 INCORPORATED
50 Galesi Drive, Wayne, NJ 07470
☎ (201) 256 79 00

QUANTRELL-MULLINS
999 Peachtree St, NE #1690, Atlanta, GA 30309
☎ (404) 874 60 48

RICE BRYDONE
512 King Street E, Toronto, Ontario, Canada, M5A 1M1
☎ (416) 864 90 94

RITA ST. CLAIR ASSOCIATES
1009 No Charles St, Baltimore, MD 21201
☎ (301) 752 13 13

ROWLAND ASSOCIATES Inc.
334 North Senate, Indianapolis, IN 46204
☎ (317) 638 24 98

RTKL ASSOCIATES
400 East Pratt St, Baltimore, MD 21202
☎ (301) 528 86 00

RYAN GIBSON BAUER KORNBLATH
90 West St 14th Fl, New York, NY 10006
☎ (212) 385 90 90

SASAKI ASSOCIATES
64 Pleasant St, Watertown, MA 02172
☎ (617) 926 33 00 - Fax (617) 924 27 48

SCHAFER ASSOCIATES Inc.
635 Butterfield Rd, Oak Brook Terrace, IL 60181
☎ (708) 932 87 87

SCR DESIGN ORGANIZATION Inc.
1114 First Ave, New York, NY 10021
☎ (212) 421 35 00

LE SEITZ ASSOC.
395 Alhambra Circle, Coral Gables, FL 33134-5003
☎ (305) 445 22 00 - Fax (305) 445 51 51

SHAW ASSOCIATES
225 Cannery row, Suite A, Monterey, CA 93940
☎ (408) 649 30 13

SILVER & ZISKIND/MOUNT
233 Park Ave So 4th Fl, New York, NY 10003
☎ (212) 727 23 83

SITE
65 Bleecker St, New York, NY 10012
☎ (212) 254 8300 - Fax (212) 353 3086

SK DESIGN INTERNATIONAL
376 Boylston St, Boston, MA 02116
☎ (617) 236 4343

SMALLWOOD, REYNOLDS, STEWART,
STEWART INTERIORS Inc.
1 Piedmont Center 303, Atlanta, GA 30305
☎ (404) 233 5453

SPACE/MANAGEMENT PROGRAMS
230 No Michigan Ave 7th Fl, Chicago, IL 60601
☎ (312) 263 2995 - Fax (312) 263 1236

STAFFELBACH DESIGNS & ASSOCIATES
2525 Carlisle, Dallas, TX 75201
☎ (214) 747 2511

ROBERT A.M. STERN ARCHITECTS
211 W 61, New York, NY 10023
☎ (212) 246 1980

STRATEGIC DESIGN GROUP
823 East Main St, Richmond, VA 23219
☎ (804) 648 9000

STUBBINS ASSOCIATES
1033 Massachusettes Avenue, Cambridge, MA 02138
☎ (617) 491 6450

STUDIOS ARCHITECTURE
99 Greene ST, San Francisco, CA 94111
☎ (301) 902 7912

SULTON ASSOCIATES
41 Union Sq West Suite 331, New York, NY 10003
☎ (212) 807 1344

SVERDRUP CORPORATION
1824 Lackland Hill Pkwy 100, St-Louis, MO 63146
☎ (314) 567 5110

SWANKE HAYDEN CONNELL
400 Park Ave, New York, NY 10022
☎ (212) 977 9696

TARDY & ASSOCIATES Inc.
1725 Montgomery St. San Francisco, CA 94111
☎ (415) 362 5555 - Fax (415) 362 5554

TDI ASSOCIATES DESIGN Inc.
1336 Notredame 2nd Fl, Montreal, Quebec, H3C 1K7
☎ (514) 937 3093

HAROLD THOMPSON ASSOCIATES
15910 Ventura Blvd, Encino, Ca 91316
☎ (818) 789 3005

THOMPSON, VENTULETT, STAINBACK AND ASSOC. Inc.
CNN Center North 12th Fl, Atlanta, GA 30303 2705
☎ (404) 688 8531

TIGERMAN McCURRY
444 No Wells, Chicago, IL 60610
☎ (312) 644 5880

ADAM D TIHANY INTERNATIONAL Ltd
57-59 E 11, New York, NY 10003
☎ (212) 505 2360

TODD LEE CLARK ROZAS ASSOCIATES
286 Congress St, Boston, MA 02210
☎ (617) 451 0066

TOFTEY CRAIG
45 Middle St, Gloucester, MA 01930-5736
☎ (508) 283 4494

TRICKETT ASSOCIATES
Russel/Trickett & Webb
584 Broadway, New York, NY 10012
☎ (212) 431 8770 - Fax (212) 431 8771

TSAO & McKOWN ARCHITECTS
41 E 42, New York, NY 10017
☎ (212) 697 0980

TUCCI SEGRETE AND ROSEN
440 9th Avenue, New York, NY 10001
☎ (212) 629 3900

URS CONSULTANTS
3605 Warrensville Cnt Rd, Cleveland, OH 44122
☎ (216) 283 4000

VALERIAN RYBAR & DAIGRE DESIGN
601 Madison Ave, New York, NY 10022
☎ (212) 752 1861

VIGNELLI ASSOCIATES
475 10th Ave, New York, NY 10018
☎ (212) 244 1919

VIVIAN/NICHOLS ASSOCIATES Inc.
311 Market St, Suite 205, Dallas, TX 75202
☎ (214) 761 9999

WALKER GROUP/CNI
320 W 13 St, New York, NY 10014
☎ (212) 206 0444

WILSON & ASSOCIATES
3811 Turtle Creek Road 15 Fl, Dallas, TX 75200
☎ (214) 521 6753

LYNN WILSON ASSOCIATES
111 Majorca Ave, Coral Gables, FL 33134
☎ (305) 442 4041 - Fax (305) 443 4276

WIMBERLY ALLISON TONG AND GOO
140 Newport Center Dr, Suite 200, Newport
Beach, California 92660
☎ (714) 759 8923 - Fax (714) 759 3473

WOMACK-HUMPHREYS ARCHITECTS
5430 LBJ Freeway Suite 1000, Dallas, TX 75240
☎ (214) 770 2300 - Fax (214) 770 2012

ACKNOWLEDGEMENTS

A great many people have contributed to the publishing of DID, Volume 1. Some have contributed directly, and others indirectly-even unknowingly! Some have played very large and significant roles, others have had smaller, but nevertheless important parts in the process.

I would especially like to thank the following people for their help and support:
Laurence Curtis, Michael Curtis, Christopher Gates, Hervé Morel, Véronique Kolasa, Yves Ferandou, John Larkin, Brian Morris, Ira Shapiro, Samia Ammar, Luc Raimond dit Yvon, Brenda Curtis, Tim Grey, Andrew Barker, Maria-Teresa Boselli, Nina Daniels, Terry Coles, Michael Cogswell, Jean-Michel Bouyer, Caroline Babeau, Mireia Massons, Alison Clayson, Christophe Gaultier, Miranda Curtis, Alex Dowding, Jean-François Genoud, Janie Blackburn, Michael Hargreave, Barbara Randall, Julie, Adam & Henrietta Curtis, Jane Gates, and of course, the directors of the DID international offices.

In addition, special thanks are due to Rovira Associados in Barcelona, for their help with the Spanish edition of DID; to Siegmund Verlag in Hanover for the German edition; to Giannino Malossi in Milan for the Italian edition... and to Le Book Editions in Paris for the French edition.

Chris Curtis, Publisher